D1588262

THE BEHAVIORAL SCIENCES TODAY

THE BEHAVIORAL SCIENCES TODAY

Edited by BERNARD BERELSON

HARPER TORCHBOOKS
THE ACADEMY LIBRARY
HARPER & ROW, PUBLISHERS
NEW YORK, EVANSTON, AND LONDON

Editor's Foreword

This collection of papers originated as a series of talks in the Forum series of the Voice of America. The Forum program, beamed in English throughout the world, was designed as a channel of communication between American scholars and their counterparts in academic and cultural institutions abroad. It covered a range of subjects in the arts and sciences. In addition to this series, Forum has included programs on biological science, architecture, chemistry, education, modern American literature, American law, music, and other subjects.

In this series, in addition to background material on the institutional organization of the behavioral sciences in this country, their applications, the state of the disciplines, and methods of inquiry, we gave attention to a number of research fields currently important on the American scene. We tried to give some coherence to the list by dealing with those fields in which there is a history of traditional work abroad and which at the same time are pursued by the methods of the modern behavioral sciences in this country. The topics included here are not all those that might have been covered in a series like this, but they will, I think, provide a reasonable sample of the present status of research work.

All of us are indebted to the USIA for the opportunity thus presented, as well as for permission to publish in this form. And we are personally grateful to Mr. Walter Nichols, the Editor of the series, for his help and encouragement.

BERNARD BERELSON

Contents

THE BEHAVIORAL SCIENCES TODAY

1 INTRODUCTION TO THE BEHAVIORAL SCIENCES

Bernard Berelson

Bernard Berelson, Director of the Communication Research Program of the Population Council, was born in Spokane, Washington, in 1912. After graduating from Whitman College, he studied at the University of Washington and the University of Chicago. A specialist in communication and public opinion, Dr. Berelson was research director of the Bureau of Applied Social Research at Columbia University from 1944 to 1946, when he joined the faculty of the University of Chicago. He is a former President of the American Association for Public Opinion Research (1951–1952), and from 1951 to 1957 served as Director of the Behavioral Sciences Program of the Ford Foundation. He has written and co-authored many articles and books, including The People's Choice, Content Analysis in Communication Research, *and* Voting. *He recently completed a two-year study of the state of graduate education in the United States, and he is senior author of a forthcoming inventory of findings in the behavioral sciences.*

The term *behavioral science* is of such recent coinage, and the field itself so new, that it is desirable at the outset to explain the meaning of the term and the way the field came to be what it is today.

Perhaps the best way to start delineating the field is to say what it is not. The core of the American university is the arts and sciences, which include the four main branches of learning: the physical sciences, the biological sciences, the social sciences, and the humanities. The term *social sciences* is usually understood to include six disciplines: anthropology, economics, history, political science, psychology, and sociology.

Actually, human affairs are so complex that academic categories, however carefully constructed, cannot contain them neatly. The broad division of the social sciences shares one of its member disciplines, history, with the humanities; another, psychology, with the biological sciences; another, anthropology, with both; and still others, economics and political science, with professional schools of business and public administration.

The behavioral sciences, in turn, center on three of the social sciences, but again not in a pure classification. At the center of the behavioral sciences are the American versions of anthropology, psychology, and sociology. But the concept includes both more and less than that. It includes less in the sense that some aspects of anthropology and psychology are not typically considered part of the behavioral sciences, e.g., certain archeological and physical interests in the former and certain technical interests like vision and hearing in the latter. And it includes more in the sense that a number of behavioral interests in other disciplines have an equal claim to inclusion: e.g., from political science and law, concern with actual political and legal behavior as distinct from the traditional formal concern with constitutions, governments, laws, and ideologies; from psychiatry, interest in deviant behavior, the motivational and emotional life, and the behavioral consequences of physiological change or chemical intervention; from geography, the behavioral implications of man's physical environment; from biology, the physiological and evolutionary bases of human behavior; from economics and business, such topics as consumer behavior, industrial morale, and the empirical analysis of businessmen's decisions; from history, broad generalizations about man's behavior under historical conditions.

To be considered a part of the behavioral sciences, a field must satisfy two basic criteria. First, it must deal with human behavior. However, some parts of psychology and biology that study animal behavior are included on the ground that they are getting at human behavior indirectly or basically. Second, it must study its subject matter in a "scientific" manner. I use the term in quotation marks because there is still so much argument over what the scientific method is as applied to human behavior, or indeed whether it can be applied at all. There is little point in arguing the question here—after all, if the several papers that follow do not make the point, then I could hardly hope to do so in a brief introduction—but it is necessary, I think, to say a few words to characterize what is meant.

The scientific aim is to establish generalizations about human behavior that are supported by empirical evidence collected in an impersonal and objective way. The evidence must be capable of verification by other interested scholars and the procedures must be completely open to review and replication. The search for broad propositions about human behavior and the effort to build knowledge cumulatively require that general categories descriptive of the behavior be set up and used more or less systematically, as will be indicated in the following papers. The ultimate end is to understand, explain, and predict human behavior in the same sense in which scientists understand, explain, and predict the behavior of physical forces or biological factors or, closer home, the behavior of goods and prices in the economic market. How the behavioral scientists go about the task, and how well they are doing, will be apparent from what follows.

Admittedly, the edges of such a broad concept as the behavioral sciences are fuzzy—people have wasted a lot of time debating whether something is or is not properly included in the behavioral sciences—but the center of the concept is, I think, reasonably clear. Nor is it any more arbitrary than other such academic combinations. Some economists and historians and political scientists, and even some philosophers and students of literature, have been put off by the term on the ground that they too are deeply concerned with human behavior. But the term does not seem to be less precise or more misleading, for example, than the term "social sciences,"

3

which does not encompass some fields that also may claim to be "social."

There is an inherent distinction between the behavioral sciences on the one hand and the other social sciences on the other. The behavioral sciences are typically more devoted to the collection of original data reflecting the direct behavior of individuals or small groups as against the more aggregative, indirect, and documentary practices of economists, political scientists, and historians. But it is not particularly useful, and usually it is downright tiresome, to argue over the definition in order to clear up every possible misconception, exception, or presumed contradiction. They cannot all be cleared up in any case, nor is there any compelling reason why they must be. For our purposes the term has a reasonably coherent meaning that distinguishes it sufficiently from related concepts, and this meaning will be increasingly communicated, I trust, by the papers that follow.

The interest in clarifying the term, I might add, has not been altogether intellectual in character. Although the phrase "behavioral science" was used from time to time over a period of years, it never caught on until about twelve years ago when the Ford Foundation used the term as a shorthand description of its program on Individual Behavior and Human Relations. For about six years in the 1950's the Foundation operated a Behavioral Sciences Program and supported this field with several millions of dollars. It was then that the term came into widespread use, and it was then that some people began to wonder whether they too were not behavioral scientists after all!

It may be worthwhile to clear up a few potential misapprehensions about this field. The newness of the field and its youthful vigor often produce unduly hostile counteractions. In the first place, to believe that there is something to the scientific study of human behavior does not imply that that is the only way to come to an "understanding" of man. And that term, too, must be put in quotes because it is used in so many different senses. There are many paths to understanding—common observation, philosophical reflection, artistic expression, intuition. All I need urge here is that the scientific approach is another way, and that for many purposes, especially those in which establishing the facts is important, it is a particularly good way. The scientific approach is distinctive in the systematic and careful attention it gives to the accumulation of objective evidence; and scientific procedures produce factual evidence that demands respect from men of reason, however skeptical they may initially be. Accordingly, I ask for my colleagues here the same detachment and sympathy that are given to students of other subjects that do not carry the emotional load of this effort to explore scientifically the nature of man.

As a summary for this background, and in order to specify the matter somewhat further, let me recall some of the more notable behavioral science productions of the past few decades in this country.

In psychology, there are the measurement of human intelligence by Terman and Thurstone; the careful building of learning theory by Tolman and Hull and then Skinner; the exploration of personality by Murray, and a later inquiry into the authoritarian personality; the development of group dynamics by Kurt Lewin; the experiments on communication effects by Hovland.

In sociology, there are the well-known community studies of Middletown by the Lynds and of Yankeetown by Warner; the intensive wartime investigations of the American soldier by Stouffer and associates; the voting studies; the inquiry into *The American Dilemma* of race relations by Myrdal; the analysis of *The Lonely Crowd* by Riesman.

In anthropology, there are the pioneering investigations of Boas and his students; the inquiries into culture and personality by Mead and Kluckhohn and Kardiner; the studies of the folk community by Redfield; the analysis of the totality of cultures of Kroeber and Benedict and Murdock.

From other fields have come the path-breaking work of Lasswell on political behavior and Simon on administrative behavior; of Roethlisberger and Dixon on industrial morale in the famous Hawthorne studies; of Kinsey on sex behavior.

Now let us move still closer to the subject by looking at the kinds of studies that behavioral scientists in America are currently conducting. Perhaps the best way to do this is the most direct way, namely, seeing what is being published in some current learned journals. That is probably a reasonably good sample of what now goes on in the field. Leading journals in anthropology, psychology, and sociology recently contained articles on the following topics, among others.

From anthropology:
  Japanese folk beliefs
  Leadership and consensus in a New Guinea society
  Statistical marriage preferences of the Ramah Navaho
  The spearman and the archer: an essay on selection in body build
  Primitive political systems: a preliminary comparative analysis
  Proto-Siouan kinship terminology

From psychology:
  The effects of high intensity intermittent sound on performance, feeling, and physiology
  Methodological considerations in the construct validation of drive-oriented scales
  The importance of time as stimulus of conditioned reflex activity
  The nature of hypnosis: artifact and essence
  Hostility in Rorschach content and overt aggressive behavior
  Effect on extinction of restricting information on verbal conditioning

The relation between mean reward and mean reinforcement

From sociology:

Anti-social sentiment and criminality

Social class and parental authority

The identifiability of Jews

The Pentecostalist minister: role conflicts and status
contradictions

Social class and size of community

Status and competence of jurors

Status integration and suicide in Ceylon

Residence and social class in Oxford

From such a list certain characteristics that distinguish
American behavioral science become apparent. In the first
place, there is no question but that the field has become
highly professionalized in recent decades. True, some ama-
teurs still do contribute to the field (for example, Whyte's
Organization Man) and some have done so with distinction in
the recent past—for example, Chester Barnard's *Functions
of the Executive* or Whorf's novel contributions in linguistics. But on the whole, the professionals have taken over.

With professionalization have come other developments.
For example, it has brought a high degree of specialization, so
that studies are done on a more and more restricted basis.
Even now, only a few decades later, the broad-ranging studies
of the Lynds in Middletown seem dated, not to mention the
even broader observations of a Bryce or a Tocqueville. And
when a current professional like Riesman or Mills does write
about such broad subjects as "the lonely crowd" or "the
power elite," he often comes under criticism from the professional fraternity for disregarding the elementary principles of scientific procedures and, in addition, for getting
rather farther out into the seas of values than behavioral
scientists in their professional capacity like to sail. And specialization, in turn, gives rise to team research and multiple

authorship, as specialists in different areas join together to get a larger task done.

Professionalization has also meant the construction of a sizable armamentarium of methods and techniques, like the sample survey and the projective test—so much so that we have felt it only proper to give separate attention here to the methods of the field. It has meant the piling up of a vast and esoteric terminology that seems so essential within the field and at the same time so oppressive, pretentious, and unnecessary from the outside. A brief list of terms taken from the journals cited above is illustrative: the situs dimension, functional differentiation, role conflicts, status integration, drive-oriented scales, response sets, suppression effects, drive strength, social perception, subjective certainty, verbal conditioning, and so on. It has meant a high degree of quantification of data, so much so that the critics are afraid that the behavioral sciences are seeking to force human behavior into a statistical straitjacket.

In sum, as I said of a sub-field on another occasion, ". . . these differences spell a revolutionary change in the field [in recent decades]: the field has become technical and quantitative, segmentalized and particularized, specialized and institutionalized, 'modernized' and 'groupized'—in short, Americanized. Twenty-five years ago and earlier, prominent writers, as part of their general concern with the nature and functioning of the society, [studied man] in broad historical, theoretical, and philosophical terms and wrote treatises. Today, teams of technicians do research projects on specific subjects and report findings. Twenty-five years ago [the field] was part of scholarship; today it is part of science."

Now all of this can be thought of as either good or bad (and is!) depending upon your point of view. On the one hand, these developments can be seen as demeaning the study of man, as reducing it to trivialities for the sake of measurement and a spurious scientificism. On the other hand, they can be seen as part of an historic effort to introduce precision and validation into another, highly complex subject. Although there is still considerable argument and disagreement within the fraternity on this set of concepts or that set of methods, still it is natural that most behavioral scientists think that there is more good than bad in these developments, and it is safe to predict, I think, that the momentum within the field is clearly in this direction. More, rather than less, science in the behavioral sciences seems indicated in the next years. The reader can decide for himself what degree of success the enterprise has achieved to this point.

Any such appraisal should take into account the history of the field. Although it is possible to trace the ancestry of the behavioral sciences all the way back to Aristotle, it is more appropriate to say that the approach to the study of man that we now designate as behavioral science did not really get under way until the latter part of the nineteenth century, with the British origins of anthropology in Tylor, Maine, and Frazer; the first experimental laboratories in psychology of Wundt in Germany and William James in this country; and the early efforts at sociological investigation growing out of the social reform movements based on the growth of cities and of industry.

The fields made slow but sure headway in this country until World War I, which gave psychology a push forward along the lines of intelligence tests and statistical measurement. The period between the wars witnessed a faster growth —everything in the universities grew more rapidly in those years, stimulated by the rise of the educational system below them and by the prosperity of the 1920's—but the growth has been even faster since World War II. During that war a large number of behavioral scientists were employed in Washington and contributed their services to the war effort —for example, the *American Soldier* series of volumes was based on the studies done at that time, as were a series on the man–machine problem and human engineering problems, a volume on the assessment of men, Benedict's *Chrysanthemum and the Sword,* and many others. Moreover, the war cut down so heavily on behavioral science activity abroad that the United States emerged as far and away the major practitioner in the field—so much so that many observers feel that the field has an overly American flavor.

This stimulus carried over and the behavioral sciences have grown most rapidly in the past decade, so that there are now thousands of professionally trained men and women at work in universities and colleges, in industry and government, in voluntary associations and foundations, and even in private practice. Indeed, a trend toward the application of behavioral science skills and knowledge to practical affairs is among the most pronounced of the postwar years.

Nor could this entire development have taken place in this country without the support and encouragement over the years of the major American foundations. The Laura Spelman Rockefeller Memorial Fund began in the 1920's and the Rockefeller, Carnegie, and Ford foundations have been active since then. Now the government, through the National Science Foundation and research offices in various departments, is providing a major part of the support.* The ready availability of research funds has no doubt turned the American version of the behavioral sciences even further toward empiricism and research and away from the reflection and study characteristic of the European version. There are those who believe that this consideration underlies the alleged tendency for major theoreticians in this field to be European and the large body of technicians to be Americans.

But these historical details are less important for our purpose here than the central point of the youth of the behavioral science discipline. We are speaking of a field that

* A special panel set up by the President's Science Advisory Committee has recently issued a report on the subject, "Strengthening the Behavioral Sciences," which appears in *Science,* Vol. 136, April 1962, pp. 233–241.

even now is not a century old in its modern form. It is really younger than that, since its great growth occurred only in the past fifty years or less. As a result it is no wonder that it has been said to have many of the characteristics of adolescence: vigor, energy, enthusiasm, a certain brashness, a faddish interest in trivialities, all coupled with a disrespect for tradition.

At the same time, I think it only fair to add these few words: The behavioral sciences are here to stay. They have already made important contributions to our understanding of man and they will make many more. They are an indispensable approach to that understanding. They have already affected man's image of himself and permanently so. They are one of the major intellectual and cultural inventions of the twentieth century.

2 INSTITUTIONAL ORGANIZATION OF THE BEHAVIORAL SCIENCES

Ralph W. Tyler

Ralph W. Tyler, Director of the Center for Advanced Study in the Behavioral Sciences in Palo Alto, California, was born in Chicago in 1902. After completing his undergraduate education at Doane College and the University of Nebraska, Dr. Tyler received his doctorate in education from the University of Chicago. A specialist in educational experimentation and achievement test construction, he has taught on the faculties of the North Carolina and Ohio State universities and was Dean of the Social Sciences Division at the University of Chicago at the time he was appointed Director of the Center for Advanced Study in the Behavioral Sciences at Palo Alto in 1953. Dr. Tyler has been a member of the Board of Directors of the Social Science Research Council (1945–1949) and is the author of numerous publications, including Constructing Achievement Tests, Appraising and Recording Student Progress, *and* Basic Principles of Curriculum and Instruction.

The recent rapid growth in the United States of the behavioral sciences can largely be understood as a response to two conditions: first, the development of the fields themselves—that is, the successful invention of new methods for studying human behavior with the resulting new knowledge arising from these methods; and second, the increasing opportunities for professional careers in the behavioral sciences —that is, the increasing demand for persons trained in the behavioral sciences to serve in colleges, universities, business, and government. As American colleges and universities have recognized the existence of new academic specialties, they have provided places in their faculties for scientists in these new fields. As young people have learned of the opportunities for professional careers in these new fields, an increasing number have chosen them for graduate study.

Hence, in the past twelve or fifteen years particularly there has been in the United States a continuing increase in the number of college and university faculty members who are behavioral scientists, a great increase in the number of students who are specializing in these fields, and a corresponding increase in the number of professional behavioral scientists employed. The purpose of this paper is to describe in more detail the recruitment and education of behavioral scientists and the organization of the institutions in which they are doing their teaching and research.

In the United States the typical child enters the elementary school at age six and almost all American children complete nine or ten years of schooling. About half of the American youth complete twelve years and graduate from the secondary school. About half of these enroll in a college. There are approximately eighteen hundred colleges in the United States, including the undergraduate colleges of the large universities. The typical student enters college at age eighteen and completes his undergraduate education at age twenty-two. Approximately one-tenth of all American young people graduate from college, but only 5 per cent of the college graduates go on to graduate school to obtain the Ph.D. degree. In 1958, there were thirty-three American graduate schools which provided programs of study in anthropology leading to the Ph.D. degree, eighty-five in psychology, sixty-three in sociology, and about fifty awarding Ph.D. degrees in biology in which specialization in the behavioral sciences could be carried on. However, most of the doctoral degrees in the behavioral sciences were awarded by less than twenty of the larger American universities.

In the American educational system, the typical student has no opportunity to study any of the behavioral sciences, as such, prior to his second or third year in college—that is, before the age of nineteen or twenty. In the secondary school, a student planning to enter college will take courses in language, mathematics, history, chemistry, and physics, but anthropology, psychology, and sociology are not commonly offered until about midway through his undergraduate study. Hence, most students who go on for graduate work in the behavioral sciences have made their career decisions later than is typical for those going on in most other fields, because they have not had an earlier opportunity to learn more directly about the behavioral sciences. In general, however, those students who select the behavioral sciences for their graduate study compare favorably in intellectual ability with graduate students in other fields. In the United States at the present time graduate students in the behavioral sciences achieve an average score on scholastic aptitude tests above two-thirds of the average scores made by graduate students in all of the academic fields.

The student who is awarded the Ph.D. in one of the behavioral sciences will have devoted the equivalent of about one year of undergraduate study and three or four years of graduate study in his field of specialization, including the time spent in the preparation of a dissertation. Typically he will have participated as an assistant in the research activities of one or more of his professors and will have conducted an independent research investigation of his own. If he is an anthropologist, he will have carried on anthropological field work, usually among the American Indians or among primitive peoples in other parts of the world. If he is a psychologist, he will have conducted experimental studies of the behavior of animals as well as of human beings, and he will have had some experience with the design of experiments and with methods of statistical analysis. Most psychologists will also have had some training in methods for measuring psychological responses.

If the student is a sociologist, he will have conducted empirical, objective studies of social organizations or institutions, or of communities. He will have had some experience in interviewing, in methods of sampling, and in methods of statistical analysis. Most sociologists will also have had some training in the formulation of mathematical models for conceptualizing the phenomena they are studying, and in methods for converting qualitative concepts into measurable indices.

The culmination of the behavioral scientist's graduate study is the conduct of an independent investigation which forms the basis of his Ph.D. dissertation. The following titles of some recent dissertations will, I hope, indicate something of their nature:

> The relation of social class to performance on psychological tests
>
> A study of the maternal role in middle class families
>
> Ghosts: an anthropological inquiry into learning and perception
>
> The effects of verbal associations on perception
>
> Religious belief and economic behavior in a central Javanese town
>
> The institutionalization of new leadership roles: an empirical study
>
> Resistance to acculturation and assimilation in an Indian Pueblo
>
> Psychotherapy as a special case of personal interaction: prediction of its course
>
> Receptivity to communications as related to personality structure
>
> Group productivity, a function of group cohesiveness

After the dissertation has been approved by the committee of the university faculty assigned to guide him on his thesis and after he has passed successfully the final oral examination on his dissertation, the student is awarded the Ph.D. degree. At that time, the typical student is between twenty-five and thirty years of age.

In the ten-year period from 1947 to 1957, American universities awarded 376 Ph.D. degrees in anthropology, 4,677 Ph.D. degrees in psychology, and 1,329 Ph.D. degrees in sociology. An estimate of the approximate number of Ph.D. degrees in the behavioral sciences which were awarded during this same period in departments of biology, psychiatry, political science, and history is 860. On this basis, it is estimated that a total of 7,242 Ph.D.s in the behavioral sciences were awarded by American universities in this ten-year period, or an average of 724 per year. Since the number of graduate students this year is larger than in 1957 and the number of Ph.D.s in the behavioral sciences increased each year from 1947 to 1957, it seems reasonable to estimate that the number of new behavioral scientists currently receiving the Ph.D. degree each year exceeds 900.

Of these 900 behavioral scientists receiving the Ph.D. degree each year about 600, or two-thirds, are obtaining employment as faculty members in colleges and universities. About 125 are going into government service at the federal, state, or local level, about 110 are accepting positions in business, and the remaining 65 are working in non-profit institutions and agencies, carrying on research or technical activities of various sorts. Some notion of the total number of behavioral scientists now employed in the United States is indicated by the membership in the professional societies. There are approximately 1,500 members of the American Anthropological Association, about 20,000 members of the American Psychological Association, about 7,300 members of the American Sociological Association, and about 4,500 behavioral scientists in the other social science fields and in biology. Of these 33,300 people, one may conservatively estimate that 50 per cent have completed their professional training and have been awarded the Ph.D. degree. From this estimate, it is safe to say that in the United States at the present time there are 16,650 professionally trained behavioral scientists.

Since the majority of behavioral scientists are in the colleges and universities of America, a further explanation of their place in these institutions is in order. Approximately half of those who are in educational institutions are employed in undergraduate colleges where their primary responsibility is the teaching of undergraduate students. This gives them only a small part of their time for study, research, and writing. Furthermore, the funds to support research in the undergraduate colleges are very limited.

Typically, the behavioral scientist in these institutions spends a few hours each week and a part of the summer on his own scholarly interests but devotes his major attention to the planning and teaching of college courses. The majority of undergraduate colleges enroll from five hundred to fifteen hundred students, and employ a total of from forty to one hundred-fifty faculty members. There is usually only one faculty in the college and it is organized into departments. Commonly there are from eight to eighteen departments, of which two or three include behavioral scientists.

At the other extreme of complexity are the large American universities, some twenty of which award most of the Ph.D. degrees in the behavioral sciences and devote major attention to research in these fields. These large universities range in size from those which enroll 8,000 students to one or two which enroll nearly 25,000 students each. The teaching and research staffs in these large institutions are organized into several faculties. Behavioral scientists will be found in the faculties of such professional schools as medicine, law, education, and business and in largest numbers in the faculties of arts and sciences. The latter faculty is usually organized into twenty to thirty departments representing the commonly recognized disciplines. Behavioral scientists are found in departments of anthropology, psychology, and sociology, and a few will also be within departments of physiology, zoology, economics, and political science.

In most American universities the graduate faculties of arts and sciences are largely the same as the undergraduate faculties and are organized into the same conventional departments. Thus, for example, the department of psychology will offer both graduate and undergraduate courses. Most of the psychology faculty members in the higher ranks will be in both the graduate and undergraduate faculties. This is generally true of all departments in the arts and sciences.

Although this is the usual organization, there are some interesting exceptions. For example, at Harvard University the Department of Social Relations includes the behavioral scientists who would elsewhere be found in social anthropology, in clinical and social psychology, and in sociology. Harvard also maintains a Laboratory of Social Relations in which and through which a great deal of large-scale social research is conducted. These research projects commonly involve teams of behavioral scientists, each team including faculty members and advanced graduate students. The projects under way are varied in nature and include studies of community change, studies of youth development, of factors influencing social attitudes, and the like.

The University of Chicago provides another example of an unusual pattern of organization. It has organized the graduate faculties of arts and sciences into four main divisions—the physical sciences, the biological sciences, the social sciences, and the humanities. There are also graduate faculties for the professional schools. Both at Harvard and Chicago there are institutes, centers, and committees which have been organized to facilitate study and research which cut across the usual departmental lines.

For example, both universities have centers for the study of human development. At Chicago, psychologists, psychiatrists, anthropologists, sociologists, educators, and pediatricians are engaged in research on the factors influencing the development of children and youth and the problems faced by older people as they move from their fifties and sixties into their seventies and eighties.

Half a dozen American universities have organized laboratories for studies of human learning in which experiments are under way in the teaching and learning of languages, mathematics and science. An increasing number of universities are including behavioral scientists in their schools of medicine and of public health, where they are not only investigating problems of illness and of therapy but are also seeking to understand the social organization of hospitals and of health centers and the ways by which organizations serve to accentuate and to negate efforts of medical and health officers. Some anthropologists and sociologists in these schools are studying the family and community influences upon health and illness. Students preparing to be physicians and health officers are spending part of their time in studying the behavioral sciences, which are increasingly recognized in the United States as among the sciences basic to the practice of medicine and of public health.

Graduate schools of business also employ a number of behavioral scientists on their faculties. They are interested in studying such problems as the human relations of people at work, the influence of working conditions upon mental health and intellectual activity, factors influencing the reception and interpretation of communications, the relation between human desires and economic choices, and the like. The behavioral scientists often include anthropologists, clinical and social psychologists, and sociologists, as well as some economists.

Several universities also have industrial relations centers where psychologists, economists, psychiatrists, sociologists, and political scientists are engaged in the study of personal, psychological, social, and political factors which influence the health, productivity, and attitudes of workers and managers. The two largest of these industrial relations centers are at the University of California and at Cornell University.

Another novel development in several of the universities is the provision of a facility for what is called "survey research." For example, the National Opinion Research Center of the University of Chicago employs a nationwide staff of trained observers and interviewers who are able to make

sample surveys of attitudes, opinions, and other social phenomena which are relevant to the research activities of behavioral scientists from many disciplines. This Center also
provides a place for training advanced graduate students in
the methods of probability sampling, interviewing, and complex analyses of statistical data.

The Columbia University Bureau of Applied Social Research and the Survey Research Center of the University of
Michigan afford facilities for similar purposes for the behavioral scientists of these universities. Also at the University
of Michigan is the Institute of Mental Health Research,
which includes behavioral scientists from several disciplines
and which publishes a new journal, *Behavioral Science*.

These novel ways of organizing the faculties and facilities
of the behavioral sciences are responses to the increasing
specialization among these disciplines combined with the
increasing recognition that human behavior is complex and
involves the interaction of many factors. Productive research
in the behavioral sciences requires both individual efforts and
collaborative efforts.

Adequate training of graduate students in the behavioral
sciences involves opportunity for actual experience in significant research activities, a chance to participate in collaborative investigations as well as to carry on individual
study, and opportunity to develop some of the requisite
specialized technical skills in the collection and analysis of
data. During the last year or two of the student's study for
the Ph.D. in the behavioral sciences he is commonly to be
found engaged in research, often as a junior colleague of
one or more members of the faculty.

Before leaving the subject of the faculty organization in
American colleges and universities it may be of interest to
explain that most academic departments, divisions, committees, and centers are governed by the faculty members
involved.

It is not common in the United States to have a "head

professor." Large departments will usually have from five to twelve full professors, a like number of associate professors, and a larger number of assistant professors and instructors. Small departments will usually have one to three full professors, two or three associate professors, and three to five younger faculty members. The department faculty, with each member having a vote, will commonly select a chairman, who, subject to the dean's or president's approval, serves as the executive officer of the department. Often, the department chairmanship is rotated after three to five years so that several of the faculty members will serve as chairman while they are in the department.

With this type of self-government and without any rigidly set number of faculty members at each level, it has been possible for American universities to expand their faculties without great difficulties when it was necessary to provide for increased numbers of students and increased opportunities for research.

While the behavioral sciences have been expanding in this way, and efforts have been made to improve Ph.D. programs, leading behavioral scientists in America have felt the need for institutionalizing opportunities for further training and education beyond the Ph.D. degree. Their recommendation was adopted by the Board of Trustees of the Ford Foundation which in June, 1952, established the Center for Advanced Study in the Behavioral Sciences by granting funds for its operation and for the construction of buildings on land leased from Stanford University, thirty miles south of San Francisco.

The Center is in an attractive physical setting, looking across San Francisco Bay to the Hamilton range of mountains in a pleasant climate for year-round work. Each year fifty behavioral scientists, forty from the United States and ten from abroad, come to the Center, where they have no responsibilities during the year except to carry on studies of their own choosing. The Center provides two important conditions for advanced study: (1) freedom to devote full time to it and (2) opportunity for free and easy communication with other scholars and scientists interested in similar intellectual problems, persons with whom they have had little previous chance for communication. The Center has no faculty separate from its students; the fifty persons who are awarded fellowships each year are both students and faculty. It is a place for mutual education, in which the Fellows learn from each other as they engage in conversation, comment on each other's writing, participate in small working groups, or engage in more formal seminars.

Since each Fellow is free to undertake studies of most interest to him and to use his time as he sees fit, there is great variation in ways of working. Typically, however, a Fellow will spend each morning in individual study, reading, writing, and thinking, and will spend some of his time on some afternoons each week in communication with other Fellows, informally or in scheduled meetings. Each Fellow has his own study room, opening on to his own patio and yet within easy access to the Center's working library, secretaries, and research assistants.

In addition to the Center for Advanced Study in the Behavioral Sciences there are other opportunities for postdoctoral study by behavioral scientists. Although the primary focus of the Institute for Advanced Study at Princeton, New Jersey, has been upon mathematics and the natural sciences, each year four or five behavioral scientists have been in residence there. Furthermore, several of the large universities have developed post-doctoral programs in fields where their faculties have been unusually strong and have invited mature scholars to join with them in research, in seminars, in lecture programs, and in special training programs devised to develop facility in the use of specialized techniques of investigation in the behavioral sciences.

The financial support of the behavioral sciences within the colleges and universities is largely derived from four sources. The salaries of the faculty members are usually obtained from the normal income of the universities. For the state and municipal institutions the normal income is an appropriation from public funds obtained by state and local taxes. For the private universities the normal income is obtained from endowment, student fees, and current gifts from alumni and other interested donors.

The funds required to carry on research in the behavioral sciences were until 1946 almost wholly obtained from grants made by philanthropic foundations such as the Rockefeller Foundation and the Carnegie Corporation. In 1951, the Ford Foundation began to make large grants in these fields. Since the end of World War II, the federal government has become an increasing supporter of research and so, too, have business corporations. Although the behavioral sciences are relatively new, funds granted for research from these three sources have grown rapidly.

We have been discussing the organization and support of behavioral sciences within the colleges and universities. However, one-third of the American behavioral scientists are employed outside of colleges and universities. Although most of them are engaged in personnel divisions, in consumer research units, and in other applied activities, some are engaged in basic research in the behavioral sciences. These are found in such government agencies as the National Institute of Mental Health, the United States Department of Agriculture, and the Bureau of the Census, or in some of the few nongovernmental research organizations. One of the most noted of these is the RAND Corporation at Santa Monica, California, which has a social science division and one or two other units largely devoted to basic research in the behavioral sciences.

The organization of behavioral scientists on a nationwide basis is accomplished through the professional societies and the Social Science Research Council. The largest of the professional societies among behavioral scientists is the American Psychological Association with about 18,000 members. This Association has headquarters in Washington with a number of fulltime staff members. It provides for annual meetings, for the publication of several psychological journals, for the organization of collaborative study of professional problems, for a psychologists' employment service, and for lobbying in the case of proposed legislation affecting psychologists. The American Sociological Association and the American Anthropological Association perform similar services for their members but since they have fewer members, the services are less elaborate.

The Social Science Research Council was organized after World War I to provide a means for cooperative action of all the social science disciplines on matters relating to research. It maintains a central staff in New York and operates through committees of social scientists. It has been a chief agent for identifying new and significant areas for research in the behavioral sciences and for encouraging and supporting their exploration. It has also been a chief factor in developing high-level research personnel through its pre-doctoral and post-doctoral fellowship programs. Through the Social Science Research Council, the professional societies, and the universities, research in the behavioral sciences has increased many fold in the past twenty years.

However, with this rapid development of research, the publication of research reports has become a problem. The journals of the professional societies in each of the fields do not provide sufficient space. New journals are being founded every year and book publishers are printing many more books devoted to research in the behavioral sciences. The problem of providing for publication is a troublesome one and for the individual scholar the problem of keeping abreast of research reports is serious. Perhaps these problems are inevitable in rapidly developing fields.

In summary, the behavioral sciences are attracting a substantial body of graduate students in American universities so that currently about nine hundred are receiving the Ph.D. degree in these fields each year. Two-thirds of them join the faculties of colleges and universities, some of which devote full time to undergraduate teaching and others of which are organized into departments, institutes, and centers for the pursuit of research and the education of graduate students. One-third of the behavioral scientists are employed in government, business, and philanthropic institutions. With strong professional associations, thriving scholarly journals, and an increasing list of published books, the behavioral scientists have developed in America an active, complex community which is growing at a rapid rate.

3 ANTHROPOLOGY: ITS PRESENT INTERESTS

Cora DuBois

Cora DuBois, Zemmuray-Stone Professor at Radcliffe College in Cambridge, Massachusetts, was born in New York City in 1903. A graduate of Barnard College, Dr. DuBois pursued advanced studies in the field of anthropology at Columbia University and the University of California. A specialist in personality and culture and in political, economic, and social studies of Southeast Asia, she has taught on the faculties of the University of California, Hunter College, Sarah Lawrence College, and Harvard University. From 1945 to 1950 she was in the service of the Department of State and in 1950–1951 served as a consultant to the World Health Organization. She is a past Vice-President of the American Anthropological Association (1949) and is the author of numerous articles and books, including the well-known People of Alor.

American anthropologists consider that their subject properly encompasses the biologic, psychologic, social, and cultural aspects of man. Nothing human is foreign to them. They have embraced enthusiastically and immodestly the literal meaning of the word anthropology—the science of man. Not satisfied with the *science* of man, they honor many in their profession who are avowed humanists.

Anthropology was formulated and acquired its designation in the full flower of late nineteenth century European optimism. To our twentieth century era a single discipline that professes to encompass all things human has a pretentious ring. For the twentieth century has given birth not only to unprecedented potentialities for man's destruction but more importantly, we can only hope, it has given birth to an unprecedentedly specialized and objective interest in man's behavior.

If man survives at all, I suspect that the twentieth century will be just as notable for the development of man's objective interest in himself as for man's mastery of atomic power. Because of this new and vigorous interest in the sciences of man, any discipline that takes humanity for its province is necessarily challenged for its presumption. As the other sciences of man develop their own bodies of specialized knowledge, as the techniques of investigation are both multiplied and refined, not only the relationship between the fields internal to anthropology but also its relationship to fellow disciplines becomes a crucial consideration.

Furthermore, until World War II, American anthropologists concentrated their empiric inquiries predominantly on the non-literate societies of the New World. Since then, and perhaps partly as a reflection of the United States' emergence from political isolation, American anthropologists have widened the scope of their inquiries. Increasingly their field research has taken them to Oceania, Asia, and Africa. In addition they have broadened their interests to include not only the non-literate societies which were their original preoccupation but also to include the high civilizations of the present and the past. The career and the work of the late Professor Robert Redfield at the University of Chicago and particularly his widely read book, *The Primitive World and Its Transformation,* aptly illustrate this broadening of interests in recent American anthropology.

In scanning the broad range of anthropology in the United States, one wonders how the discipline has maintained itself as a single profession in the face of such embracing curiosity which is cross-cut, at the same time, by the pursuit of the most arcane interests.

In sum, how has American anthropology retained its unity in the face of an almost overwhelming diversity?

Let us first consider a partial explanation which is thoroughly American in temper—namely, the matter of numbers.

Probably in no other country are there so many professional anthropologists. To be exact, in 1959 there were 826 accredited Fellows of the American Anthropological Association. Yet compared to the economists, the historians, or the psychologists, whose ranks are counted in the thousands, this is a very small number indeed. It is almost small enough to constitute what the sociologists call a primary group—a group that can meet face to face and know each other on a person-to-person basis. It is true that those of us who belong to the older generation complain that at conferences we no longer recognize the younger men and women (for about 15 per cent of the professional anthropologists in the United States are women). But there *are* conferences—regional and national, specialized and generalized, constantly scheduled and, again in a characteristically American fashion, diligently patronized. We are therefore still something of a guild, each more or less well known to the other.

Also, we have become, let us be frank, rather fashionable of late. This means that our opportunities on the whole are proportionate to our numbers (if not our aspirations). The opportunities for research, teaching, and publication, which are the life blood of a vigorous discipline, are numerous and they are growing about as rapidly as the recruitment of new personnel. The leading professors assume responsibility for finding appropriate positions for their students.

This responsibility serves as an automatic restraint on training more anthropologists than can be employed. Of course, this restraint is not an organized one. It is a covert and indirect process. But as any anthropologist knows, covert processes can be quite as effective as overt ones. The net effect is that a rough balance exists between the training and the placement of professionals. This situation reduces that bitter rivalry for a limited number of posts which existed at the beginning of the century in the United States and that still exists in countries where the challenging potentialities of anthropology are recognized by young scholars but where the institutional provisions to support them are still limited.

In sum, the first, partial explanation of unity in American

anthropology today is a sociological one and rests on a benign conjunction: on the one hand, numbers not too large to debar personal contacts and responsibilities and, on the other hand, public recognition adequate to provide opportunities.

This sociological explanation is consistent with a second and educational one: namely, the consensus that seems to exist about the training of *professional* anthropologists. Such a statement will undoubtedly astonish those foreigners who have even a casual acquaintance with American education. Possibly in no other nation is education so diversified philosophically, so decentralized administratively, so differentiated in curricula, and so unequal in quality. Nevertheless, in some twelve leading graduate departments of anthropology (to name them would be invidious), it is generally agreed that a doctoral candidate in anthropology should be well grounded in one of the internal fields and should also have generalized knowledge and a sense of problem in the other constituent fields.

For example, if a graduate student specializes in anthropological linguistics, he is expected to have also a general grasp of world ethnology and of pre-history; he should know the history and theory not only of his specialty but also, in broad terms, of social and cultural anthropology; he must not be totally ignorant of the relationship of psychology and sociology to language.

But also, just at this point, professionalism in American anthropology is reinforced by insistence on a paramount training experience: field work in a different culture. We firmly believe that the educational experience of living with, and objectively studying, a people markedly different from one's own, has intellectual and emotional impacts not easily duplicated by even the most empathic study of books.

Field work has this further effect. It inevitably faces the field worker with a mass of facts. He becomes something of a naturalist: collecting, classifying, and generalizing a wide range of data. However specialized and technical his final publications may be, he must first become an amateur of another way of life (and I use the word amateur in its French sense—"a lover of"—not in the English sense of "a superficial fellow"). Cross-cultural field work is for each anthropologist, furthermore, a re-introduction to the roots of his discipline, which lie in the natural sciences rather than the social sciences.

However, let us return to pick up the threads of our argument. We are considering why the very broad interests of American anthropology still remain within a vigorously unified discipline. First, I suggested one perhaps temporary explanation, namely, that the present relationship between the number of professional anthropologists and the opportunities available to them is optimal. Secondly, I suggested an educational reason, namely, the general agreement that exists on how to train professionals.

But, much more importantly, there is also agreement on basic assumptions. The assumptions common to our profession are, first, the comparative approach; second, holism; and third, the equal value given both synchronic and diachronic studies.

Let us examine each briefly and in turn.

First, the comparative approach. This is the assumption that all data must be seen in the perspective of other data belonging to the same universe of discourse. This view holds true even when a scholar specializes in the description or analysis of a single community or a single topical interest. Whether or not a particular research worker engages in explicit comparisons, the very fact that he has been trained to cross-cultural sensitivities and that he is usually dealing with a culture other than his own gives him a background for making comparisons. He sees the implications of his topic or of his community in these terms.

There was a period in the 1930's and 1940's when relativism was rampant. And by relativism is meant that each society or culture is considered so unique, so particular, that, logically at least, comparisons are inhibited. How can one compare unique phenomena? During those decades emphasis was placed primarily on functional relationships and on the consistency of patterns within one society. Although the assumption that comparisons were important was never abandoned, the practice of making them was in large part neglected. Emphasis was placed instead on the unique and the contextual. The search for internal coherence between institutions, or coherence between individual psychology and social form, or the coherence between belief and behavior all within a single and often arbitrarily defined unit was the fashion of the period. This emphasis was important. Valuable contributions resulted from it.

However, pushed too far, and at the expense of comparisons, such preoccupations can have also sterile implications. Today there is a corrective swing of the pendulum. Underlying all research, however specialized in time, space, or subject matter, there is now general agreement that the ultimate goal of anthropology is to recognize in human behavior, in social institutions, and in cultural beliefs what is universal, what is only probable, and what is unique.

The second unifying concept is holism. Holism is the assumption that, within any one society, behavior, institutions, and beliefs are to a greater or lesser extent integrated, that they are functionally linked one to another. It was, of course, the acceptance of this assumption, in its most extreme form, that precipitated the era of arch-relativism that we have just mentioned.

Now that a balance is being re-established between the importance of comparisons and the significance of holism, the apparent contradictions between these assumptions can be overcome. Thus, Whiting at Harvard is interested in comparing the relationship between certain child-rearing practices and varieties of religious beliefs in widely different cultures carefully selected for their contrasts. Nevertheless, he is concerned that the topics between which he is trying to find consistent linkages shall not be misconstrued by being studied out of the context of the whole society in which they lodge. In other words, anthropologists generally agree that societies are to a greater or lesser extent integrated and that the search for such linkages within any society is of equal importance with comparisons between societies. Both comparison between, and integration within, societies are major and significant goals for research.

The third commonly held view in American anthropology is that both synchronic and diachronic approaches are legitimate modes of inquiry. Generalizations that rest on timeless cross-sections of data and generalizations that rest on regularities of process through time are not considered mutually exclusive. Rather, they represent different strategies of research that depend on the problem posed. The two modes of attack, to the extent that they are accurate, can only reinforce each other.

However, it must be noted that there are also many American anthropologists working with time sequences who see their task as essentially historical. They view each developmental sequence as unique. Such investigators are respected members of the profession. The debate between history and science, between generalizing and abstracting, certainly exists in American anthropology but it is largely a sterile debate, since the empiricism that informs us ultimately requires that there be no discrepancy between the generalizations of history and the abstractions of science. The debate between historical and scientific approaches becomes essentially one of predilection for one or another method of approach and cannot, in the long run, fragment the broader goals of anthropological inquiry.

Having stressed the unifying assumptions in American anthropology, it may be interesting to sample, for it can be no more than a sample, some of the emerging trends and some of the issues in debate.

First, as I have indicated already, humanistic and historical interests are very much alive in American anthropology. Any appraisal that failed to stress those aspects of anthropology would give an impoverished picture of the discipline. The vigorous young society of ethnomusicology is only a case in point. In the same vein, there is an increasing interest among the younger anthropologists in the development and comparison of art traditions as *styles* rather than techniques. The historical interests have just been mentioned in the context of diachronic studies.

Since the old ethnographic interest in historical reconstruction based on distributional studies has been largely abandoned, it is archaeology that today provides the chief focus and valid methodologies for historical interests in American anthropology. The proliferation of techniques for dating, from dendrochronology to Carbon 14, are only examples of the technical ingenuity and specialization required by this essentially historical field. As work progresses, the general outlines of New World history, that must be reconstructed without the help of written documents, is emerging with greater and greater clarity from approximately 12,-000 B.C. to the present. The ethno-historian links his ethnographic and documentary findings to those of the archaeologist, to the mutual enrichment of both specialties.

The linguists who for several decades have been primarily preoccupied with achieving descriptive elegance and precision at the phonemic and morphemic levels of analysis have nevertheless not neglected the genetic aspects of language. Probably nowhere has a genetically, and therefore historically, based classification of unwritten languages gone farther than for the North American Indians.

But if historical interests are still very much alive and respected in various fields of American anthropology, so also is the interest in evolution—both human biologic evolution and socio-cultural evolution. For example, the Anthropological Society of Washington recently published *Evolution and Anthropology: A Centennial Appraisal.* It is a series of papers that attest to the vigor of theoretical debate on this score.

Naturally, the broad theory of *biologic* evolution has always been accepted. But biological anthropologists like Spuhler and Washburn are challenging a long-held dogma that the human organism has been essentially static since the development of culture and are advancing ingenious new arguments for the selective force of culture itself. In broadest terms, they argue that cultural selection may have operated just as potently as natural selection in the physical development of homo sapiens and his first tool-using forebears.

In socio-cultural realms, Leslie White has doggedly held aloft the doctrine of cultural evolution against attack and neglect. For many years, support came primarily from the work of that great pre-historian, V. Gordon Childe, and from the Russian school with its devotion to Morgan, who was, somewhat ironically, an American cultural evolutionist of the nineteenth century. Today, far more interested and tolerant attention is given to White's views. Rephrased as the steady accumulation of man's command over new sources of energy, and thus over his environment, cultural evolution is an acceptable high-level generalization for which Julian Steward has suggested the term "universal evolution."

Steward, on the other hand, is interested in neither unilinear cultural evolution of the nineteenth century nor in universal evolution advanced by White and others, but in what he terms "multilinear evolution." He proposes to isolate several historically independent cases in which the gradual mastery of the physical environment has resulted in population increases, which in turn resulted in closely analogous socio-political solutions. His view of multilinear evolution might be re-phrased as the diachronic study of parallel developmental processes. In archaeology, Willey and Phillips, while specifically rejecting any evolutionary implications, have also proposed sequences of development in New World archaeology which suggest, at a middle range of generalization, comparable parallel developmental sequences.

Both the historic interest and the evolutionary debates now afoot in American anthropology are balanced by a series of very different and non-historical preoccupations. In the field of social organization, the French sociologists Durkheim and Mauss and the German sociologist Weber are much in fashion. Theoretic sociology and social organization in anthropology are increasingly interrelated. For example, the systematic and provocative "theory of social action" being constructed in sociology by Talcott Parsons and his collaborators presents social anthropology with a series of new insights, of new analytic distinctions, and of new research problems that the present generation of American anthropologists will certainly not quickly exhaust. Parsons, in proposing that the individual, the society, and the culture are separate but interacting systems, opens new ways of formulating inquiries into isomorphic processes.

On a far less sweeping theoretical level, the very specialized and traditional problems that spring primarily from a preoccupation with kinship, and that have been so highly developed in the United Kingdom, continue to engage young American anthropologists. Many of them find the specialization in kinship and social structure pursued in English universities a congenial counter-poise to the theoretical indeterminism and the sometimes bewildering breadth of American graduate training.

Yet, despite the long and intensive study of kinship, there is still much to be done, particularly in the realm of the non-unilinear systems. Sahlin's work on Polynesia, Goodenough's on Micronesia, or Homans' and Schneider's work on the United States attest to a continuing interest, within American anthropology, in the growing edge of a traditional concern for kinship organization and, particularly, for questions of non-unilinear kinship systems.

The very nature of such analyses leads into the fields of

comparative jurisprudence and political science. These raise questions about the nature of authority and bring into focus the structure and function of role, status, and rank. The traditional preoccupation with social organization in American anthropology has fructified and is being fructified by a growing interest in the comparative approach among young political scientists and students of law. Even the economists, the most self-contained of the social scientists, are beginning, in conjunction with social anthropologists, to re-examine their assumptions and generalizations to determine which may be universal and which are peculiar to the Western economic situation that has primarily preoccupied them.

Just as the narrowly based approach to social organization through the analysis of kinship systems has opened new and unsuspected horizons of inquiry, so too in linguistics the decades of preoccupation with descriptive elegance are now broadening into more probing questions. A case in point is the revival of interest in the Whorf-Sapir hypothesis, which suggests that how one perceives the world is largely shaped by the language one speaks. At this point, the psycho-linguists have leapt into the fray, hoping to bridge the gap between the psychologists' concern with learning and perception and the anthropological linguists' renewed interest in semantics.

Meanwhile, the Kluckhohns and their colleagues have gone far in the comparative study of cultural value systems. This has led to new insights about the ties between psychology and philosophy on the one hand, and religion, ethics, and art on the other. Similarly, those first crude attempts to relate psychology and anthropology that received the blanket designation of personality and culture, are now achieving more precise formulations. Those broad and non-analytic notions of personality and of culture are acquiring more rigorous methods for their investigation, and in the process more convincing theoretical formulations.

It is a truism that the more one knows, the greater the number of new problems that emerges. In all this ferment almost any young and vigorous intellect may hew out new fields of research, particularly in the neglected problem areas that exist between established academic disciplines.

I shall not discuss two important and perhaps antithetical tendencies in American anthropology: at one extreme the theoretical preoccupation with models and at the other extreme the interest in the application of anthropology to practical problems. Other papers in this series will discuss theory and application for the behavioral sciences as a whole.

In conclusion, this view of American anthropology cannot presume to represent fully, or do full justice to, all my colleagues in the United States. A brief summary is not enough for exhaustive catalogues or for the fine points that preoccupy scholars concerned with widening the horizons of our knowledge of man.

The fundamental points I wish to make about American anthropology today are, first, the breadth of interpretation inherent in their common assumptions and agreements; second, the diversity of specialization; and third, the respect for such diversity that allows for new fields of inquiry, new theorizing, and for application. Indeed, no other position seems tenable for a discipline whose horizons are so wide and whose findings must be judged still so tentative.

Today, in the morality both of science and of life (for they are essentially one) those who love certitude do not love truth. A tolerance of uncertainty, and yet the constant struggle against it, is the essence of an open society and of a vigorous science.

4 PSYCHOLOGY: ITS PRESENT INTERESTS

Ernest R. Hilgard

Ernest R. Hilgard, Professor of Psychology at Stanford University, was born in Belleville, Illinois, in 1904. A graduate of the University of Illinois and Yale University, where he received his doctorate, Dr. Hilgard was an instructor in psychology at Yale before joining the faculty of Stanford University in 1933. A specialist in the fields of motivation, learning, and psychodynamics, he has taught at Stanford for the past thirty years, during which time he has been Executive Head of the Department of Psychology (1942–1951) and the Dean of the Graduate Division (1951–1955). Dr. Hilgard is a former President of the American Psychological Association (1948), and is a member of the National Academy of Sciences. He has written and co-authored numerous articles and books, including Theories of Learning, Psychoanalysis as Science, *and his well-received textbook,* Introduction to Psychology.

Psychology is a young and growing science. The first generation of laboratory psychologists, trained under Wilhelm Wundt in Leipzig, are now largely gone, but their students are still alive and active, so that psychology's origins remain in the memories of living people. We have with us today those who were students of Janet and of Freud, of James and McDougall, of Titchener and of Angell. But their lifetimes have seen an enormous expansion of the struggling little science that they pioneered.

The American Psychological Association has been growing at the rate of about 10 per cent a year—a growth which, like compound interest, has caused its expansion from 3,000 members in 1940 to nearly 20,000 now. Similar growth of psychology is occurring elsewhere in the world. For example, the Japanese Psychological Association now numbers 2,000 members, and its July, 1959, meetings had 500 papers on the program. While my remarks will deal primarily with American psychology, the field of psychology, like that of other sciences, knows no national boundaries, and what happens in one part of the world influences what takes place elsewhere.

International collaboration is furthered by an International Union of Scientific Psychology. An International Directory of Psychologists was published in 1958 to facilitate communication between psychologists all over the world. While obviously incomplete, the directory includes some 7,000 names of psychologists living outside the United States. With this growth the complexion of psychology has been changing. From a profession mainly serving colleges and universities, psychology has now become much more diversified, with half or more of the psychologists in America now serving in hospitals and clinics, business and industry, or government agencies, or self-employed as practicing psychologists.

The definition of a psychologist is not easy. Abstract definitions of psychology such as "the science of mental activity," or "the science of the behavior of men and animals in their environment" fail to convey the richness of psychological activities and fail also to distinguish between psychology and other related biological and social sciences. A 1955 poll of "elder statesmen" in psychology on the question of what defines a psychologist showed a general agreement on the pragmatic grounds that the definition had to be historical and social. That is, psychologists come to be recognized as such by each other and by their colleagues in other fields. Their interests may drift and may overlap with the interests of those in other fields, but they continue to attend the national meetings of their own association, write for psychological journals, teach courses called psychology.

This complex process yields a subject matter, a set of methods, and, to some extent, a common outlook. One problem of maintaining identity is to hold to a sense of common purpose without requiring the restraints of conformity to precedent. The present appears healthy in this respect; there are many strains owing to diversity, but not too much difficulty in knowing who is accepted as being a psychologist. The American Psychological Association with twenty-two different divisions is, of course, a big help in this social definition.

Any effort to locate psychology with precision among the various disciplines will show its strong affiliations with biological and social sciences and its weak relationship to the humanities.

The biological side is clear in the work done with lower organisms (comparative psychology) and in the work on neurophysiological problems with both lower animals and man (physiological psychology). One of the official journals published by the American Psychological Association is called the *Journal of Comparative and Physiological Psychology*. The professional relationships with medicine are close (especially in clinical psychology) and medicine is of course strongly biological in its emphasis. Psychology is accepted in the National Academy of Sciences and its National Research Council as a biological science. It is recognized as a biological science also in the National Science Foundation, and psychology majors are eligible for National Science Fellowships.

The social science side is equally clear, with psychologists at work on attitude and opinion studies, election predictions, and group dynamics. Another of the official journals is the *Journal of Abnormal and Social Psychology*. In this capacity psychology is represented as one of the family of social sciences in the Social Science Research Council. Its students are permitted to compete for special fellowships as social scientists and for the social support of the National Science Foundation.

The biological-social division is not really a sharp cleavage. Child psychology, clinical psychology, educational psychology, industrial psychology, have both their biological and social aspects; any one psychologist may act in the role of biological or social scientist, either in alternation or at once.

The relationship to the humanistic disciplines is less close, probably because of the psychologist's preoccupation with the methods of natural science and the still-too-recent divorce from philosophy. Nevertheless psychologists study esthetics, language (psycholinguistics, communication), values, and meanings. It is to be hoped that some of the beginning rapprochements with humanistic studies now taking place may be extended.

If we accept the historical process as defining a psychologist, we must be prepared to find psychology (and psychologists!) changing with the years. Institutional arrangements must remain flexible enough to accommodate these changes. The laboratory for the study of lifted weights may give way to a rat colony; the room once full of chronoscopes may give way to a modern high-speed computer; the rat colony may be displaced by a nursery school. The new may merely add to, rather than displace, the old.

In order to gain a little perspective on contemporary psychology it will be worthwhile to take a brief view of the history of topics that have interested psychology.

The break with philosophy came in the latter part of the nineteenth century when a number of Americans came back from Leipzig with Ph.D.s under Wilhelm Wundt. The first chair of psychology was created in 1888 at the University of Pennsylvania for one of these, J. McKeen Cattell. The early laboratories that sprouted in the next few years were concerned chiefly with sensory thresholds, reaction time, emotion, and memory. While in fact a number of other topics were touched upon from the start, the main problem was to prove that a laboratory science was possible. This was amply demonstrated, although some questioned what all the experiments added up to.

Alongside this experimental psychology there were developments in almost all the other branches as we know them now—studies in childhood and adolescence; in abnormal, clinical, and social psychology; in educational psychology. Stanley Hall invited Freud to lecture at Clark University in 1909—Freud's first solid academic recognition. But problems suited to the experimental laboratory—including the animal laboratory—tended to define the central interests of the official psychology.

World War I broadened psychology by drawing the most vigorous psychologists into the war effort, where, called upon to develop tests and to validate various devices, many of them learned statistics for the first time. The public acceptance of the intelligence test was very important, and individual differences became a respectable topic within the core of psychology. After World War I, there came the flurry of tests and test theories, including the developments within factor analysis.

World War II gave a second forward boost to psychology. If World War I may be said to have launched ability testing, World War II promoted clinical and social psychology on the one hand, and human engineering on the other.

Within clinical psychology we had the enormous development of interest in projective tests, personality assessment, psychodynamics, and psychotherapy. The Veterans Administration and the National Institute of Mental Health seized upon these developments and subsidized training centers for clinical psychologists and the equivalent of fellowships for trainees, thus expanding the facilities and the clientele.

The best-known of the social psychological developments are those in the survey field (consumer surveys, voting studies, attitude-opinion studies) and studies of group dynamics, leading more recently to what is called "small-group research."

Human engineering tended to draw psychologists from the fields of sensory psychology and learning—the "pure science" fields that had held themselves somewhat aloof from applications. They liked the expression "applied experimental psychology" better than the older "applied psychology." The older industrial psychology had fitted man to machine; the newer human engineering designs the machine with the human operator in mind. Now the psychologist helps not only in selection and training but in "trouble-shooting" (diagnosing and repairing defective equipment), and in designing dials, headphones, radar screens.

All of this took a little settling down after the war. The record had to be written down (nineteen volumes on psychology in the air forces, four volumes on the social-psychological studies in the army, and a number of others), and textbook writers adapted the materials for instructional purposes. Some disillusionment set in; things that seemed very exciting in the heat of war no longer seemed quite as exciting. Some of the promising leads turned out not to hold up very well when carefully tested. But much of the substance remains.

By about 1950 the settling down had taken place and some new ways of looking at things and some new topics began to emerge. This is such recent history that it is hard to evaluate it, and my selection may turn out not to be entirely representative. Nevertheless, I use it to illustrate somewhat more concretely the present interests of psychologists.

I shall discuss briefly five topics: physiological processes; learning; motivation; cognitive processes; and clinical psychology.

Physiological processes. For a time, especially in the 1930's, there was a kind of declaration of independence of physiology, as there had earlier been from philosophy. No matter whether the brain acts like a telephone switchboard, a television circuit, or a gelatinous sponge, so it was argued, habits will still be acquired as they are now acquired, sensory thresholds will be what they are, and memory functions will remain as we know them. Let us set the problems for the neurophysiologists to solve; we are ahead of them now, and we can wait for them to catch up before we go ahead. There is a measure of truth in this position, of course. One science need not wait for another. There is enough independence for each to go ahead on its own. Yet there may be interconnections that will facilitate the advance of both.

About 1950 many psychologists began to renew their interest in physiology. Hebb's influential book on the organization of behavior appeared in 1949. While highly speculative, it made a good deal of sense and proposed a kind of neuropsychology that offered promise. A number of exciting developments have taken place in neurophysiology itself. A new hormone, noradrenaline, has made interesting again the differences between fear and anger. The whole vegetative brain is being reworked, under such titles as "the limbic system." The "general adaptation syndrome" calls attention to responses to stress. A new arousal mechanism, via the reticular formation, makes possible new interpretations of sleep, waking, and energetic action. Efferents in sensory nerves modulating afferent processes make the physiology of sensation of renewed interest. The discovery of what may be a "pleasure center" in the brain fits in with an emerging neo-hedonism.

Let me illustrate this somewhat more concretely. If very small electrodes are implanted deep in the brain of a laboratory rat, in what is known as the septal area, the animal can wear them continuously without any apparent discomfort. If now the opportunity is given for the rat to shock himself by way of these electrodes, he will actually seek out opportunities to shock himself! This work, originally done by Olds and Milner, suggests that there may be "pleasure centers" in the brain as well as "pain centers." A curious supplementary finding by Miller and his collaborators is that there is a satiation effect, so that an animal that shocks itself (apparently to receive some kind of sought-after stimulation) will a little later take the opportunity to *reduce* the stimulation.

Such experiments obviously have relevance for other aspects of brain function, as in the affective disorders.

Other physiological developments, such as those in pharmacology, with the new tranquilizers and psychotomimetic drugs, have aroused additional interest of behavioral scientists. So within a few years the pendulum has swung again, and physiology is now of immensely increased interest to psychologists.

Learning. The psychology of learning has been an ascendant field of interest in psychology ever since William James gave prominence to the concept of habit, but more particularly following the work of Thorndike and Watson early in this century. The careful systematic formulations of Hull, with exciting controversies stirred up with Tolman, Lashley, Köhler, and others, have given this topic unusual prominence during the last twenty-five years. Interest in learning continues unabated, although the complexities that have turned up have now diverted more interest to motivation and other related topics.

One of the developments within learning theory, the use of mathematical models, reflects a trend toward the greater use of mathematics in all of the behavioral sciences. During and after World War II, psychologists began to share with the sociologists more complex scaling methods (e.g., Guttman's scalograms); they began to use the games-theory model of the economists and decision-theory models of political scientists; they took over information theory from communication theorists and cyberneticists; and on their own, sometimes with the help of borrowed mathematicians and physicists, they developed stochastic (i.e., probabilistic) learning models of a high order of ingenuity and complexity.

Nobody can yet tell just where all of this is going, but a young psychologist who wants to know what is happening in his field will be excluded from much of it if he cannot read literature using the nomenclature of probability and of the modern mathematics known as set theory and matrix algebra. The journal articles are not merely games with mathematics; nearly all of them use the data from experiments in order to determine whether or not there is a "fit" between the data and the model.

Motivation. While motivation has always interested some psychologists, the approach to the topic shifts, and as it shifts psychologists of different background and persuasion pick it up. For a time, early in the century, the problems of *instinct* were studied; later *drives* induced by deprivation (especially hunger, thirst, sex) came under study; the psychoanalysts contributed *anxiety* and *guilt* as motivators. The new developments, since about 1950, include such topics as the influences of needs and values on perception, perceptual defense, the expression of motives in fantasy (e.g., the achievement motive revealed in stories told about pictures), neglected drives (exploration, curiosity, manipulation, frustration-induced drives), verbally expressed values, and value systems. Another development is that of anxiety scales as related to conditioning and other forms of learning. These newer topics have brought a fresh examination of many motivational processes, signalized in part by the annual volumes of the Nebraska Symposium on Motivation.

The topic of motivation is so broad that psychologists have become uneasy about it. But this very uneasiness is a sign that the subject matter is being taken seriously. An interesting illustration of the complexities of motivational phenomena is provided by a recent book by Schachter called *The Psychology of Affiliation.* It is concerned with an old motivational problem: why people are gregarious, why they seek each other's company. He finds that when anxiety is aroused people often reduce this anxiety by seeking the company of other people sharing their anxiety. In other words, misery loves the company of other miserable people. The data become exceedingly complex. It turns out that there is a consistent relationship, for example, to birth order, the eldest child being both more anxious than the later-born and more eager to seek the company of others when anxious. Turning to alcohol appears to have an opposite relationship:

more alcoholics come from the later-born children. Thus the problems of motivation get tied up with parent-child relationships and with social psychology in an interesting manner.

Cognitive processes. The so-called higher mental processes (i.e., thinking, creating, problem-solving) have been subjected to renewed study by a great variety of methods. An old set of topics, they nevertheless proved resistant in the past to systematic study. As psychologists have gained in confidence they have again begun to study language and thinking, meanings, concepts, and values, risking failure to do anything significant, but determined to make the effort to succeed. The methods include those of factor analysis, group and individual experimentation, comparative studies of animals, children, and adults. Personality and motivational influence are assessed with intellectual capacities. Studies are done in applied contexts (e.g., "trouble-shooting") as well as in the laboratory.

Clinical psychology. Among the several fields of application of psychology to problems of social welfare, clinical psychology has a unique place both because of its importance and because of its rapid development since World War II. More narrowly defined, clinical psychology relates to research and practice in diagnosing mental or emotional disturbances, in treating illnesses with psychological causes, and in studying causal factors, prevention, and the promise of cure. I call this the narrow definition because the emphasis is upon illness. (The word "clinical" implies illness, as it does in clinical medicine.) Many clinical psychologists are, in fact, associated with clinics and hospitals dealing with the mentally ill. A broader conception of clinical psychology includes, however, practices enhancing mental health, so that some clinical psychologists use their training in connection with vocational adjustment, marital counseling, and so on, where the question of mental illness need not arise.

The practical tools of the clinical psychologist fall chiefly

47

into two classes: psychological tests and procedures of psychotherapy. In addition to these practical tools there are, of course, the research tools of experimental and statistical methods, as well as the methods of family history studies and population surveys.

In the team of workers concerned with mental health and mental illness the psychologist affiliates himself primarily with psychiatrists and social workers. While many roles are shared in common, his main contribution often comes from his training in quantitative research methods.

If one were to characterize the research activities of clinical psychologists today he would arrive at some such classification as the following. First, the development and standardization of various tests for understanding personality differences and for diagnosing personality difficulties. These include some question-and-answer tests, in which the client or patient reports his difficulties or troubles, and also the so-called projective tests, in which the person "gives himself away" in a more subtle fashion, by telling what he sees in an ink-blot (as in the Rorschach test) or by inventing a story to fit a picture (as in the Thematic Apperception Test).

A second class of activities would include the study of the process of psychotherapy, both in the individual relation of a patient and therapist and in the group relationship in which several patients participate at once in psychotherapy. One of the distinctively American contributions to this process is that method developed by the psychologist Carl Rogers, known as "client-centered therapy." However, a variety of methods are under study.

A third class of activities would be the study of causal factors, especially those in early childhood, leading to difficulties later on. These studies include child-rearing practices (nursing, toilet-training, punishment), the effects of parent loss and separation from the parents, rivalry among brothers and sisters, and so on. Other studies concern the effects of brain lesions, hormones, and drugs. These illustrations are mere suggestions of the many things going on.

These examples of the changes brought by two wars and by an exciting postwar period suggest that psychology has not yet settled down. Perhaps it never will settle down. Instead there may be cycles of interest in which old questions again get asked because of fresh approaches to their answers, while other questions, still unanswered, are temporarily no longer asked. Such a cycle of emphasis and de-emphasis can conceivably go on for many years, as it has, in fact, gone on in sciences better established than psychology.

So much of modern psychology rests in the twentieth century that it is perhaps fair to say that psychology is just coming of age. To some extent the vigor and excitement of the profession during World War II and the early postwar years completed psychology's adolescence, and the sober re-thinking of the 1950's and 1960's, wiser but a little less confident, represents the beginning of adulthood. Laws respecting the title of psychologist and the practice of psychology are beginning to be passed in many of the states. This is a recognition that the psychologist is someone the public knows and that psychological services are here to stay.

The big advance for psychology as a science has been to achieve an objective approach that is at the same time comprehensive. An unwise adherence to operational and probabilistic notions (replacing the earlier mechanistic ones) could have led to sterility. Instead they have been used to domesticate Freud's quaint metaphors, to make possible the collaboration between ethologists and comparative psychologists, to further rapport between anthropologists and psychologists. This tolerant acceptance of subject matter coming from a variety of sources is healthful, especially because of the serious efforts being made all along to cast the new problems into scientific form.

The major forward surges of psychology have not come

in the form of "discoveries"; the gain has been, rather, in achieving a stance toward our problems that gives hope of future progress. Our tools are sharper because of the contributions from many fields; stimulus controls, vacuum tubes, photographic recording, electromagnetic tape, survey methods, statistical and mathematical advances.

The background figures from the nineteenth and early twentieth century fade somewhat as we study present gains, yet there they are, and their influences are still perceptible. William James and G. Stanley Hall gave psychology a certain robust quality that still suits the American temper. Fechner contributed psychophysics, Pavlov conditioning, Galton and Binet the study of individual differences, Freud the dynamic conception of personality.

Contemporary American psychology, because of the diverse streams of historical influences upon it, has an eclectic character, so that one coming upon it from outside must be confused by the diversity of interests and theories within American psychology.

What unity exists can be attributed, at least in part, to a common logic of science. This is the logic that scientific disputes can be arbitrated by an appeal to objective facts—objective in the sense that the relationships can be reproduced or observed by other competent people who do not share the initial biases of the one who first calls attention to the facts. The pragmatic tradition of William James and John Dewey, in the form of modern positivism or operationism, can cover both the "pure science" and the practical interests of American psychologists. The extreme objectivism of the behaviorism of John B. Watson had its useful influence as a background for the more tempered objectivism of the present. Thus both the biologically oriented and the socially oriented psychologists see themselves as in the natural science tradition, in which the search for new and communicable information is equivalent to the search for truth. This common stance, rather than leading all psychologists to do similar things, provides for a tolerance of diversity. Out of this diversity it is hoped that new knowledge may be forthcoming that will help man to understand himself and come nearer to a solution of his problems.

5 SOCIOLOGY: ITS PRESENT INTERESTS

Harry Alpert

Harry Alpert, Dean of the Graduate School at the University of Oregon, was born in New York City in 1912. A specialist in research methodology, social psychology, and inter-relations of the natural and social sciences, Dr. Alpert took his academic training at the College of the City of New York, the University of Bordeaux, France, and Columbia University. He has taught on the faculties of the College of the City of New York, Yale University, Queens College, the American University, and the University of Washington. He is a former President of the American Association for Public Opinion Research (1955) and is the author of many articles and books, including Emile Durkheim and His Sociology.

To George Bernard Shaw is attributed the remark that America's youth is its oldest tradition. The observation is applicable with equal cogency to sociology, the science of society. Many of the limitations of sociology are frequently excused on the ground that it is a very young discipline. And, indeed, as scientific studies go, sociology is quite youthful: just 120 years old, if we may date its origin, somewhat arbitrarily, from the first appearance of the newly-coined word "sociology" in the forty-seventh chapter of Auguste Comte's *The Positive Philosophy*. Comte invented this barbaric cognomen in order to designate by a specialized name the scientific study of the fundamental laws of social phenomena.

Although sociology had its birth in the nineteenth century, chiefly in response to the immediate practical requirements of social reconstruction and societal amelioration, its major contemporary features—rigorous methodology, empirical emphasis, behavioral orientation, and conceptual consciousness—are largely a product of the past half-century.

In terms of its present interests, sociology may be defined as the scientific study of society, its structure, functions, and processes. In this over-all view of the discipline, I shall attempt to identify the general areas of sociological concern and comment briefly on selected specialized fields of sociological inquiry. Some of these special fields will be described in greater detail in later papers in this series.

In the broadest sense, sociology studies society in terms of its structure, organization, change, and relation to environment. Professor Robert M. MacIver's definition of the field is a useful formulation of the major interests of this discipline. "Sociology seeks to discover the principles of cohesion and of order within the social structure, the ways in which it roots and grows within an environment, the moving equilibrium of changing structure and changing environment, the main trends of this incessant change and the forces which determine its direction at any time, the harmonies and conflicts, the adjustments and maladjustments within the structure as they are revealed in the light of human desires, and thus the practical application of means to ends in the creative activities of social man."

As a scientific discipline, sociology may be divided into three broad, analytical fields: the study of groups; institutional analysis; and the study of social structure in general.

Group analysis is currently one of the fields of research in which sociologists are most active. Social groups are viewed as individuals regularly in contact or communication who, for certain purposes, identify themselves with each other. Small intimate groups may range from a family to a play group or a neighborhood. To distinguish such groups from larger and less closely associated aggregates, such as an urban community, some sociologists use the terms primary and secondary. Other sociologists have developed the concept of quasi-group to cover social classes, publics, and other aggregates or portions of the community which have no recognizable structure, but whose members have certain interests or modes of behavior in common which may at any time lead them to form themselves into definite groups. The nature and types of social groupings, the bases of group formation, the processes of group cohesion, the conditions of group action, and the structure and patterns of intergroup relations are among the major problems with which this area of sociology is concerned.

Suggestive ideas have been developed in analysis of group behavior from a consideration of the way in which members of the same group regard each other as against all outsiders. This in-group versus out-group distinction has supplied clues to the understanding of intergroup relations. The concepts, first formulated by William Graham Sumner in his famous *Folkways,* refer to the fact that group relations affect ethical judgments and ways of thinking. Thus, a particular action by a member of one's own political party will be viewed as an excusable error, while the same act by a member of the opposition is deemed to be a gross betrayal of trust. An extreme form of group attitude is represented by ethnocentrism, which is the view of things in which one's own group is the center of everything and all others are scaled with reference to it.

But ethnocentrism is only one aspect of the process by which groups develop conceptions of themselves and of others. Group images, that is, the typical mental pictures that members have of themselves and others, serve to define their relations to one another and play an important part in determining the nature of intergroup contacts. In this connection, the study of stereotypes or fixed mental images is especially important.

Social groups have also been analyzed as "sifting devices" whereby people in a large urban population are organized in associations having recognized positions of prestige or power, such as churches, exclusive clubs, or boards of directors. The role of groups in determining the status and power structure of modern American communities is effectively presented in the *Yankee City* series directed by Professor W. Lloyd Warner. Professor Robert S. Lynd, among others, has analyzed power relations in American society, but in general the study of who belongs to what, for what reason, and with what effect is still in its early stages.

Recent research on industrial morale, clique behavior, voting behavior, consumer buying, sociometric patterns, and group dynamics has tended to reaffirm the sociological conception of the influential character of the small, direct, face-to-face group and has increased understanding of the nature of interpersonal relations in the small group. Professor Paul F. Lazarsfeld and his associates at Columbia University have made significant contributions in this area.

Institutions are a second major field of sociological interest. Institutions are variously defined by the different social sciences, but the accent among sociologists is on an organized system of practices and actions and the machinery evolved to maintain the system of rules or norms of expected behavior. Institutions are seen as established, determinate forms in accordance with which men enter into relations with one another. The major social institutions such as marriage, kinship, law, property, education, religion, recreation, welfare, art, science, health, government, warfare, and political and economic institutions are the subject of specialized sociological disciplines (sociology of law, sociology of religion, sociology of art, sociology of the family, and so forth).

Among the numerous ideas that have developed from institutional analysis, the following five may be singled out for special mention: the persistence of certain basic institutions like the family as universal features of social organization; the transference and shifting of functions over time from one institution to another, such as the transfer of welfare functions from the family to the state; the interdependence of institutions so that changes in one create changes in others; the operation of a principle of congeniality or a "strain towards consistency" among institutions in a given society;

and the operation of a principle of institutional inertia, or the tendency of institutions to persist through organization for self-perpetuation.

In addition to a specific concern with particular social groups and institutions, sociologists study the over-all framework within which groups and institutions function, namely society itself. Society may be viewed as the whole complex of social behavior and the total network of social relations. An especially fruitful area of investigation has been the analysis of the nature of the social bond, the modes and types of social cohesion or integration. Sociologists such as Carl Taylor, the late Professor Louis Wirth, and the late Professor Robert Redfield have been particularly successful in identifying the characteristic features of rural society, urban society, and folk society.

Central to an understanding of a social structure is knowledge of the manner in which it is organized into groups with differential status positions, that is, social classes. Sociologists have traditionally stressed the importance of status even in democratic societies, and it is interesting to recall that the non-fiction "best seller" in the United States a few years ago was *The Status Seekers* by Vance Packard, a popular summary and interpretation of the not inconsiderable research by sociologists and others on the American status system. Status is considered as part of a system of social stratification by which the members of a society rank each other in terms of prestige and other types of social rewards.

Social classes may be defined as aggregates of individuals, often without specific inherent differentiating characteristics, who enter into and maintain relations with one another on a basis of equality, in contrast to other members of the community from whom they are distinguished (for the moment at least) by socially recognized standards of inferiority and superiority. Members of a given class characteristically develop a similar mode of life and similar attitudes and patterns of behavior and, with varying degrees of explicitness, a sense of belonging together. The sociologist is concerned with the bases of class differentiation (that is, the criteria that determine the class position of individuals), with the analysis of the patterns of behavior characteristic of different classes, including speech and language behavior, and with the types of stress that arise between classes.

Special attention has been given to vertical social mobility, or the movement of persons from class to class in the social hierarchy. When, because of differentiating characteristics that can be acquired only by birth, such as Hindu religious status or brown skin, the degree of vertical mobility approaches zero, the class structure may be called a caste system. On the other hand, if there is a large degree of vertical mobility, as for white persons in the United States, that part of the society is said to have an open-class system. Research has identified the extent to which social change depends on the caste and class structure in a given society, and the frequency of movement in an upward or downward direction.

Sociologists have addressed themselves to such questions as who moves up and who moves down, and whether such movements take place within relatively small ranges of the social scale, or involve relatively long-range movements, as from the lowest to the very highest class stratum. In addition to studying the extent, direction, and nature of the movement of individuals up and down the social scale, investigations are made into the channels of mobility. What are the characteristic career patterns in the society? To what extent do church, school, army, political parties, and other institutional groups serve as "elevators" through which individuals move up and down?

In a stratified social situation, those at the top level with respect to power and influence are called the elite, regardless of desirable or undesirable qualities or the efficiency with which they play their roles. Analyses of elites, by the late Professor C. Wright Mills and others, have included studies of their composition, their personality characteristics, their methods of maintaining power, their basic thought patterns, and their "circulation" or permanency.

Age and sex categories are another central feature of social structures. Numerous investigations of the role of age-sex categories have been undertaken since the late Professor Ralph Linton, some twenty years ago, called attention to this neglected aspect of social organization. Stressing the vital importance of age and sex categories in defining the relationship of an individual to his total society and its culture, Professor Linton called these categories and their derivatives "the building blocks of the society." Age and sex are standard variables in practically all surveys of opinions and attitudes and other sociological investigations.

Sociologists have deepened our understanding of the behavior of man in society in other ways. If space permitted, attention could be given to the sociologist's concern with value orientations and social ethos, his analysis of the forms and patterns of social control, his more recent preoccupation with social roles and positions, including deviant roles that induce social change, and his development of related concepts which provide ways of analyzing behavior and motivation in complex social situations. Sociologists are thus able to contribute to the behavioral sciences a distinctive sensitivity to the intricate patterns of social interactions and relationships that in large measure govern human conduct.

In addition to these matters of general interest to all sociologists, there are more specific areas of study that constitute special sub-fields. Urban and rural sociology, the sociology of race and ethnic relations, demography, communications research, public opinion and attitude studies, collective behavior, the study of occupations, the sociology of medicine and social psychiatry, and social disorganization and deviant behavior are among the sub-fields in which considerable research and study are undertaken in the United States. Substantial attention is also given to such sub-disciplines as political sociology, industrial sociology, the sociology of law, family sociology, the sociology of religion, educational sociology, the sociology of art, the sociology of knowledge, and the sociology of science and invention. We can do no more than deal briefly here with a few of these sub-fields.

The city was among the earliest of the "natural laboratories" exploited by American sociologists. In Chicago, in particular, urbanism as a way of life has been thoroughly examined. The shift from rural to urban patterns of living has been well documented in terms of its effects on family relations and social roles, and the development of new types of impersonal, secular relationships. Special attention has been directed to the study of human ecology, or the relations between man and his environment. Urban ecological studies have viewed the city as an arena of competition for the use of valuable land and of other forms of competition between adjacent groups. This has led to an emphasis on studying the city in terms of its distinctive socio-economic subareas. More recently, urban sociologists have shown considerable interest in comparative, cross-cultural urban studies and in urbanization as a worldwide phenomenon.

At the same time, with continuing governmental support, rural sociologists have been investigating the nature of rural communities and the social aspects of farm living. A recent analysis of trends in rural sociological research suggests a growing interest in such topics as education, suburbanization, the aged, health, and diffusion of technical practices.

Population study or demography is another focal area of sociological interest. Professors Philip M. Hauser and Otis D. Duncan define demography as the "study of the size, territorial distribution, and composition of population, changes therein, and the components of such changes, which may be identified as natality, mortality, territorial movement (migration), and social mobility (change of status)." In addition to their traditional concern with these formal aspects of population study, demographers today are exploring increasingly such topics as fertility levels in industrial and underdeveloped countries, especially the connections between fertility and basic attitudes and social institutions. Other promising areas of study, as identified by Professor Kingsley Davis, are: population change in relation to social and economic change; the labor force with respect to population structure and social organization; and the family with regard to demographic behavior.

We may also note the sociologist's interest in race and ethnic group relations and in the social, cultural, and personality variables involved in understanding the nature of prejudice and discrimination. A major study by Professor T. W. Adorno and his associates on *The Authoritarian Personality* has stimulated a large amount of research on the intricate interconnections between personality and social situations in determining responses to contacts with racial and cultural groups. Another area of research concentration is the role of legal and administrative processes in effecting changes in intergroup relations. The earlier view that law is impotent to change interracial relations has given way to a systematic analysis of the factors and conditions involved in the varying effectiveness of legal and administrative action.

Still another sub-field is communications research. Communications research has developed as a result of the manner in which radio, television, motion pictures, the printing press, the mimeograph machine, and related inventions have profoundly affected the patterns of interindividual and intergroup relationships through the creation of new methods of communication, new patterns of social control, and new techniques of wielding social power and influence. The rapid development of the media of mass communication, their institutionalization, and their central position in the presentation and manipulation of symbols have led sociologists to investigate the role of these media in contemporary society with particular reference to their impact on the formation of public opinion, their use in psychological warfare, and their influence on intergroup relations.

Research in this field has been defined by Professor Harold Lasswell in terms of the question: "Who—says what —to whom—in what channel—in what style—and with what effect?" Accordingly, the field of communications research has moved forward simultaneously on five fronts: communicator analysis; audience or recipient analysis; content analysis; response analysis; and social control analysis, that is, the study of the interrelations of communications and the social system.

Closely allied to communications research are studies of public opinion and attitudes. The creation of public opinion polling organizations in the United States and other countries (Gallup, Roper, Crossley, International Research Associates, National Opinion Research Center, Survey Research Center, and so on) has stimulated much research into the nature and measurement of public opinion, the factors influencing it, the role of opinion leaders, the techniques and processes of opinion and attitude formation, and the dynamics of opinion change. A major difficulty in the utilization of poll data has been the failure of many consumers of such data to appreciate the methodological limitations of poll materials.

Questions need to be raised concerning the reliability of the sampling techniques used; the extent of interviewer bias, bias of non-response and other types of survey bias; the influence of question-wording; the reliability of coding and tabulating procedures; errors in interpretation and biases in the presentation of results. The critical user of polling information is often compelled to compare the results of polls with the data obtained by other techniques of opinion measurement. Intensive interview surveys, standardized scaling techniques, mass observation methods, panel procedures, content analysis of newspapers, magazines, and other media of opinion, and leadership surveys are among the established methods used by sociologists and other gatherers of opinion and attitude data.

As a matter of fact, an abiding and concentrated interest in methods of social research is a distinctive feature of sociology in the United States. A French mathematician once remarked impatiently that sociology is the science with the most methods and the least results. Yet the concern with rigorous methods of empirical observation, and accurate recording of these observations, with reliable techniques of data collection, and with logically sound modes of analysis is the *sine qua non* of advance and progress in the scientific study of social behavior. It is only as a result of the rigorous character of its methods that sociology can claim superiority for its findings over common-sense judgments, folklore, everyday observations, popular conceptions, and ingrained stereotypes and prejudices. The *science* of sociology has had to wage a continuing uphill battle against the widespread belief that everyone, by virtue of living in a society, can be his own sociological authority.

One of the most significant developments in social research methods in the United States has been the introduction of the sample interview survey as a basic social science tool and as an instrument of governmental policy. Improvements in sample design, coding procedures, and interviewing techniques have led to the forging of an efficient, reliable, and relatively economical instrument for obtaining valuable data on people's desires, needs, problems, opinions, behavior, knowledge, reading and comprehension, consumption patterns, and motivations. Simultaneously, we have witnessed equally impressive results in the effective employment of the questionnaire as a research tool. Scaling devices, multivariate analysis, panel techniques, projective tests, and standardized instruments of measurement have also contributed to American sociology's high level of methodological sophistication. The electronic computer is making possible rapid analysis of complex data heretofore inaccessible to the sociological investigator. Laboratories are being constructed which permit the making of controlled, reliable observations of interactive behavior. Statistical methods have been devised which insure proper measurement of the contributions of complex variables. In brief, the zealous preoccupation with methodology has paid dividends in terms of improved accuracy of observations, increased reliability of measurement devices, better scientific research and experimental designs, more logical methods of analysis, and increased confidence in the validity of the generalizations and conclusions drawn.

I must now conclude with an emphatic "and so on and so forth." I have barely begun to describe the numerous accomplishments of sociological thinking and research in the United States. I trust, however, that I have succeeded in conveying the image of a vigorous scientific discipline in which substantial progress is being made on a variety of fronts. Sociology in the United States is both a firmly established academic discipline with numerous chairs in every major university, and a body of specially trained, skilled professional personnel to whom industrial and business organizations, governmental agencies, health and welfare institutions, and other groups turn for expert practical advice, consultation, and service.

Membership in the American Sociological Association this past year exceeded 7,350. According to reports received by the *American Journal of Sociology* from 68 departments of sociology in the United States and Canada, 156 doctoral degrees and 305 master's degrees in sociology were conferred in the calendar year 1960. And in 1961, 179 doctoral dissertations were newly begun. Sociology is, indeed, a well-rooted feature of American cultural and intellectual life.

Although proud of their indigenous accomplishments, American sociologists are acutely aware of their indebtedness to colleagues in other lands. Max Weber and Georg Simmel, German sociologists, Emile Durkheim, founder of the French school of sociology, Vilfredo Pareto, an Italian author of a major sociological treatise, and Leonard T. Hobhouse of England are among the world-renowned sociologists whose works are systematically studied in the United States. We are also conscious of the direct gains American sociology has made through the contributions of those who came here as refugees from totalitarian oppression.

For example, Professor Pitirim Sorokin, forced to flee from Russian communism, has written major sociological books and played a major role in establishing sociology at Harvard University. Dr. Hans Speier, who left Germany when the Nazis came to power, has become one of our foremost authorities on psychological warfare and military sociology. And the late Professor Florian Znaniecki, unable to return to his native Poland at the outbreak of World War II, stayed in the United States and was later elected president of the American Sociological Society. In close collaboration with our colleagues from abroad, we are dedicated to providing positive evidence that rational intelligence and scientific method can contribute to a better understanding of man and his social environment.

6 METHODS OF RESEARCH USED BY AMERICAN SOCIAL SCIENTISTS

Samuel A. Stouffer

Samuel A. Stouffer, late Professor of Sociology at Harvard University, was born in Sac City, Iowa, in 1900. After completing his undergraduate education at Morningside College, in Iowa, Dr. Stouffer pursued graduate studies in sociology at Harvard University and the University of Chicago. Before he joined the faculty of Harvard University in 1946 as Director of the Laboratory of Social Relations, he had taught at the universities of Chicago and Wisconsin, and during the wartime period (1941–1946) had served as Director of the Research Staff of the U.S. War Department's Information and Education Division. Dr. Stouffer served as President of the American Sociological Society (1952–1953) and of the American Association for Public Opinion Research (1953–1954). A specialist in research studies applying quantitative methods in sociology, Dr. Stouffer wrote and co-authored numerous articles and books, including Communism, Conformity and Civil Liberties, *and the famous* American Soldier *series.*

The purpose of this paper is to make some observations on the methods and techniques used by American behavioral scientists in testing hypotheses or nailing down facts in sociology, social psychology, and anthropology.

In the space available, I am compelled to be selective rather than comprehensive. My emphasis will be on some of the newer developments, to which Americans have made significant contributions. Some of these newer techniques are American originals; some of them—notably in the adaptation of modern statistical theory—are fresh applications or elaborations of basic ideas originating in Great Britain or on the continent.

Therefore, I will do less than justice to many of the conventional methods which characterize some of the most important research here and abroad—for example, the use of historical materials to illustrate or document an argument; the use of published bodies of statistics, as in the official reports of the Census Bureau or other governmental agencies; the use of personal documents, such as case histories, to provide clinical illustrations; and straightforward observation, either direct or through the medium of informants. Much of the research which by any definition would be included within the scope of the behavioral sciences is of this character. To pass this over quickly is certainly not to deprecate or minimize its importance, particularly in the exploratory stages of our inquiries. Most of us at one time or another use one or more of these conventional approaches; indeed, in some instances no other approach is as yet suitable.

The methods I wish to discuss fall under four main heads: advances in measurement; development of survey methodology; the design of experiments; and some contributions to the analysis of complex social and personal data involving many variables simultaneously.

Before this is undertaken, however, a brief word is appropriate as to why these particular techniques have received so much attention and use. In America, especially since World War II, there has been an increasing appreciation of the practical value of the behavioral sciences in applications to a wide variety of everyday problems. In the medical field, for example, clinicians in the field of mental health need instruments for measurement and diagnosis of personality disorders. In education, the whole guidance process in the primary and secondary schools and the selection and guidance process in the colleges calls for reliable and valid tools. At the same time there is pressure for the development of research designs which will test the effectiveness of new teaching techniques, of which educational television is just one recent example. In government, there is much use of behavioral science techniques, notably those attempting to assess public opinion. In spite of considerable resentment of and resistance to public opinion polls, the fact remains that neither of our major parties is likely to nominate for the presidency a man who shows up badly in national polls compared with others in the same party.

But it is in the field of business that, in terms of dollars spent and effort put forth, the behavioral sciences have perhaps their greatest application—in marketing, in public relations, and in the selection and handling of both employee and management personnel. Business is spending many millions of dollars annually in these areas of research, and is becoming increasingly sophisticated in demanding high standards of quality—even though, admittedly, there is still much poor work and there are, I fear, some charlatans. The point, of course, is that research which is done to establish facts important for practical decisions needs to be searching and accurate and there is money to pay for it because so much depends on it. Some of the best work to improve techniques in these applied areas has been done outside the halls of our colleges and universities, and has been fed back, influencing academic research on more basic theoretical studies in the behavioral sciences.

Now let us look at some of these techniques. First, measurement.

In the analysis of aptitudes, abilities, and achievement, we have come a long way in a generation. In this work there has been much interchange of ideas between Europe and the United States. The already fairly sophisticated body of test theory available to psychometricians is being augmented continually by new studies. At the same time the invention of new electronic scoring machines has made it possible to process hundreds of thousands of tests in a very short time and to print automatically scores and sub-scores which can be passed back to schools or to individuals.

In the area of personality measurement, there have been movements in two directions. One, using the manifest content of the responses as basic data, closely resembles the standard psychometric methods used in measuring abilities or aptitudes. These tests are open to the danger that some responses are transparently more socially desirable than others, thus encouraging bias or even faking. One way around this is the use of forced choices. The subject has to indicate which of two statements he prefers and, though different, they are equated for social desirability. For example, "I like to have friends" and "I like to be successful." The second road which personality measurement is taking is through the use of what are called projective tests. These devices owe much to psychoanalytic theory. Some of the most widely used, such as the Rorschach ink-blot test, were developed first in Europe.

But there are now a very large number of such tests, all of which are devices to get a person to reveal aspects of his personality or his needs indirectly, so that the examiner can infer what he is like when his guard is down. Quite well known, for example, is the Thematic Apperception Test, in which the subject describes what he sees in a standardized series of pictures. There are difficult and debatable problems of interpretation and scoring. The enthusiasm of clinicians for these diagnostic tools has often met a rude shock when the validation of tests has failed under careful psychometric scrutiny. But there is encouraging progress in improving the reliability and objectivity of scoring. There also has been considerable work in America in using the machine called the polygraph to measure a wide variety of physiological reactions concomitant, for example, to states of fear and anger. The polygraph can generate thousands of measurements in a brief span of time, and it was not until the new electronic computers came along that it became feasible to summarize and correlate them without too formidable labor.

Another area in which there has been increasing attention to measurement problems is the study of opinions, attitudes, and values. Techniques borrowed from sensory psychology—for example, the discrimination between lifted weights—were adapted to the scaling of attitudes some two or three decades ago. These techniques have been supplemented in recent years by other models of scaling, which have advantages of simplicity without entailing a loss of rigor. The amount of invention, as well as of criticism, in this field has been quite considerable, especially in the last decade.

There are other specialized measurment problems which should be noted, such as that of reporting and summarizing the interaction within small groups. However, I shall close this section by mentioning only one other area which involves, at the least, enumeration—namely, that of content analysis. Here the problem is to classify the contents of a communication, such as a printed page or a radio broadcast, into categories relevant to the problem at hand, and to determine the frequency of content within each category. This method has numerous practical applications, as in propaganda analysis. But it can also be used in the historical or comparative analysis of cultural values—for example, a current content analysis of primary school readers is seeking to compare and contrast recurrent themes in a large number of both Occidental and Oriental cultures.

Now, having provided an all too hurried glimpse of the attention being paid by American behavioral scientists to problems of measurement, let me take up a second topic, namely, the development of survey methodology.

Surveys quite commonly involve the construction of questionnaires, which are administered by interviewers to representative samples of the public. Although such sample polls have spread throughout the world, the American experience is particularly versatile. This is due in no small part to the fact, already mentioned, that American business is spending millions of dollars annually in market research, much of it using one form or another of survey techniques.

There are several different types of methodological problems involved in surveys and on each of them there has been much written in America in recent years. Mention may be made of just three—sampling, questionnaire design, and interviewing.

There are two principal methods of getting a sample of respondents. One is what is called the probability method. All geographical units in the population are put on punch cards and a sample of such communities drawn at random, mechanically. Within each of the sample communities, the process is repeated. For example, all the city blocks or street segments in the community may be listed and a small sub-sample drawn at random from this list. Again, the process may be repeated. Within each small sub-sample, all households may be listed, and just a few of these households selected at random to be interviewed. Ideally, this procedure, because it is as random and unbiased as the flip of a coin, guarantees that each household in the population will have an equal chance of ending up in the sample. Of course, there will still be error, even if the sample is extremely large, but this error, which is a chance error, can be calculated in advance quite accurately. Hence, whatever the degree of accuracy we need, we can know in advance how large a sample is required to get this accuracy.

The probability method of sampling is used by United States government agencies to obtain current and quite accurate data on such things as unemployment, internal migration, consumer savings, consumers' intentions to buy new houses or new automobiles, and the incidence of chronic illnesses. Behavioral scientists in universities also use this method, though more often on a local or regional than on a nationwide basis, to collect data bearing on hypotheses they wish to test. While the probability sampling method is ideal, it is not foolproof. Some people are away from home and cannot be reached. A few stubborn holdouts exercise their right as democratic citizens not to be interviewed. A practical American contribution has been to devise appropriate formulas for evaluating the flaws in the ideal and for making workable corrections.

As might be guessed from my description of the probability method of sampling, it is rather an expensive business—particularly if high-priced interviewers must call back several times before they find a sample household at home. Also, if one wanted information overnight, as election pollsters might on the eve of election, one couldn't get it this way.

So a second method, called quota sampling, is frequently used. Communities or even neighborhoods may be chosen at random, but the selection of households within that area is left to the discretion of the interviewer himself—except that he must try to get a preassigned proportion of males and females, old and young, rich and poor, and so on. This method is cheaper and faster than the probability method, since callbacks to homes are eliminated. But lazy or not too resourceful interviewers can introduce considerable bias. For example, slum dwellers or remote farmers are likely to be under-sampled.

The design of questionnaires is an art about which there has been much accumulation of wisdom in recent years. Schedules to be used on a large survey are usually pretested on one or more sub-samples and revised before being used in the field. There has been a good deal of study of the effect of biases in the phrasing of questions and even in such matters as the context of other questions in which a given item appears. Often a slight, subtle twist in wording will make a difference of 10 per cent or 20 per cent in the proportions agreeing or disagreeing with a question. Sometimes this fact can be turned to good advantage, in order to evaluate the stability with which an opinion is held. One can ask several forms of the same question, one deliberately biased in the positive direction, one deliberately biased in the negative direction, and one thought to be neutral. The more salient and clear-cut the opinion, the less difference question bias should make.

Since so many surveys rely on interviewers, there have been many perceptive studies of the ways in which the personalities and opinions of the interviewer can color a person's answers. For example, Negro interviewers in America often get quite different responses from Negroes than would whites from these same Negroes. The selection and training of an interviewing staff and the preparation of instructions to the staff with respect to any field survey is no small undertaking. In addition to the many polling and market research organizations which now maintain their own nationwide field staffs, there are also organizations, consisting of a field staff only, whose services are purchased by clients who wish to put a questionnaire into the field. Such facilities can be especially useful to academic researchers, since only a few college-based research institutes maintain field staffs of their own.

The costs of personal calls on households are so high that very serious efforts are being made to see how cheaper methods, such as telephone interviews or mailed questionnaires, can be substituted under what conditions and with what results. Some of this experience has been quite encouraging, particularly with respect to telephone samples. Most American families now have phones. A special advantage of the telephone method is that the man of the house is more likely to be at home in the evening. A dozen such men can be interviewed over the phone in the time it might take a personal caller to make contact with just one of them. The mail questionnaire is possibly beginning to enjoy a revival, after a period in which it became rather discredited because its biases were not properly evaluated. Now that it is possible to estimate better some of the biases and correct for them, more studies are using the mails.

A special kind of survey is one which is made from a panel of persons—that is, a sampling of people who agree to fill out and mail back questionnaires on a variety of topics over an extended time period, say for a year or two. Many such panels are operated commercially, and some have up to five thousand regular respondents. The importance of such data is obvious in the marketing field. It is the only reliable method, for example, by which one can learn about loyalty to products or brands. There are many technical problems peculiar to these panels, especially as they relate to biases introduced, because some personality types may be more co-operative than others in reporting. Such problems, as might be expected, are receiving careful study.

In general, university researchers in the behavioral sciences have not had the resources to maintain permanent panels of their own. But surveys based on second or third visits to the same households have led to some of the most important academic studies of the past decade. Particularly notable have been panel studies of voting behavior, where attitudes of a panel of individuals are studied at several points throughout a political campaign. The shifts in these attitudes relate in interesting ways to the social and personal characteristics of the people. Also, academic research on consumer behavior, using the panel technique, has thrown light on factors explaining discrepancies between the intention to purchase something, say a new home, and subsequent market behavior.

I have now made some comments on measurement and on surveys. A third field of increasing attention is the design of experiments. The classic experimental design, used in every branch of science, involves experimental and control groups. Both groups are measured; one group then receives a certain treatment, another does not. Afterward both are remeasured, and the effect of the treatment is shown as the changes in the experimental group differ from whatever changes may occur in the control group. There are, of course, many variations and elaborations of the basic design. Controlled experiments have long been staples of much of the research in individual psychology, but until recently have been rare in sociology or social psychology and their applied fields. Now experimental designs are frequent.

Broadly, there are two types of use. One is in tests of

specific hypotheses; the other is in what might be called program testing. Hypotheses testing has been quite fruitful in experimental studies of communication and persuasion. You can prove, for example, that a fear stimulus in a message has an effect and how much, and this is not a mere inference or hopeful guess. Also in small group studies it is possible to alter the roles of participants and measure the changes in group interaction with considerable rigor.

The aim of program testing is to see whether one complex way of doing things is more effective than another. For example, if television is used in the schoolroom how much more do children learn than by conventional teaching methods? Some of the most elaborate experimental designs to test programs are now used in business and are often very costly. For example, a firm will set up two or more parallel test markets and will try one advertising and marketing program in one, while it tries a different program in another. Such studies, if they are to yield valid results, may require an intricately careful design and execution. Unfortunately, many such commercial studies are confidential, and the profession as a whole does not learn as much from the experience as it should. Those who have never been involved in the design and execution of controlled experiments of human behavior can hardly imagine the myriad things which can go wrong. Here, even more than in most types of behavioral science research, there is a special need for wider dissemination of experience.

As my fourth and concluding illustration of research progress, some words are needed about the analysis of data, particularly data involving several variables and permitting statistical treatment.

In the past decade or two there seems to have been a drift away from some of the conventional techniques, like correlation, in spite of some of their mathematical advantages. The tendency has been more in the direction of subdividing and resubdividing the data successively as additional variables are introduced, often treating each variable as having only two or three broad categories. This usually requires a lot of cases to begin with. For example, if each one of four variables contains three categories, the number of subcategories resulting through successive subdivisions is three to the fourth power, or eighty-one. Fortunately, data numerous enough to permit the analysis of so many separate cells are more often becoming available.

Such a situation can be a happy one. One can see what is going on and can also apply very simple but adequate significance tests, based on order statistics. For example, if out of twenty-seven possible matched comparisons twenty-two are positive and only five are negative, one may not need anything but the most rudimentary statistical theory to demonstrate that this positive excess is not likely to be attributable to chance.

There is another trend in analysis, however, which may lead in other directions. I refer to the increasing use of high-speed electronic computing machines, which are now readily available to behavioral scientists. Training in programming the new computers is now part of the experience which many of our graduate students are getting. One of these IBM monsters in an hour produces huge matrices of correlation coefficients which might have taken a clerk with a desk calculator a year to do. Of course this can be bad as well as good, especially if it encourages too much lazy empiricism in analysis. The temptation may be to take twenty or thirty variables and dump them into this electric hopper with little if any prior speculation as to what they may mean. If something happens, fine. If not, one has lost only a few hours at most. But let's not be pessimistic about this. The same fears have been expressed by scholars for years as every new gadget has been introduced into our tool chest. What seems to happen in the long run is that the machine never takes over the man, but definitely vice versa. At every stage of the research process, whether one is working at home with a slide rule or standing in front of the blinking lights of a fast computer, there is need for imagination.

The chemist in his laboratory is both scientist and artisan. So is the behavioral scientist. The mastery of some of the techniques described here involves much more than routine learning. It involves judgment, imagination, and dexterity of many kinds, and these attributes are not acquired merely by reading books on methods. They are learned through the fingertips, as it were, in actual practical experience. This is why the major American universities training a new generation of behavioral scientists are providing practical experience in research institutes, bureaus, or laboratories which are closely allied to the academic departments.

The techniques of research which I have described, are, of course, not ends in themselves. They are tools—tools which are helping in the thrilling quest after better knowledge of man and the society in which he lives.

7 COMPUTER SIMULATION IN THE BEHAVIORAL SCIENCES

Carl I. Hovland

Carl I. Hovland, late Sterling Professor of Psychology at Yale University, New Haven, Connecticut, was born in Chicago, Illinois, in 1912. A graduate of Northwestern University, Dr. Hovland received his doctorate in psychology from Yale University and was associated throughout his professional career with the faculty of that institution. During the more than twenty-three years that he served on the Yale University faculty, he was Director of Graduate Studies in Psychology (1941–1946) and Chairman of the Department of Psychology (1945–1951). From 1942 to 1945 Dr. Hovland was also Director of Experimental Studies in the Information and Education Division of the U.S. War Department. A former President of the Eastern Psychological Association (1950), he was the senior author of Experiments on Mass Communication *and* Communication and Persuasion.

It is commonplace in the history of science for developments in one field of knowledge to have profound effects on other related areas. The dramatic influence of advances in atomic physics on biology, genetics, and medicine is a good case in point. We are currently witnessing a similar phenomenon in the repercussions of high-speed computer technology on research in the behavioral sciences. The initial impact came from the computational efficiency of these devices, which permitted calculations formerly prohibitive in terms of time and effort. A more recent and less direct effect has been in stimulating machine-like methods of analysis of human thought and behavior through simulation on high-speed computers. It is these newer techniques and their applicability to the behavioral sciences that I should like to discuss.

The analogy between the high-speed computer and human thinking has long been noted. We frequently see large-scale electronic computers referred to in the popular press as "giant brains" or "thinking machines." In most uses of high-speed computers, however, there is an attempt to attain objectives beyond the scope of human capabilities, either because of their speed or their extensive storage capacity (called, interestingly enough, their "memory"). But in the investigations I shall be describing, the utilization is quite different. Here, we are primarily concerned with the use of computing machines to simulate in exact fashion the way a human solves a problem. Both human weaknesses, such as limited and fallible memory, and strengths, such as ability to choose an efficient solution out of innumerable alternatives, must be represented. We say that we can simulate human problem-solving when we are able to specify both the prior information a human possesses and the sequence of steps by which he utilizes this information in the solution of a problem. We are then able to set up a computing machine to carry out this same sequence of operation.

Those of you familiar with the operation of high-speed computers will readily understand the way in which simulation proceeds. Just as in the ordinary operations of a computer, one gives the machine a set of "instructions" to execute. These constitute what is called a "program." In arithmetical operations these are statements like the following: "square the product of the first and second number," "store the product in memory." Or such instructions as: "find the number of dollars paid to the individual last month," "add to this amount the number of dollars earned this month," and so forth. The machine then executes each of these instructions through an intricate electronic system, printing out its answers on an electric typewriter.

The nub of the simulation problem involves the use of similar types of "programs" of "instructions" to the machine in order to reproduce the steps an individual goes through in thinking out the solution to a difficult problem. One specifies the steps the individual uses by stating them in an unambiguous way so that a computing machine is able to carry them out. These may be instructions like: "store the answer to the last problem," "determine whether you have stored in memory any similar problems," "if so, what are the differences between the past problem and the present one," "see if applying rule *a* will convert the old problem into the new one," "if so, apply rule *b* to convert the answer to the former problem into the solution to the present one." Thus the computer can be given information which is exactly equivalent to that of the human problem-solver, as well as a specification of the way the human goes about processing that information to reach a solution.

The obvious point is that if we can be precise enough about a process to describe it in terms which can be programmed and executed by a machine, we indeed know quite a bit about that process. And if we can specify singly each of the sub-processes involved, we can determine the effects of combinations of them and of variations in order of execution of the steps.

Simulated thought, a new and promising technique, is currently being used by a wide range of behavioral scientists —psychologists, sociologists, linguists, and political scientists —to simulate thought processes, interpersonal interactions, the learning of language, and the structure of complex organizational patterns.

Let me begin by giving a concrete example of the new techniques, namely, simulation of the solving of geometry problems. We certainly think of the solving of theorems in Euclidian geometry by a high school sophomore as constituting a clear-cut example of intelligent human behavior. But two researchers, Gelernter and Rochester, have now successfully developed a program whereby a high-speed computer is able to solve many of the theorems in Euclid's geometry—for example, the one stating that the diagonals of a parallelogram bisect one another. A human learner who tries to solve such a problem has usually been taught a series of fundamental

principles, or axioms, together with a set of rules for in-
ferring relationships by which the basic symbols in the system may be manipulated. He is then asked to prove a new
theorem. He tries to find a way of transforming and combin-
ing previous axioms through the set of rules until he achieves
the proof of the new theorem. Typically he starts out in
rather routine fashion, then has a flash of insight as to a possible means of solution, and then methodically tests the adequacy of the solution.

The geometry computing machine is set up to operate in
an analogous fashion. It is given a set of basic formulas and
axioms, together with rules as to possible ways of manipulating them in order to form new theorems. The new theorem is
then presented to the machine to prove. The machine is
equipped with a number of rules of thumb for possible ways
of solving problems. For example, it is instructed that if the
proposition to be proved involves parallel lines and equality
of angles, there is a good chance that it may be useful to try
the theorem which states: "If two parallel lines are inter-
sected by a third line, the opposite interior angles are equal."
This instruction constitutes a short cut which often works
well but is by no means sure to be of value. The use of short
cuts differs from the typical operation of high-speed computers, which methodically go through every possible solution in a deliberate way. Rules of thumb, however, permit
the use of likely and plausible methods of solution—just the
way a clever high school student would proceed.

Successful solution typically involves setting up a series of
sub-goals which are then worked on in succession. Once the
sequence of sub-goals leads from the initial axioms to the
theorem to be proved, the machine tests the accuracy of the
proof. This it can do in an exhaustive manner, since once one
has a possible proof, checking it is largely a clerical matter.
When the proof has been verified, the machine prints
"Proved." Throughout the entire operation the machine
prints out on paper a complete tracing of the steps it tries—

this is analogous to an individual's account of the way he solves a problem in geometry. Some of the machine's failures in finding proofs closely resemble those made by beginning geometry students.

This geometry computer solves problems but does not really learn to solve them, in the sense that the machine would solve the same problem in the same way on a second trial. Humans, of course, improve through practice. So the interesting task is to build into the computer this capability as well.

A number of different types of learning are currently being simulated. The first involves what is called stimulus-response learning, the type made famous by Pavlov's experiments on the conditioned response. It is rather simple to simulate this type of learning, in which rewards are given when certain types of behavior occur and are not given when other types of responses are made. The probability that the response followed by reward will occur on later trials of the machine can then be made to increase. Failure of reward, simulating punishment, can be made to lead to a decreased probability of response.

At a somewhat more complex level is the type of learning involved in recognizing patterns embedded in complex stimuli. It seems a simple thing for a human to respond to a triangle as a triangle whether it is large or small, short or tall, tilted or upright, and to distinguish it clearly from a square. But to specify rigorously the criteria in such a way that a machine can learn to recognize it invariably is quite a job. And the difficulty clearly hints that there is a lot we do not understand about the phenomenon even at the human level where we take the process for granted. Selfridge and Dinneen have worked most extensively on this problem and have been able to develop methods for getting the salient features of patterns to stand out so that a uniform response is given to a particular pattern.

The third type of learning is made possible by having the

machine keep records of success and failure attained when different methods are pursued and using these records to improve performance. Thus, in the case of the geometry computer it is possible to store theorems which have already been proved. It is also possible for machines to be selective in their choice of theorems for permanent storage, rejecting those which do not seem sufficiently general to be useful later on.

The most highly developed simulation of this type of learning is that incorporated in a checker-playing machine developed by Samuel. His machine utilizes a type of rote learning which stores all of the checkerboard positions it encounters in play, together with the outcomes following each move. In addition this machine has some capacity to generalize on the basis of past experience and to store the generalizations themselves. With these learning mechanisms it appears possible for the computer to learn in a short period of time to play a better game of checkers than can be played by the person who wrote the program.

In the work in our own laboratory, the emphasis is on understanding and simulating the processes involved in acquiring complex concepts through experience. The learner acquires a particular concept when he is told which of a series of specific instances presented to him belong in the concept class and which do not. This is similar to the way in which a child learns the concept of "animate" through experiences in which parents and teachers label some things as "animate" and others as "inanimate."

Our type of problem is illustrated by a situation in which there are a large number of slides of cancer cells, some of which are known to be malignant and others non-malignant. The task of the individual (or the machine) is one of inducing the basis of difference between the two types and subsequently labelling correctly new slides previously unidentified. Medical pathologists have just such a task and have achieved considerable success, although not 100 per cent accuracy, in making such distinctions.

It is of interest to note in passing that there is a machine available which can make such a distinction on the basis of slides presented to it; but here the combination of characteristics (the "concept") was formulated by the scientists who developed the instrument. The machine's task is simply to see whether the new specimen conforms to certain specifications, that is, whether on the basis of density and structure the cell belongs in the "malignant" or "normal" category. Thus it has the "concept" built into it, obviating the need to start from the beginning in order to induce it.

The input to the type of concept learner in which we are interested is a series of geometric figures, some labelled "positive" instances (or examples of the concept) and some labelled "negative" instances (that is, examples of what the concept is *not*). The geometric forms on cards can be transformed into symbols for processing by the machine by using a television camera which converts the visual image into electrical signals. These signals register their impulses as input to the machine. Thus, the picture images become converted into a string of symbols representing the characteristics which constitute the instances of the concept, while another string of symbols represents instances of what the concept *is not*.

Potentially, a machine can then consider combinations of all of these characteristics as possible ways of categorizing and distinguishing between the class of "A" and the class of "not A." Typically, human learners attend to only part of the potential set of characteristics because of perceptual limitations. We have devoted considerable research effort toward determining just how attention and perception vary during the course of learning. We have incorporated in the machine simulation a selective scanning of possible aspects of the complex stimuli with provision for the fact that some individuals see only some of the characteristics while other individuals pay attention to different aspects.

Human subjects, at least at the adult level, operate on material of this type by developing strategies involving some generalization as to what concepts are like. The strategies may be different for different types of concepts. Logicians describe some concepts as being of the *conjunctive* type, where all the members of the class share certain common characteristics. For example, rubies share the characteristics of hardness, translucence, and redness.

A second type of concept is called *disjunctive,* in which possession of either of two characteristics makes the instance subsumable under the general class. This is illustrated by the concept in American baseball of a "strike," which is either a pitched ball across the plate between the batter's knees and shoulders *or,* alternatively, any pitch which the batter strikes at but fails to send into the field. A third type of concept is *relational,* where the instances of the concept share no common fixed characteristics but do have certain relationships in common. A sample would be the concept of "isosceles triangles." All instances of this concept involve triangles with two equal sides. But any fixed characteristics, such as lengths of the equal sides, lengths of the third side, or sizes of angles, are not an adequate basis for inclusion or exclusion in the concept class.

In preparation for later simulation, we have carried out extensive experimentation to determine the order in which these various types of concepts are considered by human learners. We find in our experiments that conjunctive and relational concepts are considered much more commonly than disjunctive ones. So our present machine will have built into it a hierarchy of responses in which the first attempts to organize the material will be in terms of shared characteristics—conjunctive type concepts. Alternatively, the machine will consider concepts which are based on relationships between the stimuli. Only when these have been extensively and unsuccessfully explored will the machine try disjunctive concept patterns.

Tasks of even greater complexity are now being programmed for machine simulation and study. I have already mentioned the checker-player machine. Several other groups of researchers are working on the more difficult task of simulating *chess* playing. In principle, a machine can play an excellent game of chess if it is provided with mechanisms for considering and evaluating the consequences of every move each player can make in order to evaluate its own best move. However, the calculation of each of the alternatives one, two, three or more steps in depth becomes an enormous task and could be executed only if unlimited time for analysis were available.

Various investigators, notably Berstein, have developed simplification methods which permit certain short cuts. A Dutch scholar named DeGroot has supplied interesting reports concerning the procedure of experienced chess players. Partly on the basis of DeGroot's data, a machine has been developed which simulates these human strategies in chess. The short cuts and rules of thumb which experienced chess players find effective are built into the machine. At present such machines can beat only amateur chess players but, again in principle, they may ultimately have all of the techniques of the master chess player.

Finally, I should like to mention in passing several other areas in which machine simulation is being applied in the behavioral sciences. One area is machine simulation of the process of learning grammar. In ordinary life an individual learns that certain combinations of words are grammatical and others not. Can this learning process be simulated? In recent years linguists have carried the formal analysis of rules of grammar to an elegant length. Their studies provide a good foundation for developing machines which can simulate the process by which the child acquires his patterns of grammatical speech.

There have also been several recent attempts to simulate social interaction patterns on high-speed computers. When two- or three-man groups carry on a discussion or work on solving a problem, typical patterns of interaction between the members develop. Certain individuals adopt one role, for example, that of synthesizer or summarizer, and others develop other roles, perhaps that of originator or idea-proposer. Attempts are being made to simulate the interaction process so that one can specify all of the principal determinants of how each individual is going to respond to the total situation and to the actions of the others in the group. One can then introduce other variables and study their effects, such as how familiarity with the members of the group influences behavior, or how pressure on the group to reach decision affects the responses of the individuals.

I hope that the foregoing discussion has suggested some of the advantages of these new techniques. Let me briefly summarize the potentialities. First, simulation methods have a tremendous role in sharpening our formulations concerning mental processes and phenomena. It is one thing to say, as earlier students have said, that problem solving involves a number of different stages—for example, those of preparation, incubation, illumination, and verification—and quite another for one to specify exactly what is involved in each stage. The pioneering studies by Newell, Shaw, and Simon on the General Problem Solver indicate the great forward strides which result from specifying the nature of these processes in such complete detail that a computer is able to solve problems by following the sequence of steps programmed into the machine.

Closely related is the second advantage of the computer, the emphasis which it places on developing theories that have both descriptive and predictive power. The program written for the computer to describe a particular process constitutes a theory which, if successful in carrying out the process in the same way as the human, is highly efficient in predicting the effects of changes in conditions and in specifying what other individuals will do under particular conditions.

Lastly, the simulation of human responses has the same overwhelming advantages for our understanding of behavioral phenomena as similar methods in other sciences. For example, the use of the wind tunnel represents a complex set of interacting conditions whose effects could not be predicted from theory alone. Analogously, in the present case, for single factors one can analyze effects without simulation, but when one seeks to understand the combined action of a number of factors interacting in complex ways, no satisfactory way of predicting the exact outcome may be possible. Researchers working on the geometry simulator, the General Problem Solver, and the chess- and checker-playing machines, all testify to the fact that many of the moves made by the computer greatly surprised their inventors.

I hope that my remarks on the importance of simulation methods do not give rise to the feeling that these methods automatically lead to quick success in areas which have been investigated for decades using other techniques. Two examples of the difficulties confronting us may be mentioned. The first is the complexity of the process to be simulated. At present we consider ourselves fortunate if we can simulate on a machine the typical performance of a single individual in solving a particular problem. This is indeed a great step forward. But for simulation to be maximally effective, we would like to be able to predict machine solutions which simulate not only a single individual under some specified condition but also the effects for different individuals under different environmental conditions and after various amounts of experience.

The second difficulty of machine simulation is attributable to the nature of the process with which we are concerned. Simulation methods have most successfully been employed where it is possible to define the final performance of a task as an outcome of a succession of single steps. Thus, where the mental process involves steps in a sequence, one can synthesize the process by having the computing machine work first on stage one, then stage two, and so forth. Much more difficult are those processes where a number of stages are going on simultaneously, in parallel fashion. It certainly appears that much of our perceptual process operates in this way. Under these conditions, it is much more difficult to untangle the processes at work prior to simulation.

Despite the difficulties mentioned, work on simulation of complex psychological and sociological processes is yielding results of increasing importance. Processes which were thought to be understood turn out to require much more explicit statement. But along with the increased explicitness comes new understanding and precision. At present most computer programs grapple with only one phase of complex processes, but we are beginning to see common features in a number of different programs, permitting the construction of comprehensive programs from simpler sub-programs.

Let not this enthusiastic report on the scientific potentialities of simulation research arouse anxieties of the sort raised by the speculations of science fiction writers that machines will take over our civilization and supplant man in the near future. Rather, I think, there is great hope that detailed knowledge of how humans learn, think, and organize will redound to human welfare in removing much of the mystery which surrounds these processes and in leading to better understanding of the limitations of current ways of solving problems. It may, of course, then become possible for us to build machines which will work out solutions to many problems which we now consider distinctively human and to do so in a manner surpassing present human performance. But that this will lead to the machine becoming master and the designer becoming slave seems to me most unlikely. On the contrary, it will free man for novel, creative tasks which are progressively beyond the capability of machines designed by man.

8 THE EVOLUTION OF BEHAVIOR

George Gaylord Simpson
Anne Roe

George Gaylord Simpson, Alexander Agassiz Professor of Vertebrate Paleontology at Harvard University, was born in Chicago, Illinois, in 1902. Dr. Simpson received both his undergraduate and doctoral degrees from Yale University. From 1927 to 1959 he was associated with the American Museum of Natural History in New York City, and from 1945 to 1959 was Professor of Vertebrate Paleontology at Columbia University. He joined the Harvard faculty in the fall of 1959. Dr. Simpson is the author of numerous books, including The Major Features of Evolution *and* Life. *His wife, the psychologist Anne Roe, also on the Harvard faculty, is the author of numerous works, including* The Making of a Scientist.

All the resemblances and all the differences among organisms have a historical basis. They are the results of evolution. Evolution thus underlies and provides a historical explanation of all the activities of living things. That is the broadest, most literally unifying of the principles of biology.

Among the activities of most organisms are those that we call "behavior." Behavioral activities are minimal, indeed usually absent, in plants, but in most animals they are not only especially striking to us as observers but also particularly important to the animals themselves. Behavior is like all other biological phenomena in having a historical, evolutionary basis. Behavior also has evolved, and study of its evolution is essential for any real understanding of the animal kingdom in general and of the human condition in particular.

In what follows, we shall not attempt to trace the factual

history of behavior among the millions of different kinds of animals, past and present. That is obviously too large a subject for this brief paper. Moreover, those facts are very incompletely known. Biologists have been giving some explicit attention to the subject for over one hundred and fifty years now, but only quite recently has a real synthesis of modern evolutionary science and modern behavioral science been attempted. This is at present one of the more promising and interesting frontiers of research.

We shall attempt to summarize a few of the principles and relationships currently known or surmised, and believed to be important for research on the evolution of behavior.

First of all, some thought should be given to how one can actually go about studying this subject. In this connection, and indeed in the natural sciences generally, the old distinction between observational and experimental methods is not very helpful. The data of natural science are always observations. The circumstances under which the observations are made are always selected and frequently manipulated by the observer. The extent of the manipulation, and hence the extent to which experiment is involved, varies so largely and so continuously that it is seldom realistic to try to make a sharp distinction.

The observations that can be made on any animal are, broadly, anatomical, physiological, and behavioral. That distinction is useful, and yet it also is largely artificial as the three aspects are never completely separable. Anatomy is the substrate for physiology and behavior, and it is meaningless unless it is related in study, as it is in reality, to those functions of the whole organism. Physiology (including biochemistry and biophysics) simply cannot be studied apart from the anatomy that is its necessary and sufficient condition. Behavior, in turn, arises from and acts by means of anatomical organization and physiological processes. A first conclusion is that study of the evolution of behavior cannot be successfully pursued without simultaneous study of the evolution of all other aspects of organisms as wholes.

A broad, synthetic approach to the evolution of behavior is a comparatively recent development. It has been advanced especially in America by several conferences and symposia in recent years. The number of workers involved is in the hundreds, but just a few may be mentioned by way of example.

Alfred S. Romer, a paleontologist at Harvard University, has followed the crucial influence of locomotory behavior as revealed by vertebrate fossils over several hundred million years. Frank A. Beach, an animal behaviorist, long at Yale University and now at the University of California, has made extensive comparative studies of sexual behavior and the evolution of endocrine glands and secretions. Geneticists Ernst Caspari, now at the University of Rochester, and Herman T. Spieth of the University of California are among those who are studying the genetical basis of evolution with emphasis on behavioral concomitants. Ernst Mayr of Harvard University is one of many zoologists who are concerned with the importance of behavioral evolution for the science of systematics.

In anthropology, the evolutionary approach had for a time fallen into disfavor, but it is now being revived by some ethnologists such as Margaret Mead of the American Museum of Natural History, experimentalists such as S. L. Washburn of the University of California, and anatomists such as William Straus, Jr., of Johns Hopkins University.

Comparative psychology, the core science for this approach, was curiously inadequate as regards evolutionary concepts and principles until rather recently. A truly evolutionary approach was developed by the late Henry W. Nissen of the Yerkes Laboratories and Harry F. Harlow of the University of Wisconsin, among others.

It is this breadth of attack, the application of evolutionary concepts to every discipline and specialty touching on behavior, that especially characterizes much American work on the subject at present. In this country, that is more significant than the rise of any one school, as, for instance, the ethological school of Tinbergen, Lorenz, and others in Europe. The current approach involves, but is also much wider in scope than, numerous intensely specialized studies, such as those on social insects by von Frisch in Europe and Schneirla in the United States, among many others.

Evolution is history, and the direct approach to history is by means of original documents distributed through time in a known sequence. In this case the pertinent documents are fossils. There is a surprisingly large absolute number of fossils that yield directly observable physiological and behavioral data, but the number is still relatively so small that these exceptional fossils are not sufficiently enlightening as to the evolution of behavior. The fossil data are overwhelmingly anatomical and quite incomplete even with respect to anatomy, usually including only hard parts, skeletal elements.

Incomplete as it is, the fossil record does bear on the evolution of behavior in two important ways. First, its anatomical evidence permits many conclusions as to the processes of evolution in general that are, with suitable precautions, also applicable to the evolution of behavior. Second, a considerable part of the behavior of animals can be inferred from their skeletons and hence from fossils. That is particularly true of locomotion, which depends so characteristically on skeletal parts that it can often be worked out in great detail from these alone. This has, for example, been done for the horse family, in which some of the most important evolutionary changes were in locomotory behavior. Changes in locomotion were also essentially involved in the origin of man, and something about these is also being learned from fossils. In suitable instances, much can also be determined from fossils about other behavioral traits such as food-getting, attack, and defense.

At this point it is necessary to recognize that there are different (although intergrading) levels of behavior and that the directly historical data are for the most part confined to a relatively basic or primary level. A bird, for instance, is capable of certain motions of the jaws, the head and neck, the wings, the legs and feet, and so on. The nature and extent of these motions are closely determined by the skeletal elements involved, and they can be quite precisely inferred from a well-preserved fossil. This already tells us a good deal about the behavior of a particular bird, but only about what may be called elemental behavior. In life those basic elements of behavior are frequently compounded into definite sequences and combinations. For instance, in many birds courtship involves elaborate behavior based on the elemental motions but programmed in ways characteristic of each species and different in distinct species. Such programmed, compound, or second-order behavior is certainly vitally important for evolution, and it cannot, as a rule, be inferred from anatomy alone or from the directly historical evidence of fossils.

We will later refer briefly to the still higher order of behavior involved in human cultures. The point here is that much behavior above the elemental level can be studied only in living animals. We are therefore without directly historical evidence on many important aspects of the evolution of behavior. For this part of the study, we have only the results and not the record of the historical events. In fact, the same limitation applies to much of anatomical and most of physiological evolution. The situation is far from hopeless, however. Comparative study of recent animals can, in skilled and scientifically sophisticated hands, reveal the essential antecedent historical events.

It must be admitted that many comparative studies of animal behavior have been relatively unskilled and naive from an evolutionary point of view. It is naive, for instance, to assume that a rat is a primitive animal and that its behavior, by and large, is phylogenetically anterior to that of a man. A rat is a highly specialized animal, divergently adapted to a way of life, and hence to behavioral patterns, quite different from any that ever occurred in an ancestor of man. It would, however, be equally wrong to conclude that no historical inferences can be drawn from careful comparison of human and rat behavior. What is needed is a more complex and more careful application of historical principles and concepts, many of which are available from better documented aspects of evolution. It is here that the current rapprochement of behavioral and evolutionary research can be expected to be especially fruitful.

We have been speaking mostly of historical events and their reconstruction. Fuller understanding of evolution also requires knowledge of the mechanisms and processes involved in, and in a sense producing, those events. In turn, such knowledge helps to put inferences about the events on a sounder basis. Here the science of genetics is especially pertinent, and some attention must now be paid to the relationships between genetics and behavior.

The study of these relationships was long obscured by a wrong approach embodied in the false dichotomy between "inherited" and "acquired" characteristics, equated in earlier behavioral studies with "instinctual" and "learned" behavior. It took a long time for biologists and psychologists to realize that very few characteristics are strictly and completely either inherited or acquired, and that perhaps even fewer items of behavior are 100 per cent either instinctual or learned.

Among higher animals at least, and with exceptions not important to us here, characteristics, whether anatomical, physiological, or behavioral, are not inherited as such. What is inherited is information, a set of plans that guide the development of an organism and that determine the eventual nature and limits of its structures, functions, and activities. In some respects, mostly of a biochemical nature and far below the behavioral level, the genetic determination is highly precise and specific. The biochemical blood groups are an example. More often, especially as regards behavior, genetic determinants set a narrower or wider range to which development is limited, but do not determine the exact point within the range that the organism will in fact reach.

In such circumstances, the developmental range, which always does have limits, is inherited, but the point within that range is acquired. That is why the strict statement that something is *either* inherited *or* acquired often becomes meaningless. Human speech is a striking and familiar example. The specifically human capacity for true speech is completely determined by genetic control of development. The particular language spoken by any one man is acquired; it is learned. The songs of birds provide similar examples over a broader gamut. In some species a particular, quite precise song is genetically determined. In others only the capacity to sing is so determined and within that capacity almost any song may be learned.

Another way of looking at this matter is that behavioral and other characteristics are more or less modifiable according to the life experiences of the individual. Some are hardly modifiable at all, and it does make sense to call them rather strictly inherited or instinctual. Others are modifiable over a wide (but never limitless) range, and with some reservation it is then fair to think of the particular modification that develops as acquired or, in behavioral terms, learned.

It is well known that Lamarckian and neo-Lamarckian theories of evolution envision an especially direct and firm kind of interaction between behavior and genetics. Lamarck supposed, and his followers continued to maintain, that the behavior of an organism—especially but rather crudely its use or disuse of organs—modifies its organization and that such modifications eventually become heritable. Although that view still has some adherents, it has been widely discarded for three main reasons (among others). First, the genetic mechanism is now fairly well known, and it seems to provide no possible means for the inheritance of acquired characteristics as postulated by Lamarck. Second, neither laboratory experiment nor observation in nature has produced a single properly controlled and confirmed example of Lamarckian inheritance, and the results of many careful and extensive studies have all been negative. Third, an alternative theory that is based on modern genetics and is confirmed by many studies adequately explains the known phenomena.

The alternative theory stems from Darwin, although it has developed so far beyond him that it is no longer informative to call it Darwinian or even neo-Darwinian. According to this theory, the basic directive process of evolution is the action of natural selection on the mutations and recombinations of genetic factors in populations. The theory is far more complex and subtle than that bald statement allows, but we cannot here go into its myriad details beyond one main additional point especially pertinent to our present subject.

On the face of things, it might appear that this theory excludes reciprocal relationships between behavior and genetics. If true, that would be an almost fatal flaw in the theory, because there is abundant evidence that such relationships are at least probable. However, it was long ago suggested, and has lately been firmly demonstrated, that mutation-recombination-selection theory does provide a potent mechanism for reciprocal influence between the behavioral and the genetic systems. In the terms preferred by some electronically-minded biologists, there is mutual feedback or a cybernetic relationship between the two systems.

Again the details are so intricate that we cannot present them adequately. Perhaps, however, we can convey the central idea in an oversimplified way. We start from the basis of the genetically determined behavioral reaction range. As a concrete though mildly speculative example, we might take a Devonian crossopterygian fish. It normally lived in the water, but its reaction ranges included the possibility of coming out on land, breathing air, and stumping along on its axially-stiffened paired fins.

It is a fair assumption that by no means all crossopterygians took advantage of this possibility. Most of them were, so to speak, content with entirely fishlike behavior. But the more amphibian-like behavior was genetically possible as a matter of choice—we think the word "choice" here is justified and informative even though it must be understood in a non-anthropomorphic way.

The next element in the process is that the behavior that was marginal or atypical, but still within the reaction range, was quite advantageous for survival under some local and perhaps temporary conditions. That is demonstrably true in some recent minor experimental examples and is at least reasonable in our major historical example. Natural selection would then act strongly and in two main ways. In the first place it would tend to narrow the reaction range, to reinforce, intensify, and eventually stabilize the particular part of the range that had special survival (hence reproductive) value for these particular animals. Eventually it would probably eliminate the former norm, the strictly fishlike part of the range. The amphibian-like behavior that was formerly facultative, "chosen," or "learned" would become obligatory, "inherited" or "instinctive." Behavior has effectively fed back into the genetic system, which in turn has fed back into the behavioral system by stabilizing it around a new norm.

At the same time, selection would have an important second effect. It would favor other mutations and recombinations that were disadvantageous in relation to the original norm but advantageous as the new norm became established. For instance, selection would tend to retain fins in our Devonian fish as long as it was behaviorally a fish even part of the time. But when it became behaviorally amphibian, selection would favor genetic variation toward the development of legs. The combination of these processes in our example is, indeed, how amphibians evolved from fishes, a major transformation in the evolutionary line that eventually produced mankind.

That, in brief, is a clear and factually based theory of reciprocal interaction between behavior and genetics mediated by natural selection. Once this interaction theory is grasped, it illuminates many of the events of evolutionary history. There is little doubt that this sort of process has been common throughout the history of life, and that it is still occurring today. That is not to say that it is the *only* pattern of behavioral evolution, which has certainly been more varied on the whole. It is evident that in some instances the link between behavior and genetics has been more direct, not in the Lamarckian way, but by more immediate and more narrowly determinate effects of genetic factors on behavior. There is, for example, some evidence that biochemical changes directly mediated by genes can have specific effects on behavior.

Many considerations strongly suggest that most behavioral evolution is adaptive, even though inadaptive changes are not excluded. It is, indeed, a general conclusion that sustained evolutionary trends of any kind, behavioral or otherwise, are adaptive while they are occurring. The once popular idea of orthogenesis, in the sense of an internal tendency to change regardless of adaptive advantage, is no more than a dismal blunder that we should long since have left behind us.

Indeed there is some danger of circular reasoning in the statement that behavior and its evolution are normally adaptive. "Correct" behavior in a natural sense is correct precisely because it favors survival and reproduction, hence is by definition adaptive. "Incorrect" behavior, in the same sense, if widespread and persistent, can only lead to extinction. Behavior is more directly open to the action of natural selection than the structural and functional patterns that underlie it.

As to broad trends, it is obvious that the fundamental dichotomy of organisms into plants and animals is behavioral as well as structural and functional. Plants have very simple behavior or none at all. Animals usually show much and commonly quite complex behavior. More than to any other one factor this is surely due to the fact that most animals are mobile, at least during some phase of their lives. This mobility is evidently related to the fact that so many animals actively seek their food.

Among animals, there has been a constant interplay not only of innumerable specific behavioral patterns but also of more basic tendencies. In part this involves a balance between narrower and wider reaction ranges or less and more modifiable behavior. Increasing behavioral complication may arise in either way, or in both at once. The opposite tendencies are well exemplified by the two widely divergent terminal groups that have, on the whole, the most elaborate behavior of all: the insects and the mammals.

Most insect behavior is comparatively stereotyped, governed by genetic programming. Most mammalian behavior is highly modifiable, its details, at least, learned. Yet even in this well-known contrast the distinction is not absolute. Insect behavior is somewhat modifiable; many insects are capable of some modest learning. And on the other hand, even man, the greatest learner of all, has some unlearned behavior. Birds, another group with unusually complex behavior, may have a more even balance of more and less modifiable behavior.

It has often been remarked but cannot be too strongly emphasized that in man there are two parallel and interacting evolutions, one biological and one cultural. Both were involved in man's origin and both are certainly proceeding today, although in directions that only the foolhardy would venture to predict. From our present point of view, it is to be noted that the *capacity* for culture (the ability for speech, the complex sensory and associative mechanism, the hand-eye coordination, and the rest), was the result of strictly biological evolution. All these characteristics are plainly under genetic control and all certainly evolved in just the same way as birdsong or frog-hop or, for that matter, the tapeworm's remarkable reproductive capacity. But what in fact made for culture and for cultural evolution was the extraordinary latitude of these mechanisms, the great width of their reaction ranges, which also evolved biologically through natural selection.

Certainly there are marked genetical differences in the ranges of behavior of human individuals in any one population. There are also probably some such, but lesser, differences in the average ranges of different racial populations, although that is as yet more a matter of inference and of probability than of trustworthy data. By and large, however, the behavioral differences among human populations occur within almost the same reaction ranges. Most special and differential traits of human behavior are culturally determined. We all share nearly the same biological capacities, and our behavioral diversity is almost entirely cultural. Cultural evolution is both more rapidly and more easily controllable than biological evolution. Even though "rapid" and "easy" are quite relative terms in this connection, these considerations do give some basis for moderate optimism about the future course of human evolution.

9 NEUROPSYCHOLOGY IN AMERICA

Karl H. Pribram

Karl H. Pribram, M.D., U.S.P.H.S. Research Professor of Physiological Psychology at Stanford University, was born in Vienna, Austria, in 1919. A graduate of the University of Chicago Medical School, Dr. Pribram began his professional career as a neurological surgeon, in which capacity he served on the staffs of the Chicago Memorial Hospital, St. Luke's Hospital, and the Yerkes Laboratory of Primate Biology. In 1948 he was appointed Research Assistant Professor of Physiology and Psychology at the Yale University School of Medicine. Dr. Pribram served as Chairman of the Department of Neurophysiology at the Institute of Living in Hartford, Connecticut from 1951 to 1956, and in 1956 was appointed Director of the Institute's Research and Laboratories. Dr. Pribram joined the staff of Stanford University in the fall of 1959.

A time-honored pursuit of philosophers, of psychiatrists and neurologists, and of physiologists and anatomists has been a study of the neural mechanisms that critically affect behavior. But in America during recent years new impetus to discovery has been provided from several fresh sources. These are experimental psychology, electrophysiology, Russian neurophysiology of the Pavlovian type, psychosurgery, and psychopharmacology. The aim of this presentation is to trace briefly the effects that each of these tributaries has had in the development of a body of knowledge that has sufficient scope and unity by now to have acquired the label "neuropsychology."

American experimental psychology is characterized by the precision of its techniques and theories. Theories of learning and decision-making are couched in mathematical language. Factorial analyses of individual differences are used not only in the laboratory but also as standard techniques in the evaluation of competencies. Devices have been perfected that allow precise recording of the number, latency, or rate of responses in various problem-solving situations. Programming an ever increasing array of schedules of stimulus, reward, and punishment presentations has become an art. These devices allow tremendous flexibility in the type of problem set to human and animal organisms.

Still more recently, data analysis by computer has become a frequent concomitant of the ever increasing amount of data that can be gathered per unit time. These are only some of the everyday events that a visitor to American psychological laboratories would find in abundance, and, here and there, these techniques and theories are combined with those aimed at a study of the nervous system.* On these occasions, a reevaluation of earlier concepts invariably results.

The older views were usually derived exclusively from clinical and neuroanatomical observation. Often the new data, because of their quantitative character, show up old notions as fuzzy. Precision in theory construction makes possible a restatement of fact and hypothesis which is at the same time more definitive and broader in scope. And the interdisciplinary referents from which these data and concepts are derived promise to bridge the gap that now exists between the physical and biological sciences on the one hand and the behavioral sciences and humanities on the other.

The single most pervasive advance in analysis of neural mechanisms has been electrophysiology, the development of electrical techniques to amplify and measure potential changes that can be recorded from brain and nerve. Whether or not the electrical manifestations of neural activity reflect accurately the essential processes within the nervous system that affect behavior remains to be proved. Nonetheless, elec-

---

* K. H. Pribram, "Toward a Science of Neuropsychology," in *Current Trends in Psychology and the Behavioral Sciences* (Pittsburgh: University of Pittsburgh Press, 1954).

trical techniques have been used to study the organization of the nervous system and, more recently, to demonstrate that at least something is going on within the brain while an organism responds behaviorally in particular situations.

That the brain is critically involved in the determination of behavior has been man's faith for some time, a faith based mainly on observations made on patients who have suffered brain injury. To prove that the brain *is* actually concerned in the regulation of specific aspects of behavior has been the task that has occupied the neurophysiologist, and at last he has the tools to make the demonstration.

An extension of these preliminary results stems from the impact of Russian neurophysiology, which has pursued in several directions the techniques initiated by Pavlov. In combination with the methods of experimental psychology and of electrophysiology, some beginnings are being made in the analysis of the differences in neural processes that accompany differences in behavioral manifestations.

Pavlov's conditional reflex technique, a very simple way to demonstrate a change in behavior with experience, is combined with electrical recordings made from a variety of locations in the brain. And correlations are demonstrated between the behavioral changes and those that occur in the brain. Some of these, such as the mechanisms that allow the organism to be sensitive to "error" when it attempts to solve problems, are of fundamental importance to theory and clinical practice. These early results do show promise and should prove interesting to pursue during the next decade.*

Psychosurgery has fallen into a secondary place in therapy in the United States. However, the stimulus that the psychosurgical procedure has had in providing research funds and in interesting young people in the effects of brain lesions on complex behavioral processes is almost unmeasurable. The

* Proceedings of the Macy Conferences on "The Central Nervous System and Behavior," 1958 and 1959.

fact that man can interfere in a human being's psychic life is at the same time frightening and challenging. Contrary to what one would expect, the most important results for research have not been the study of the effects of psychosurgery in man, but study of the effects of brain lesions on the more complex behavioral processes in animals, especially primates. Advances have been made in the description of the strategies that monkeys develop to solve problems and of what constitutes a "problem" in the first place.

The hitherto silent areas of the brain cortex have yielded some of their mystery to these explorations, and the advances in knowledge have been sufficiently great to warrant a thorough recasting of currently held notions. Interestingly, the impact of these explorations is at the moment felt most in engineering laboratories devoted to the construction of computers. Problems of memory storage and retrieval, of perception and programming, of computation and logic are common to those interested in the brain—whether it be made of metal or of tissue. What the offspring of this marriage between the communication and computer engineer and the neurobiologist will be like, it is too early to say—but hybridization in this instance, as in most others, promises vigor. If the noise and heat generated by the mating is any index, the lusty cybernetic infant will have a lasting impact not only in the behavioral sciences but in the way man makes all of his science in the future.*

In the immediate present, psychopharmacology has replaced psychosurgery as the practical focus around which basic research is crystallized. The challenge is: How do the psychopharmacological agents produce their effect? The assumption is almost universally held that the effect is mediated through neural mechanisms, and the search is on to determine what these mechanisms might be. So the visitor would

* G. A. Miller, Eugene Galanter, and K. H. Pribram, *Plans and the Structure of Behavior* (New York: Henry Holt and Co., 1960).

find pharmaceutical houses supporting research laboratories wherein the techniques of experimental psychology and those of biochemistry and pharmacology, as well as those of electrophysiology and even psychosurgery, are combined. At the moment this area of convergent endeavor is so new that prediction of future results is risky. Chances are that empirically useful data will emerge—here the medical clinician rather than the communication and computer engineer may reap the practical benefits.*

So much for technical advances. Now, what are some of the substantive gains which these combinations of methods have made possible? Only a few of the most striking facts and most interesting advances can be mentioned here. Of course, one never knows whether a finding that at this time appears to be of minor importance may not in the proper hands grow into something that overshadows those which now seem more significant.

Some age-old questions important to the behavioral sciences have recently received definitive answers. One such question is whether the brain is or is not a *tabula rasa* upon which experience is etched. What happens when brain tissue is completely isolated? Does it, much as does the heart, show evidence of intrinsically generated activity, or is the brain essentially quiescent? The answer, as is so often the case, fully supports neither the notion that brain activity is basically spontaneous, nor the axiom of a passive matrix. Even in the unanesthetized preparation, the isolated brain slab remains silent unless stimulated, but any brief excitation will cause electrical discharges to persist for long periods of time.

Thus, though the brain is quiescent in the absence of input, the tissue is easily aroused to prolonged activity; hence, at rest it may be conceived to be in a state just below the level for continuous self-excitation, and in the intact animal

* Abraham Wikler, *The Relation of Psychiatry to Pharmacology* (Baltimore: William and Wilkins Co., 1957).

a mechanism exists to insure excitation beyond such a resting level.* This mechanism is a spontaneous discharge of receptors and sense organs in general. Gradually, the investigations of the past several decades, involving especially the techniques of electrophysiology, have forced upon us the idea that spontaneous activity is an integral part of the performance of sensory instruments.†

Evidence has accumulated that this spontaneous activity of sense organs makes them, through their connections, one of the brain's most important activators. Sensory receptors and the brain, then, together make an active unit which interacts with the environment, and this interaction is intricately determined. Even in such simple organisms as the sea urchin, the intrinsic activities of the nervous system are patterned, not just homogeneous and generalized.

The effects of interaction depend on the ongoing neural activity and the differences between such activities at different locations in the nervous system of the organism. Differences in environmental conditions are, therefore, reacted to in terms of these differences in neural activity.‡ The response of the organism is the resultant. If this is true of the sea urchin, how much more must it be true of man?

Another important contribution made primarily by electrophysiology is the finding that in the core of the central nervous system there are tissues characterized by their relatively diffuse organization. These reticular tissues serve the organism by changing the state of excitability of the entire brain. The spontaneously active sensory receptors discharge directly into this diffuse tissue and, therefore, tend to keep

---

* B. D. Burns, *The Mammalian Cerebral Cortex* (London: Edward Arnold Publishers, Ltd., 1958).

† R. Granit, *Receptors and Sensory Perception* (New Haven: Yale University Press, 1955).

‡ T. H. Bullock, "Evolution of Neurophysiological Mechanisms," in *Behavior and Evolution* (New Haven: Yale University Press, 1958), Chapter 8, pp. 165–177.

the brain "awake." In fact, destruction of this reticular sub-stance of the core of the brain results in an interminably sleeping animal.*

Equally exciting has been the finding that animals with electrodes placed deep within their brains will turn on a switch in order to stimulate themselves with electrical current. Only certain areas of the brain make the animal respond in this way, and the inference has been drawn, correctly or incorrectly, that these areas serve as "reward centers" for the organism. Mechanisms of reward and punishment have fascinated not only neurophysiologists but also experimental psychologists.† And so the varied techniques described earlier have been brought to bear on the problem, and with this increase in sophistication our areas of ignorance have expanded.

No longer can we say simply, "here is a pleasure center, here is a pain center in the brain," for stimulation of one and the same spot may produce behavior quite different depending upon the situation in which the organism finds itself. The arguments of the philosophers are taken out of the realm of the speculative and into the laboratory. The arguments remain the same, but now tissue is involved and the behavior of organisms studied. This new solidity has a two-fold effect. First, it shows that the arguments of the philosophers were not just "hot air," and secondly, it shows that the naive materialism which has served the biologist so well thus far must be amplified, if not totally discarded, if his data are to make any sense to him or to anyone else.

The advent of the study of the effects of drugs on these same neural mechanisms may throw some light on just what is experienced as pleasurable or unpleasurable by an organism. But as yet only the techniques are available, and fer-

---

* H. W. Magoun, *The Waking Brain*, (Springfield, Ill.: Chas. C Thomas, 1958).
† James Olds, "Higher Functions of the Central Nervous System," in *Annual Review of Physiology*, 1959.

ment is in the air. What will come out of all this activity remains to be seen.

A closely related area of investigation has been the exploration of the core structures of the brain: the reticular formation of the brain, already mentioned; the hypothalamus and thalamus; and the limbic systems of the endbrain, which lie along the innermost edge of the cerebral hemispheres. Anatomically, these structures are closely interrelated. Current theory holds that the core structures regulate the drives of the organism by mechanisms similar to the thermostat that regulates the temperature of a building.

The term homeostats is used to designate these biological regulatory mechanisms.* Each mechanism has certain components, including a receptor element which is sensitive to the hormone or metabolite that it regulates, just as the thermostat is sensitive to the temperature which it controls. In addition, each mechanism is so constructed that there is a reciprocal connection or "feed-back" loop between the sensitive mechanisms and another unit that operates in such a fashion as to increase or decrease the amount of the substance regulated. In the thermostat, this is the control mechanism of the furnace that turns it on when the temperature in the room drops and turns it off when the temperature has risen beyond a certain point.

And finally, each mechanism has a bias or setting device which controls the level around which the homeostasis takes place. In the thermostat, this setting device is usually a small dial that can be controlled by hand. In the biological homeostats, this setting device is probably the excitability level of the reticular substance of the brain stem core, to which reference has already been made.

The limbic systems are linked by multiple reciprocal connections with the internal core homeostats. Some of these connections are long and conduct impulses from one place to

* K. H. Pribram, "A Review of Theory in Physiological Psychology," in *Annual Review of Psychology*, 1960.

another without any discontinuities. Other connections have several discontinuities intercalated, and still others have a great many. The functional result of this type of multi-linking can only be guessed at the moment: when electronic models are constructed with these characteristics, an ultra-stable system results. In the face of externally initiated perturbations, such a system shows a "disposition" to return to its prior level of excitability. Such stability is necessary to an electronic or biological organism if it is to be sensitive to error. Could it be, then, that the limbic formations of the endbrain control the dispositions of organisms, dispositions that depend on the functions of the homeostatic mechanisms that regulate the organism's internal environment?

Neuro-behavioral investigations support such a notion. "Instinctive" behavior is most obviously disturbed when lesions are made in the limbic systems. Mechanisms of feeding, fleeing, fighting, maternal, and mating behavior are disrupted when portions of the limbic systems are surgically ablated. But more basically, sensitivity to error is decreased when organisms are faced with problems to solve, and electrophysiological evidence shows that the activity of certain formations within the limbic areas changes when errors are made by organisms performing certain tasks. No wonder that neurophysiologists and experimental psychologists are so excited by these findings that they are overcoming major technical difficulties and pursuing their explorations into the deepest recesses of the brain.

As a last point, considerable progress has been made by a combination of the techniques of psychosurgery, experimental psychology, and electrophysiology in delineating the functions of the so-called association areas of the brain in cognitive behavior. Two large categories can be discerned, one dealing with knowledge and information. The posterior portions of the forebrain deal with this type of cognitive activity. The other, served by the frontal areas of the brain, is more difficult to specify.* The American term "know-how" comes closest, perhaps, to characterizing this form of activity. Wisdom is a more hallowed term for the same processes when they deal less with the immediate physical environment and more with the social aspects of situations.

To know and to know how are certainly different, and experimental evidence is now available that these differences have their roots in differences between neural mechanisms. Many other things could be mentioned. The story of the simulation of brain activity by computers is one. Another would deal with the studies of the differences in chemistry between different portions of the central nervous system and how these differences are related to mechanisms of drive. Equally fascinating are the investigations, only just beginning, of memory storage in the brain. And the related problem of retrieval or recall of this stored material has as yet hardly been formulated as an experimental problem. And so one could go on and on.

In summary, then, what can be said of the past, present, and future of neuropsychology's contributions to behavioral science in America? In the past half century, the important advances have been of method and technique. Even in the realm of theory technical precision has characterized the advances. Currently, a change is taking place. There is ferment. There are new applications and combinations of already available techniques. Thinkers are beginning to range freely again and not be tied to their technical, logical rigidities.

There is some danger that the neuropsychologically-oriented behavioral scientist may lose himself in the wealth of data and the free-ranging speculations that are now possible to him. But this danger is counterbalanced by the promise of a fresh view of man by man. Western thought has alternated between two views of man's relations to his universe. One view holds that he is an essentially passive organ-

* K. H. Pribram, "On the Neurology of Thinking," in *Behavioral Science,* October, 1959.

ism shaped by the exigencies of his environment. The other emphasizes his active role, manipulative and selective not only of artifacts but of sense data as well. The American neuropsychological contributions to behavioral science point to a resurgence of the dignity of man as a scientific as well as a political and humanistic tenet.

10 ANIMAL STUDY

Harry F. Harlow

Harry F. Harlow, Professor of Psychology at the University of Wisconsin and Director of the Primate Laboratory and the Wisconsin Regional Primate Center, was born in Fairfield, Iowa, in 1905. Dr. Harlow received both his bachelor and doctoral degrees in psychology from Stanford University. He joined the faculty of the University of Wisconsin in 1930 as an assistant professor of Psychology. After further advanced study from 1939 to 1940 as a Carnegie Fellow at Columbia University, he returned to the Wisconsin faculty, with which he has been associated throughout his professional career. A specialist in primate psychobiology, the cortical localization of function in monkeys, and learning and motivation, Dr. Harlow is a member of the National Academy of Sciences, the American Philosophical Society, and the American Academy of Arts and Sciences. From 1950 to 1962, he served as editor of the Journal of Comparative and Physiological Psychology.

At the present time the behavior of animals is being actively studied by scientists both in Europe and America. The European investigators have been for the most part zoologists with a background and interest in problems of behavioral evolution and taxonomy. Their tradition has been to study animals, most often birds, fish, or insects, in their natural or semi-natural environment. Many of the European workers use the term "ethology" to refer to their animal behavior studies, and they describe themselves as "ethologists."

In America zoologists have been primarily interested in the adaptations of animals to their environment rather than the direct study of animal behavior, and most animal behavior studies have been made by the comparative psychologists. For the most part these researches are experimental studies conducted in the laboratory, as contrasted with observational studies under natural conditions. The American behavioral scientists have been much more concerned with learning than with unlearned or instinctual responses, and a large part of their investigations involve the analysis of various kinds of learning, or the determination of the way in which other variables, such as hunger, thirst, age, or past experience affect learning.

In the past, even the recent past, a majority of the American studies were conducted on a single animal species, the rat. Experiments, by their very nature, usually require many subjects if there are to be adequate experimental and control groups. Limitations of both laboratory space and funds necessitated the use of a relatively cheap and small animal, and the rat became this standard animal. Although the rat has some advantages as a research animal and has lent itself to some excellent behavioral studies, the preponderant use of the rat limited psychologists in the kinds of behavioral problems they could investigate. Fortunately, the trend to concentrate research on the rat has been reversed, and the animal studies presently being conducted involve many different animal species. The percentage of investigations in which other animals, including chimpanzees, monkeys, cats, dogs, raccoons, mice, pigeons, chickens, ducks, fish, worms, and even more primitive forms, are used as subjects is steadily increasing. Actually, most of the research on subhuman primates, particularly rhesus monkeys and chimpanzees, has been done in America during the last thirty years.

Although differences in interest, emphasis, and methods exist between the European ethologists and the American comparative psychologists, they should not be considered antagonistic. Dr. Otto Loehler's studies of complex learning in birds, particularly in regard to number concepts, are imaginative investigations conducted under rigorous laboratory conditions, and Dr. Karl von Frisch's studies in communication among bees represent experimental studies of unsurpassed excellence under naturalistic conditions. Furthermore, progressively greater attention has been given by many ethologists to experimental alteration of field conditions and to laboratory testing and refinement of theories based on naturalistic observations.

Conversely, excellent naturalistic studies have been made by American psychologists. Noteworthy are investigations by Dr. Theodore Schneirla on the army ant, and by Dr. Ray Carpenter on howler monkeys, macaques, gibbons, and orangutans. Nor are such interests declining, for in the past few years there have been four American groups conducting field studies on the mountain gorilla, the baboon, the rhesus monkey, and the howler monkey.

Neither have the American psychologists ignored the study of basic responses, frequently described as instinctive. There is a wealth of studies on fundamental behavior patterns, including sexual behavior in rats, guinea pigs, monkeys, and chimpanzees and nest building, maternal, and food-hoarding behavior in rats. By and large, the Americans differ from the Europeans in that the Americans have given more attention to the role of internal variables, such as the endocrines, and of learning variables, than have the ethologists. The different emphasis on learning probably stems in part from different interests, but in large part it results from the fact that the Europeans have studied non-mammalian forms, whereas the Americans have worked with mammals, whose basic behavior patterns are much more influenced by learning.

One of the primary contributions of the American workers to the study of animal behavior is the development of useful and reliable test apparatus and test methods. Unfortunately, it is possible to mention only a few. The Hampton Court Maze was the prototype for one of our most widely used instruments, and a host of mazes of diverse forms and kinds has been employed. During the developmental period, mazes became progressively more complex, and mazes with fourteen or more cul-de-sacs have been widely used, in part because of the high reliability of such devices.

A large number of variables influencing maze learning were studied, including massed vs. spaced practice, whole vs. part learning, active vs. passive learning, order of elimination of errors, the effects of hunger, and introduction of preferred vs. non-preferred incentives. The effects of many physiological variables have also been measured, including inadequate diets, hormones, drugs, enzymes, electroconvulsive shock, destruction of various receptor systems, and cortical and subcortical lesions. By and large these maze studies gave useful learning information. The techniques that produced efficient classroom learning in man produced efficient learning in rats also, and the complex maze has proved to be an effective instrument for assaying the effects of brain lesions and of physiological and pharmacological agents.

Although the multiple-unit maze is still frequently used in psychological experiments, it has been replaced to a considerable extent by simpler forms of apparatus, by single cul-de-sac mazes, a single T or single Y unit, and by the straight runway, an apparatus consisting only of a starting box, a straight runway, and a reward chamber. Obviously, learning is achieved very rapidly in such instruments, and in many experiments they are used to determine the variables that are essential to maintain performance or running activity, rather than learning per se.

The rationale for their use lies in the fact that it is difficult to maintain efficient performance in the complex mazes unless a relatively high motivational state is maintained in the animal. By using the simpler single T or Y mazes and the straight runway it is possible to study the effects of a wider range of motivational states on learning and the maintenance of previously learned responses. Very brief as well as very long periods of food and water deprivation and very small as well as large amounts of food and liquid rewards will maintain ongoing behavior, enabling the psychologist to study the effects of the full range of motivational states on problems relating to spaced and massed practice, infrequent as well as consistent rewards at the end of every trial, and second-order or derived reinforcements as contrasted with the primary reinforcers of foods and liquids. Furthermore, the effect of all these conditions on extinction as well as on learning may be measured.

An entirely different apparatus and method was created by Dr. B. F. Skinner and has been widely used. In its simplest form the Skinner box is a small chamber with a single lever at one end. Pressing the lever, or pressing the lever at a predetermined rate or frequency, automatically presents the subject with a reward. Learning is not measured by correct and incorrect responses but by the rate or increase of rate of lever-pressing, and forgetting or extinction is measured by a decreasing rate of lever-pressing. It has been demonstrated repeatedly that rate of response is a function of the particular schedule of reinforcement that is provided the animal; for example, the greater the number of responses required to obtain a single reward, the more rapid the rate of responding. A relatively unlimited number of different reinforcement schedules may be established, and each evokes a characteristic pattern of responsiveness whether pigeons, rats, or monkeys serve as subjects.

This rate-measure technique has proved to be an efficient measure of the effect of many variables on learning. Since many responses, that is, lever presses, can be elicited to produce a single reinforcement, satiation with the reward, usually food, is held to a minimum and prolonged work periods can be studied. Precise measures of unlearned and learned fears are reflected in changes in response rate, and the technique has proved to be unusually effective in measuring the effects of drugs and in screening new drugs for possible medical application. The method is also being used as a measure of psychotic behavior in mental patients, and it was the prototype for Dr. Skinner's teaching machines, automatic devices designed to train human beings, from nursery school through college, independently of a human instructor.

By the introduction of multiple levers, Skinner's technique may be used to measure discrimination learning, and it may also be complicated by rapid transitions from one schedule to another, either signaled or not signaled by some sensory cue. To date the apparatus has been primarily effective with rats or pigeons on relatively simple learning problems. Its usefulness in measuring complex learning abilities remains to be demonstrated.

Psychologists have long attempted to use the rat as an experimental animal for the study of complex learning, such as concept formation, reasoning, and insight. However, major efforts by the late Professor Edward Tolman and by Professors Paul Field and Norman Maier failed to demonstrate such abilities in these animals, and it would appear that we must turn to higher forms for such analyses. The remarkable studies by Dr. Wolfgang Köhler and by the late Dr. Robert Yerkes and associates on tool-using abilities in chimpanzees represented one such approach. The results indicate that the chimpanzee learns by trial and error to use tools. There is no evidence of problem-solving by insight or reasoning.

Fortunately there have been developed during the last thirty years very effective standardized learning-test techniques which measure, or come close to measuring, the full range of subhuman primate learning and thinking capabilities. These techniques have been developed on chimpanzees at the Yerkes laboratories and on monkeys at the Wisconsin Laboratory and represent modifications of basic techniques used by Dr. Nadigen Kohts in Russia. Effective scaling of problem difficulty has been achieved at the University of Wisconsin by separating more than one hundred monkeys from their mothers at birth, and testing the growth and development of the monkeys' learning abilities from the first day of life until they attain, or approximate, full intellectual development at about four years of age.

It is now possible to make effective comparisons of learning ability both within the primate order and between the primates and other mammalian forms. One of the most useful and reliable of these tests is that of multiple-problem learning. It was first demonstrated at the University of Wisconsin that rhesus monkeys, presented a sequence of similar discrimination problems, solved the early problems by a slow trial-and-error procedure. However, when they were tested on problem after problem, they showed progressive improvement in their efficiency and eventually solved any new discrimination problem with no errors or very few errors. This capacity to transfer information from successive problems of a given kind is probably basic to the formation of concepts.

Comparable data exist for multiple-problem learning on a wide variety of primates ranging from the primitive marmoset to the human being, and the efficiency of this learning is closely related to presumed status within the primate order and to known facts concerning anatomical and physiological data relating to cerebral cortical development. Thus, progressively greater learning efficiency has been demonstrated as we pass from marmoset, to squirrel monkey, to cebus monkey, to spider monkey, to rhesus monkey, to chimpanzee, and to man. Also, some information concerning the status of the rhesus monkey may be inferred from the fact that he learns these problems more efficiently than the human idiot or low-grade imbecile, but he is inferior to other human subjects.

Although the data outside the primate order are not definite, it would appear that even the marmoset is superior to the cat or raccoon, and that these animals are superior to all rodents; indeed, precise and efficient multiple-problem learning has not been demonstrated in rats or pigeons, although many attempts have been made to train these lower forms.

Obviously, it takes more than one test or test technique to arrange animals along a learning-capability continuum, and no doubt many animal forms have special learning capabilities. It may be noted, however, that simple kinds of learning, the kinds which newborn and infant monkeys master readily, do not differentiate animals at various phyletic levels; this is achieved only by more complex learning problems.

Another major area of research interest for the American animal psychologists has centered around problems of motivation. The early investigators were primarily concerned with the role of the homeostatic motives of hunger, thirst, and sex. Evidence was presented by Dr. Kurt Richter and Dr. G. H. Wang that these drives gave rise to recurring cycles of activity, measured in terms of free running in a revolving drum, and in terms of goal-directed behavior of eating and drinking, and of mating for the female rat.

More recently the effect of various periods of food and water deprivation on performance in standardized learning situations has been extensively investigated. In both the Skinner box and the straight runway, performance, as measured by speed of behavior or resistance to extinction, is enhanced by increasingly long deprivation periods. It is doubtful, however, if deprivation facilitates learning per se since discrimination learning by monkeys and rats is either not affected or is little affected by the amount of food deprivation.

Pioneering researches by Dr. Edward Tolman and by Dr. P. T. Young and their associates had indicated that the amount and kind of reward, that is, the incentive, was an important motivational force regardless of the period of food or water deprivation, and American psychologists have given increasing attention to the role of incentives in learning. A classical experiment by Dr. Leo Crespi showed that it was not the absolute amount of reward, but the amount of reward expected, that was the prime determiner of performance. Thus, if the amount of reward was decreased, performance abruptly suffered; if the amount was increased, performance abruptly improved, and these conditions were independent of absolute amount of reward.

A large body of research has been completed on the development of secondary motives or learned motives, as illustrated by a well-known study by Professor Neal Miller. Rats were trained to run from a white compartment to a black compartment to escape electric shock from the grid floor of the white compartment. It was subsequently shown that they would run from the white to the black compartment even if no shock were given, and, even more striking, they would learn to turn a wheel which opened a door blocking their escape from the white to the black chamber. Thus, the sight of the walls of the white compartment became a persisting motive for escape.

Equally striking results were obtained by Dr. Richard Solomon, testing dogs in a similar apparatus. Not only did the dogs learn rapidly to escape from the threatening chamber, but once this response was learned, it persisted over an almost unlimited number of extinction trials.

During the last ten years there has been a revival of interest among American psychologists in motivational mechanisms other than the homeostatic drives and their associated incentive systems. The late Professor Kay C. Montgomery conducted a series of studies demonstrating persistent exploration by rats as measured by locomotion in a goal-less maze, and showed that this activity was enhanced by such variables as novelty and complexity, and inhibited by fear and hunger. Furthermore, Montgomery demonstrated that rats could learn both spatial and non-spatial discriminations with no other reward than that of exploration.

Experiments were being concurrently conducted at the University of Wisconsin on the strength and role of exploratory motives in monkeys. The monkeys demonstrated a compulsive need to solve puzzles for no other reward than puzzle solution. Professor Robert Butler demonstrated intense and persisting visual exploration motives—monkeys placed in a dimly illuminated box would open a window hundreds of times for hours on end for the sheer pleasure of looking out.

The exploratory motives of chimpanzees have been investigated by Dr. Walter Welker at the Yerkes laboratories. Chimpanzees, like monkeys, have strong exploratory motives, but the chimpanzee satiates on a single object or plaything, demonstrating a compulsive need to explore different or changing stimuli. Furthermore, the chimpanzee differs from the monkey in one other way: the chimpanzee occasionally puts puzzles back together after taking them apart.

Professor Harry Harlow and associates have demonstrated that the affectional tie between the newborn monkey and its mother is more dependent upon contact motives than upon the satisfactions obtained from sucking and the elimination of hunger and thirst. Groups of newborn monkeys were separated from their real mothers and placed in individual cages, each with two artificial or surrogate mothers. One mother surrogate was made of welded wire and the other was of wire also, but covered with a terry-cloth sheath. Half the monkeys received milk from a small nursing bottle in the wire mother's body and half the monkeys received milk from the cloth-covered mother. The wire mothers offered no security, even for the babies that received all their milk from the wire mother. This and subsequent studies have pointed to the conclusion that nursing per se is a minor variable in the development of affection in infant monkeys.

The very fact that the American psychologists have conducted most of their animal behavior studies in the laboratory and have developed experimental laboratory test techniques no doubt accounts for the emphasis on psychophysiology that has characterized many of the American programs. The late Professor Karl Lashley's epochal work, which demonstrated the relative non-specificity of cortical localization of intellectual function, was the first of the many major programs that now exist. Lashley, himself, believed that all learned or intellectual functions were equally represented throughout all parts of the cerebral cortex and coined the phrase "equipoteniality of function" to describe the phenomenon. Whether or not this is strictly true, Lashley's research ended any belief in precise localization of specific learned functions within the cortex.

Twenty-five years later, researches concurrently conducted by Dr. Karl Pribram at Yale University and by Professor Harry Harlow at the University of Wisconsin indicated that a certain specificity of cortical localization of function probably existed. Using monkeys as subjects, and the refined learning tests that had been developed, they were able to show that solution of both simple and complex visual discrimination problems is adversely affected by partial removal of both temporal lobes and unaffected by partial removal of both frontal lobes. The converse was true for delayed-response tests, which presumably measure either immediate memory or some form of attentive processes. Less definitive researches suggest that learned responses mediated by body-sense information may be primarily affected by lesions of the parietal lobes in monkeys. However, in a very real sense these researches are extensions rather than contradictions of Lashley's thesis, since no investigator has discovered precise cortical localization for any complex learning or intellectual task or function.

These researches are merely representative of many programs that presently exist. Their success has been dependent upon the use of laboratory methods, the development of increasingly precise techniques for measuring different kinds of learning, and the use of monkeys as experimental subjects.

A number of years ago Dr. Heinrich Klüver and Dr. P. C. Bucy discovered that total removal of the temporal lobes in monkeys led to a remarkable pattern of behavior characterized by loss of fear and aggression, hypersexuality, and compulsive mouthing responses, with little or no loss of intellectual capability. These findings have led to many researches on the role of the primitive cortical and subcortical centers in the regulation of emotions, confirming the earlier work of Klüver and Bucy, and suggesting that there may even be differential subcortical localization of the various components of this behavior syndrome.

One of the most challenging ongoing programs correlating animal behavior with subcortical mechanisms stems from the original work of Dr. James Olds and Dr. Peter Milner at McGill University. These investigators discovered that the frequency of lever responses made by rats placed in a Skinner box could be greatly augmented by repetitive stimulation of subcortical centers which had previously been implanted with electrodes. In other words, there were brain centers which would reward lever-pressing responses, independently of food and water. Further researches showed that these subcortical centers were widely distributed, though all were not equally efficient. Stimulation by electrodes planted in the hypothalamus might induce continuous, repetitive lever presses until the rats stopped from sheer exhaustion, whereas satiation was induced more rapidly through electrodes implanted in the amygdaloid and septal areas. Furthermore, Olds demonstrated that rats could be trained to traverse straight runways and even learn multiple-unit mazes for no other reward than that of subcortical stimulation, and he has explained these results by postulating that pleasure centers are being activated.

The results obtained through the multiple researches by Olds have been confirmed in other laboratories and have been demonstrated to hold for other species, including the cat and the rhesus monkey. It has been shown that, under certain conditions, electrical stimulation of specific hypothalamic areas may produce antagonistic effects. Short intervals of stimulation may be positively reinforcing, that is, the rat will repetitively press a lever to obtain brain stimulation, whereas long intervals of stimulation may be negatively reinforcing in that the same rat will learn to select the left or right alley in a T maze to escape from the effects of ongoing brain stimulation.

The researches which we have described are merely illustrative of the way in which comparative psychologists have utilized their experimental laboratory techniques for the purpose of unraveling the difficult problems of psychophysiology. A great deal of our knowledge about the functioning of the reticulo-activating system, the system so intimately related to wakefulness and attentiveness, has come through the development, in large part by psychologists, of appropriate behavioral measures, both electro-encephalographic and conditioning.

Similar methods are bing used to measure directly both the cortical and subcortical centers that are the essential links in the formation and elicitation of conditioned responses. Finally, a wide range of learning techniques has been utilized to assess the effects of X irradiation and gamma irradiation on the central nervous system, with results that clearly demonstrate the radiation-resistant properties of the central nervous system. Learned behaviors ranging from the simplest to the most complex typically show no loss until the subjects, rats or monkeys, are near death from radiation illness.

In summary, laboratory experimental techniques in the study of animal behavior are, in and of themselves, both interesting and valuable. Beyond this, however, they appear to be the techniques of primary value for interdisciplinary research involving psychology on the one hand and pharmacology, neurology, or physiology, on the other.

No research method, however, has any exclusive priority. Laboratory researches will always have limited generality if we do not know the life history of the animal and its behavior under naturalistic conditions. Naturalistic studies have value in their own right and are indispensable for suggesting laboratory research problems. Laboratory methods may be adapted for naturalistic studies, even including pharmacological and physiological manipulations.

For these reasons, we see ever-increasing rapport and

cross-fertilization between the European ethologists and the American comparative psychologists. The ethologists have become progressively more laboratory-oriented and more interested in interdisciplinary research, and the animal psychologists have come to recognize that the full significance of laboratory animal studies can be understood only in terms of the social and even cultural variables regulating the behavior of animals within their natural environments.

11 LANGUAGE AND LINGUISTICS

Joseph H. Greenberg

Joseph H. Greenberg, Professor of Anthropology at Columbia University, was born in Brooklyn, New York, in 1915. An alumnus of Columbia University, Dr. Greenberg received his graduate degrees from Yale and Northwestern universities after advanced studies in anthropology which included research in Nigeria as a Fields Fellow of the Social Science Research Council. He began his teaching career as an instructor in anthropology at the University of Minnesota and later joined the faculty of Columbia University. Within recent years he has been the recipient of a Ford Foundation faculty research award (1951) and a Guggenheim award (1954–1955). A specialist in the ethnology of Africa, the classification of African languages, and general linguistics, Dr. Greenberg is the author of Studies in African Linguistic Classification, Quantitative Approach to a Morphological Typology of Language, *and* The Influence of Islam on a Sudanese Religion.

Language is unique to man. No other species possesses a truly symbolic means of communication and no human society, however simple its material culture, lacks the basic human heritage of a well-developed language. Language is the prerequisite for the accumulation and transmission of other cultural traits. Such fundamental aspects of human society as organized political life, legal systems, religion, and science are inconceivable without that most basic and human of tools, a linguistic system of communication. Language is not only a necessary condition for culture, it is itself a part of culture. It, like other shared behavioral norms, is acquired by the individual as a member of a particular social group through a complex process of learning. Like other aspects of human culture, it characteristically varies from group to group and undergoes significant modification in the course of its transmission through time within the same society.

It might have been thought self-evident that linguistics, the science which deals with this most characteristically human of traits, would always and indisputably have been considered a social science. Yet in the mid-nineteenth century, August Schleicher, a linguist of eminence, declared linguistics to be a *Naturwissenschaft* rather than *Geisteswissenschaft* (and, of course, he was not alone in this). More specifically, he conceived of language as an organism and of linguistics consequently as a biological science.

This view of course has long been abandoned. Yet it is worth asking why a thesis which to one generation is obviously false could have been seriously entertained and in some cases adopted by highly intelligent men, among the leaders in their science. For the grounds of this belief, some explicitly stated, some implicitly assumed, must be symptomatic of the state of the science itself and likely to leave traces in the thinking of succeeding generations of scholars.

We ask, then, why the view that linguistics was a natural science—and, more specifically, a biological science in a literal and not merely analogical fashion—should once have proved so attractive. A brief glance at the history of linguistic science will prove illuminating. Linguistics is, with the possible exception of economics, the most precocious of the behavioral sciences. The historic or comparative branch of the subject, which was the first to become prominent, achieved remarkable successes in the early part of the nineteenth century. The discovery that the vast majority of the peoples of Europe and western Asia spoke related languages derived from a common ancestral form was followed by the successful reconstruction of many of the phonetic and grammatical features of the Indo-European parent speech. This achievement threw a flood of light upon periods before the beginning of written history and stirred the historical imagination of educated men in the nineteenth century far beyond the confines of professional linguistics.

A further incidental aspect of this development impressed some thoughtful people as being of perhaps even greater ultimate significance than the specific historical results. This was the discovery of so-called "sound laws," that is, that under given phonetic circumstances, a particular sound changed regularly to some other sound. The most celebrated instance was that according to which certain sound-changes occurred in the course of development of the ancestral Germanic tongue from the earlier common Indo-European; this became known as Grimm's Law. It was, indeed, striking that in this apparently trivial aspect of human behavior, in which no one had suspected that there was any orderly principle, such regularity should exist. Kroeber, the eminent anthropologist, once remarked in conversation that in moments of discouragement regarding the prospects of the scientific study of human behavior, he took comfort in thinking of Grimm's Law.

A consideration of some aspects of this law, however, will show why, viewed in a certain light, it and similar phenomena might lead quite naturally to the view of language as a completely self-contained structure with laws of its own, quite detached from consideration of the other aspects of its speakers' behavior. For example, according to Grimm's Law, an original consonant *t* (which did not change in classical Latin, for example), would be changed to *th* in Germanic, where, in English at least, it has continued essentially unmodified to the present time. Thus *th* in English *three* corresponds to the Latin *t* in *tres,* with the same meaning; or again, English *thunder* is cognate with Latin *tonare,* "to thunder." In some cases, it appears that we have an exception. For example, English *stand* and German *stehen,* show a *t* against Latin *stare* "to stand," instead of the expected *th.* However, in this and other examples, the *t* is preceded by *s.* Therefore the law must be qualified by the statement that Proto-

Indo-European *t* changes to Germanic *th* when not preceded by *s*, but remains when preceded by *s*. Note that these and other qualifications that might have been mentioned are likewise stated in terms of sounds. The meanings and grammatical functions of the words in which the changes occur seem irrelevant to the operation of the law.

It is the apparently self-contained nature of the linguistic domain exemplified in this historically important case that leads, even after the rejection of the notion of language as a quasi-organism developing according to its own internal laws, to the demand that language be studied autonomously and that linguistic phenomena be explained only by reference to other linguistic phenomena.

This view of language as an autonomous domain with its own immanent laws, widely held by linguists, has indeed so far proved to be a valuable methodological rule. It may be viewed as an exhortation to cultivate one's own garden first, and as a standing warning against the facile employment of principles of explanation based on a superficial knowledge of other sciences, such as psychology, which in the view of many linguists are less well developed scientifically than linguistics itself and thus, far from being able to aid in the solution of linguistic problems, stand rather in need of help themselves.

It is possible, however, that an outside observer, interested in language as a general human phenomenon—for example, in the wider contexts of the psychology of language, the role of language in communication, and the relation of language to other aspects of human cultural behavior—and being unaware of the outstanding success of linguistic science in its own circumscribed domain, might, on glancing at the titles of articles in a professional linguistic journal, remark, paraphrasing the well-known remark of Clemenceau about generals and war, that language was much too important a matter to be left to linguists.

As a matter of fact, in the United States, as elsewhere, the tendency to see linguistic problems in these varied and wider contexts *has* developed alongside of and supplementary to an entirely legitimate continuation of traditional linguistic concerns.

In one respect, at least, a broader approach to linguistic problems is well established in the American scientific scene. Because of the basic role of languge in making other cultural behavior possible, earlier alluded to, and because it is itself a most important aspect of culture, linguistics can, from one point of view, be considered not only a behavioral science, but specifically a specialized sub-science within that branch of anthropolgy which considers human cultural, as distinct from physical, traits, namely, cultural anthropology. This view is reflected in American academic organization. Ever major department of anthropology in the United States offers courses in general linguistics, considers linguistics a basic branch of anthropology, and usually has a professionally trained linguist on its staff. Historically considered, this situation is chiefly due to the influence of the late Franz Boas, doubtless the key figure in the development of anthropology in the United States. In the extensive investigations of American Indian peoples which he sponsored and in part carried out himself, he found it indispensable to include the scientific study of their languages. This field had been relatively neglected by the more traditionally oriented linguists of the period, who were chiefly interested in the languages of people who had left written records of historical value or a literature worthy of study and humanistic appreciation.

The close integration of linguistics with general anthropology in the United States does not of course mean that linguistics cannot be and is not pursued from other points of view. Indeed the majority of linguists in the United States are not affiliated with anthropology departments. However, when some of the specific lines of this inquiry, and the substantive contributions of American linguists, are considered, it will be evident that to a considerable degree the most pervasive characteristics of linguistic science in the United States owe their ultimate origin to this intimate connection with anthropology.

Linguistics as traditionally practiced has two main branches: descriptive linguistics, whose task it is to study languages as functioning systems in a single community at a single time, and historical linguistics, which investigates languages under their dynamic aspect of change through time. Thus, a grammar of English as spoken about 1800 would fall within the province of descriptive linguistics, while a comparative study of the changes undergone by the various Romance languages in their development from Latin would belong to the historical subdivision of the subject. It was only from about 1920 onward that such questions as the nature of the categories employed in describing language, and the requirements to be met for a scientifically adequate grammar, ceased to be taken more or less for granted and became a center of theoretical interest. A number of approaches, which have been called structural, emerged both in Europe and the United States at about this time. While not denying the validity and importance of historical considerations, all have in common an interest in interrelationships within a language as a structure functioning on a single time plane. The problem of describing American Indian languages, highly varied among themselves and differing greatly in type from the Indo-European and other languages of Europe and neighboring areas, raised in a particularly acute form the question of the nature and the universal validity of grammatical categories. For example, the traditional parts of speech based on Latin grammar had hitherto been employed in more or less modified form in describing the grammatical structure of all languages.

The difficulties of the traditional method, which is based on semantic definitions presumed to reflect universally necessary categories of thought, may be illustrated in the instance of adjectives. In school grammars, adjectives are defined as words which designate qualities of substances. For example, "green," "large," and so on. But in many languages of the world, not only American Indian languages, such concepts are frequently expressed by formal means which are in some cases identical with those used to express actions and other ideas which are semantically characteristic of what are commonly called verbs. In such languages the sentence, "The leaf is green," would be literally translated as something like "The leaf greens." To put those members of the formal class which translate as action words in our language into one grammatical class and call them verbs, and others which translate adjectives into another grammatical class, is an imposition of categories derived a priori on a situation in which they do not apply. It will lead to inefficient grammars which, from the point of view of the language itself, arbitrarily group together things which are separate and separate things which belong together.

The treatment of this problem has tended therefore toward the setting up of categories on a purely formal rather than a semantic basis. As a matter of method, meanings are disregarded, and those forms which function similarly—in that one can substitute for the other and produce a grammatically possible utterance—or which exhibit other formal features in common, such as similar inflections, are put in the same class. Thus *boy* and *man* are members of the same class because one can be substituted for the other and the resulting sentence remain grammatical rather than because, in the traditional terminology, they stand for "a person, place, or thing."

This view of grammar leads squarely to the notion of a language as a calculus, that is, a structure to be described by a mathematics having to do with classes or sets of elements, their membership, and their relations of sequencing and combination. Such a mathematics is non-quantitative, since it is not concerned with the numbers of elements involved but rather with their relational structure. From this point of view, linguistics might be considered part of a wider subject matter, such as semiotics or the study of sign systems in general. For example, the formulas of mathematics or symbolic logic seem to display a certain analogy with language. From a limited number of elementary symbols, sequences of finite length are constructed according to certain rules which might be called the "grammar" of the system. Thus it is part of the grammar of mathematics that an open parenthesis must sooner or later be followed by a closed parenthesis, just as it is part of English grammar that an adjective preceded by an article must ultimately be followed by a noun.

Semiotics, the general study of such systems, is not a subject matter or discipline in the academic sense but rather a common interest still very much in its infancy, developed in common by logicians, linguists, and communication engineers, among others. This development, which in the case of linguistics has perhaps gone farther in the United States than elsewhere, is remarkably parallel to the formalization of logic, although most probably without historical connection with it. For in logic the notion of implication—that is, that one statement follows from or is the logical consequence of another—came to be looked upon among certain logicians as not primarily resulting from the meaning of the statements. The rules of logical deduction are then formulated as a set of transformations following certain rules and operating on a string of symbols without regard to their meaning.

This tendency toward formalization, which has the twofold advantage of overcoming the bias inherent in an a priori semantic classification and of allowing the application of non-metric mathematical methods, calls for certain further general observations. Reverting to the specific example of the traditional parts of speech treated earlier, we see that for further development of linguistics it is necessary that it transcend its status as a merely descriptive science which produces grammars adequate to the idiosyncratic structure of each language described. For such a method, whose validity

THE BEHAVIORAL SCIENCES TODAY

as a technique for the description of individual languages is not here in question, would tend to overlook the great similarities which do in fact exist among all languages. Such similarities are a reflection of the basic biological unity of man as a behavioral animal and the fundamental similarity of the functional task that a communicative system must perform in any society. Thus, were we to follow to its ultimate consequences the logic of the formal approach, we would divorce ourselves completely from the traditional terminology of grammatical analysis and instead of noun, verb, adjective, and the like, talk about classes A, B, C, and so forth for each individual language. Since such designations would be quite arbitrary, the affixing of the same label A to grammatical classes in different languages would not equate them as we do tacitly in the traditional approach when, for example, we call a certain class of words nouns in both English and Turkish. The lack of comparability would disguise the fact that there are important correlations and similarities among languages reflecting the common factors mentioned earlier. So, although we would quite rightly decide upon the specific membership and the number of classes by rigorous combinatoral methods, we still must note that a particular class of words involves notions which from the semantic point of view exhibit a general similarity to classes in other languages. Such similarities are, in some cases, of universal scope and occur in all languages. Thus, although details will differ, a class corresponding to nouns and another distinct class corresponding to verbs, and their combination to express a proposition, are found everywhere; and here, as so often, we return again on a higher level to an apparently abandoned viewpoint—that of a universally valid set of general concepts embodied in language and reflecting the universal requirements of human thought. But now, instead of imposing such a scheme a priori and based on the single arbitrarily selected pattern of Latin grammar, we arrive at it by inductive comparisons of results obtained from the most diverse languages and by a rigorous methodology. It should be stated, of course, that what is sketched here as the last step is at present a program and direction of development rather than in any sense a fully formulated set of results. It is evident, though, that the promise of such conclusions is of the highest importance for general psychology as showing which features of human thinking are universal and necessary and which are transient and accidental.

What might be termed the calculus approach to language calls, perhaps, for one more comment. The role of meaning in contemporary linguistics has been the subject of much discussion and controversy. It should be emphasized that several distinct questions are involved. The rejection of semantic criteria as defining properties for grammatical class does not necessarily involve the rejection of meaning itself as a proper subject for linguistic science. In fact, it cannot be avoided if linguistic descriptions of individual languages are to have any practical or scientific usefulness. The prominence of formal methods in grammatical analysis in the United States should not lead to the mistaken view, as it sometimes has, that the semantic aspect of language is being rejected as part of linguistic science.

Turning to the historical branch of linguistic science, its most characteristic achievement, as has been noted, is the reconstruction, with a high degree of plausibility, of many features of extinct languages through intensive and careful comparison of the descendant languages. It has been widely thought that success in this enterprise is only possible where, as for Indo-European and Semitic languages, there are written documents which can help us by giving direct evidence of the earlier periods of the languages being compared. However, a precisely similar method has been applied with success to the comparison of languages without earlier written records, for example, the Bantu languages of Africa and the Malayo-Polynesian languages of the Pacific. Here again, in the United States, the intimate tie with anthropology asserts itself. The archeologists and historically oriented ethnologist seek to integrate the results of their work with that of comparative linguists in the American Indian and other fields and to profit by the contribution which linguists can make in this area, a contribution which becomes all the more important where early written records are very nearly absent.

The most important desideratum in coordinating such results has been a means of dating the period at which earlier extinct languages have been spoken by an absolute rather than a merely relative chronology. In recent years there has emerged in the United States a method, associated chiefly with the names of Swadesh and Leese, which promises for the first time to furnish such an absolute time scale for linguistic reconstructions. Although there are still important difficulties to be overcome, the method has already been applied to problems of prehistory with some success.

The basic notion is that if we compare related languages, certain elements of vocabulary are extremely stable in that they are not easily replaced by borrowed words from a foreign language, such as terms for low numerals, parts of the human body, fire, water, and so on. The more closely languages are related, the more of those related elements they still have in common. For example, English and German, being more closely related to each other than either is to French, have more such related terms in common. For example, the word for "arm" in German is *Arm* but French for the unrelated form is *bras*. The percentage of such terms held in common by two languages is thus a measure of the remoteness of their relationship, that is, of the period of time elapsed since they were once the same language. The assumption is that over a given period of time a certain proportion of a standard list of one hundred terms will be replaced. This is still a relative chronology. However, the replacement rate in terms of absolute time has been established empirically by considering languages for which there are written records over a considerable time span. The most recent determination of this rate gives the result that a language will retain approximately 86 per cent of this list in a thousand years with an error of 6½ per cent at the 5 per cent confidence level.

Glottochronology may be considered to have developed to a certain extent as a method which is of interdisciplinary interest since it concerns archeologists and cultural historians as well as linguists. This interdisciplinary aspect is important in a number of other relatively recent developments in linguistics, of which only brief mention can be made here.

The study of acoustics of speech sounds, which may be considered a border area between linguistics and physics, has made important advances in the last decade or so, largely through the invention of the sound spectograph, which permits a very exact study of the acoustic characteristics of speech sounds. This invention was developed in the Bell laboratories out of a general interest in communication and as a specific aid in teaching deaf mutes to speak. The subsequent invention of a speech synthesizer by which sounds are produced from hand-painted spectograms allows manipulation of features of the sound waves which can be systematically studied. This line of experimentation, which is obviously of great importance for the general psychology of perception, has already produced interesting and significant results. It has been discovered, for example, that a basic cue for distinguishing one stop consonant from another is the direction and size of transition to or from the main resonance frequencies of the vowel which precedes or follows, rather than in the consonant itself.

Finally, to mention but one more characteristic area of interest, in the relatively unexplored area between language and other aspects of culture, known as ethnolinguistics, and that between linguistics and psychology, known as psycholinguistics, the sharpest issues have been raised through the largely posthumous interest in the writings of Benjamin Lee Whorf. This writer's basic viewpoint, often called

Whorfianism or linguistic relativity, is one which has strong parallels in certain European writings on the subject. The general notion is that the grammatical categories of a language determine or at least influence strongly the general manner of conceiving the world of those who speak it. This general thesis has given rise to much theoretical discussion. An extensive program of research involving monolingual and multilingual speakers of Hopi, Navaho, Zuni, Spanish, and English in the southwestern part of the United States was begun in 1954. The basic design of the studies has been to test limited and specific aspects of the general Whorfian thesis by administering the same psycholinguistic tests to speakers of the different languages. In such studies the speaker's language is intended to be the only independent variable. As yet only partial results have been published. An examination of these data as well as the unpublished materials of the project points to the over-all conclusion that agreement in fundamentals of human behavior among speakers of radically diverse languages far outweighs the idiosyncratic differences to be expected from a radical theory of linguistic relativity.

Linguistics is at the moment in a phase of vigorous expansion in the United States. The realization is gradually gaining ground that linguistics is a behavioral science and one of basic importance. Beyond the study of specific languages as tools of research and communication, there is the science of language in general which studies a phenomenon so basic to human cultural, social, and individual behavior that no adequate body of theory having to do with behavior in general is ever likely to emerge without a consideration of the key role of language in its interrelations with other aspects of this behavior.

12 THINKING, COGNITION, AND LEARNING

George A. Miller

George A. Miller, Professor of Psychology at Harvard University, was born in Charleston, West Virginia, in 1920. Dr. Miller received his undergraduate education at the University of Alabama and pursued graduate studies in psychology at Harvard University. After receiving his doctorate, he continued at Harvard as a resident fellow and joined the faculty in 1948 as an assistant professor. After five years as an associate professor at the Massachusetts Institute of Technology (1951–1955), Dr. Miller rejoined the Harvard faculty. He is a member of the American Association for the Advancement of Science, the American Psychology Association, and the Linguistic Society of America. A specialist in audition, perception of speech, and the psychology of communication, Dr. Miller is the author of the book Language and Communication.

A scientist is a man who goes and looks. If he wants to study fish, he catches some and looks at them. If he is interested in stars, he gets a telescope. But where should a scientist go and look when he wants to study the human mind? A psychologist seems to be at a disadvantage in this business of going and looking, because the traditional subject matter of psychology—the mind and its various attributes—has a troublesome way of remaining invisible. We know what a brain looks like, but nobody has ever seen a mind. Where does a psychologist find the thing he is supposed to study?

Several years ago a large sum of money was given to create a new institution in the United States, a place where scholars and scientists could go to sit and think about any problems that interested them. One skeptic, when told of the plan, commented drily, "Well, I can see how you would know they were sitting." His comment is a succinct description of the psychologist's problem. How, indeed, could you tell they were thinking?

You could ask them, of course. That was one of the first things that psychologists tried. People were told that they would have to perform some simple mental task. Then they would be asked to describe the thoughts they had had as they carried it out. The tasks were short and simple. For example, "What is the first word you think of when I say 'animal'?" After the person answered—"plant" or "dog" or "vegetable" or whatever—he tried to describe exactly everything that had happened in his mind between hearing the question and giving his answer. What surprised the psychologists was that people often had nothing to report. During the time the person was searching for a reply, his mind was blank. Usually the interval was filled with a tense, imageless nothingness. It seemed preposterous, but there it was: The processes of conscious thought are unconscious! As Karl Lashley once put it, "No activity of mind is ever conscious."

You probably never noticed before that the operations of your mind are all unconscious. It is only the end products of those operations that appear in consciousness. Are you surprised? The psychologists were astonished. But perhaps you are not convinced? In that case you are in good company. Many psychologists refused to believe it. Remember that they were working around the turn of the century, before Sigmund Freud made the unconscious mind a household word. In those days "unconscious mind" was a contradiction in terms! Little wonder that the young science of psychology was torn by violent disagreements. Within a short time the most distinguished psychologists were insulting each other about what they saw or didn't see when they examined their own minds.

Those bitter controversies came at a time when psychologically oriented philosophers like John Dewey were helping to create in America a more pragmatic conception of human nature. The younger men were finding the conscious minds of well-educated, adult human beings to be too special and restricted to hold their full attention. Robert M. Yerkes and Edward L. Thorndike were turning to the study of animals. G. Stanley Hall pioneered in the study of children and primitive peoples, H. H. Goddard and Lewis M. Terman studied the mentally retarded, and many others became interested in the insane. They studied them, necessarily, without benefit of introspection. If introspection leads to disagreement, said the younger men, then consign it to the flames. There are other ways to create psychology.

In its most extreme form the rejection of introspection led some Americans to denounce consciousness as pure superstition, to banish the mind from the world of science, and to set up new shrines to worship the truly visible, namely, brains and behavior. The behaviorists, especially their outspoken leader, J. B. Watson, attracted a great deal of attention. For a while during the 1920's their materialistic philosophy seemed a wholesome antidote to the subjective bickering of the introspectionists.

But behaviorism went too far. It is one thing to say that the operations of the mind are not accessible to introspection; it is quite a different thing to say there is no mind at all. Yet it took American psychologists a long time to realize that behaviorism went too far. In my opinion, one reason for its survival in the face of criticism—even in spite of growing indifference from some quarters—is that behaviorism did introduce one essential idea that earlier psychologists seemed to ignore, the idea that *the mind has a job to do*. The first scientific psychologists were so deeply engrossed in dissecting the anatomy of consciousness that they were frequently in danger of overlooking the function it performs.

But what is the function of consciousness? Obviously—I say "obviously" because it is obvious to me—the function of consciousness is to guide action. Let me see if I can make this important point as obvious to you as it is to me.

Imagine that by some impossible, Druidical magic a new

kind of tree is created. This tree, like an animal, has sense organs connected by sensory nerves to a large, well-organized brain. But the tree does not have any motor nerves or any muscles or glands. It must stand immobile, moving only with the wind, as trees have always stood. Now, here is the question: Does this remarkable tree have any advantage over an ordinary tree?

Whatever knowledge a tree might accumulate would be quite useless if the tree could not do anything about it. When the forest burns there is little virtue in feeling pain if you cannot run away. When lumberjacks approach what good does it do an immobile tree to see them coming?

But even that is too much. I asked what good it would do for the tree to know something. But I am not persuaded that the tree could know anything, even if it had all the wonderfully complex machinery of receptors, nerves, and brain that you and I are blessed with. The difference is that you and I can *move*—not only to approach things we want and avoid things we fear—you and I can move our sense organs from one place to another. A tree with eyes might see a house nearby, but the tree could never suspect that the house had another side concealed from view. In order to discover the thickness of reality it is necessary to move around in it. We must be able to walk around the house and then, somehow, miraculously to construct an object that explains all the different views we had of it. A tree with eyes but lacking movement would not need such an explanation and so would never see deeper than the flat surface of appearances. Moreover, the tree would not distinguish size from distance and so could never learn that it takes a long time to move a long distance. Without motions through distances, the tree would have no conception of time and hence no way to date its memories. In short, a sentient but immobile intelligence would not, could not, develop anything resembling the state of consciousness that you and I recognize as our own.

That is why I say it is perfectly obvious that the function

of consciousness is to guide action. Or, to put it the other way around, mobility is a necessary precondition for the development of consciousness. To insist that a psychologist must study behavior, therefore, is not to deny the existence of mind. Quite the contrary. It is the only path available to a deeper, as well as a more objective, understanding of what a mind is and how it works.

A conception of space and time is reserved for creatures that can move about in space and time, that need space and time in order to reduce and simplify the confusion of appearances reported by their moving sense organs. Of course, the implication is that people *learn* the concepts of space and time, that these concepts are not given a priori to every intelligence, but are constructed in order to account for the experience of creatures with movable sense organs. To attain the conception of a stable environment of objects when the only evidence we have is the haphazard flow of energies into our receptors is one of the greatest triumphs of childhood. Yet it happens so naturally and inevitably that we scarcely notice that it happens at all.

Let me give you an example. Select some object across the room. Take two points, one on either side of it. Now move your eyes back and forth from one of those points to the other. What happens to the object? Nothing. Isn't that amazing? Is it not a true wonder that the object sits there firm and solid when you move your eyes across it? But perhaps you are not amazed. Perhaps familiarity has dulled your appreciation of this interesting fact. Let me see if I can help you recapture a proper sense of wonder at the great delicacy and beauty of the mechanisms that support your cognitive life. Try to remember the last time you looked at a scene through binoculars. Then, if you recall, you moved your head and the landscape went spinning by in the opposite direction. What causes the world to slip its anchor and float about in the lenses of the binoculars? The trouble is that the magnification in the lenses disturbs the familiar ratio between the movements of your head and the change in your visual image. With this familiar ratio altered, you no longer see objects as firm and stable, as fixed in space. The stability of your visual world depends upon the accuracy with which a delicate adjustment of movement to sensory change has been learned. In recent years J. J. Gibson and Hans Wallach have both made important contributions to our understanding of this interesting problem.

But why, you may ask, do I keep insisting that this sensory-motor relation must have been learned? Why could it not be inherited? There are several reasons. In the first place, the discrepancy between your movements and the changes in your perceptual image would not be apparent to you unless you knew the appropriate sizes of the objects— hills, trees, houses, streets, whatever—that you were looking at. You could scarcely be born knowing how large a house must look. That is something you must learn for yourself after you get here. And, in the second place, you can learn a new ratio very quickly. If you strap the binoculars to your head and wear them all the time, the world will soon steady down for you. As G. M. Stratton demonstrated many years ago, you can even wear prisms that turn the world upside down, or reverse it left for right, and learn to move about as well as before. The new visual world becomes quite natural. But, you may ask, would you continue to see the world upside down or backwards, or would it suddenly flip right? The subjects who have tried it have no clear answer to that question. How could they have? All they can say is that their visual world comes to look quite natural and that they do not feel at all disoriented. They learn which way to reach for objects, which way to move their receptors to bring objects into the center of the visual field. And eventually they learn to feel that things are where they see them to be. That is all anyone can say about his perception of space. He can say that it is self-consistent and that it is sufficient to guide his movements in space.

These skills that are so essential to our cognitive world become transparent by familiarity. We forget that the firm and solid reality we see around us is, after all, a hypothesis, something we have learned, a mental construction that we use to simplify our cognitive housekeeping. As Jerome S. Bruner has pointed out, we are all constantly "going beyond the information given." We look at some familiar object and seem to recognize it as immediately as our eyes encounter it. It is difficult to realize how much skilled activity is involved just in that simple act of recognizing an object, and how much of ourselves we project into the world around us. It was the recognition of this personal component in perception that enabled psychologists like J. S. Bruner and Hadley Cantril to demonstrate the importance of personality and cultural factors in the way all of us learn to see the world we live in.

Notice, if you will, how the terms "skill" and "learning" have crept into my sentences. Almost everyone who begins his consideration of the human mind with a moving, behaving organism, rather than with a passive, receptive organism, seems to run very quickly to discussions of learning. Perhaps it is just an accident of history, but the American psychologists who have argued that the mind has a function to perform—Clark Hull, Edward Tolman, Edwin R. Guthrie —are the same men who argue that the mind must learn how to perform it. This attitude can lead to disputes about the relative importance of heredity and learning that I do not wish to go into, except to say that the problems of nature and nurture are a great deal more complex than we originally imagined and that no simple generalization could possibly summarize the true state of affairs. When I say that the human mind could not develop the way it does without an intensive program of learning by an active, participating organism, I do not wish to deny in any way the importance of heredity. I wish to state merely what is open and obvious to common sense.

A child must learn even so simple a skill as how to recognize an object. But really, you know, recognizing objects is not as simple as it sounds. At the Massachusetts Institute of Technology, there is a group of research workers—Marvin Minsky, Oliver Selfridge, John McCarthy, and several others —who are trying to explain to a large, high-speed electronic computer how to recognize simple pictures. The machine is learning slowly, but it certainly is not a simple process. Where does a child get his conception of objects, of things that continue to exist even when he is not looking at them? He could, for example, imagine that every view he has of a human face is a separate experience. Why doesn't he? He could even learn that some faces are similar, that some of his experiences with faces are essentially equivalent. But he goes further than that. The child jumps to the conclusion of identity. The faces that feed him are not just equivalent. They are—or it is—all one identical face. He is not waited upon each time by a different but similar, new but equivalent woman. There is only one woman, and she appears and disappears at irregular intervals. But that is not all the child must learn. Once he has discovered mother's identity, he must next learn that she persists, that when she vanishes from view she has not been destroyed, that each reappearance is not a new act of creation. To the child who is just learning this lesson, peek-a-boo is a dangerous and exciting game. But when the lesson is finally learned, he will have taken one of his most important steps toward the creation of a universe out of a collection of haphazard stimulations. The creation of the concept of an object out of a sequence of different exposures to it is a skill we learn quite early in life and perform quite automatically and unconsciously ever after. If you grant the fact, you have mastered one of the most important propositions in the psychology of cognition.

Once a child has mastered the skill of recognizing objects, he has the prototype for a great variety of other intellectual accomplishments. One of the simplest, no doubt, is the process of searching. The child knows that an object exists and that the object is not present. Two alternatives are open: either he can look for it himself, or he can cry for help. Consider first the search process.

In its simplest form, searching involves more of the business of moving the sense organs around. The sense organs are directed at an object that is then examined and either accepted or rejected. If it matches up to some inner representation of the object, it will be recognized and accepted. If it does not match up, it will be rejected and the sense organs will move on to another object, where the inspection will be repeated. Eventually, either the receptors are pointed at an object that passes the inspection or the search is halted as a failure. The critical component in this search process, of course, is the matching up of the present perception of an object with the remembered conception of the object that is sought. This matching-up process is what we normally regard as a *test;* the object is tested and either passes or fails, is recognized as the desired object or is rejected and forgotten.

Testing a series of things until we find the right one is the pattern behind many of man's most complicated intellectual activities. That was how Edison, for example, discovered a substance that he could use for the filament in an electric light: he tested one thing after another with dogged persistence until finally he found one that would work. Carl Hovland, by his "communication analysis of concept learning," has demonstrated how cognitive processes can be described in these terms. In the experimental studies of concept learning done by Hull, Hovland, Bruner, and many others, the subject searches through a set of alternative hypotheses to find one that correctly describes all the known instances of the concept. A mathematician searches for the unknown value of x that will satisfy his equations. The chess player searches through dozens of possible continuations of the game, testing to see which one gives him the greatest advantage. A thief may try many sequences of numbers hoping to find one that will open the combination lock and let him into the safe. Or a logician searches for some sequence of steps that will enable him to go from his axioms to the theorem he wants to prove.

Not all our thinking should be reduced to searching, however. Sometimes it is much better to talk in terms of the problem of prediction, instead of the problem of location. When we predict, we must build a conception of what is going to happen. Once this is formulated, we can then compare it with reality. We can move our sense organs into positions to observe whether or not the prediction we made came true. You recognize, I am sure, that the same test procedure is involved in checking the prediction as in recognizing the desired object in a search situation. It is our ability to test that keeps our minds anchored in what we ordinarily call "the real world."

What happens in situations where no test is possible? Certainly there are problems that we think about, that we think hard about, where there does not seem to be any test. Sometimes the test may be possible but we are, like the child, too ignorant or too confused to see what it would be. At other times the test simply may not exist. Ethical questions seem to have that character. By what test do we settle the problem of living a good life? But whatever the reason for the lack, the kind of thinking we do without a test is quite different from the kind of thinking we do with one. The man without a test is not able to recognize the solution to his problem even when he sees it. He literally does not know what he is looking for. In that situation he can only continue to explore, to experiment, to learn, to accumulate, to try to clarify his image of the situation. If he is lucky, he may develop what Edward Tolman calls a "cognitive map" that will enable him to define the problem, to translate a felt difficulty into an explicit puzzle that can then be solved.

I said that the other thing the child can do when he wants

a missing object is to cry for help. Here again we find that men have developed marvelous elaborations on the childish response. Just as the impulse to look develops into the probing curiosity of the explorer and the scientist, so the impulse to cry for help develops into the cooperative communications of the teacher and the politician. The missing object must be identified by name, and from these first vocalizations grow the wonderful patterns of linguistic communication that evoke in us everything that separates us from the other animals. Men talk, and so they share their experience. Each builds for himself a larger universe than he will ever see. Each exploits the great minds and the great discoveries of his cultural tradition. Each sets his goals and plans his life and anticipates his rewards in the way he does because he has linguistic symbols. Almost nothing I could say about the importance of language—of verbal symbols—in the cognitive life of the adult human being could be too extravagant. The effects of verbal behavior on the individual form the subject of a new research area called "psycholinguistics." The effects of verbal habits on the social group form the subject of a new research area called the "communication sciences." Both of these new areas illustrate the advantages of an interdisciplinary approach to problems of the behavioral sciences.

These are some of the things psychologists study when they try to understand how the mind works. How do we formulate our universe out of the scraps of experience life gives us? How do we search through the universe to discover the things we want? How do we communicate our discoveries to our fellow men? These are the large over-arching questions that give direction and meaning to thousands of particular studies, experiments, and investigations that psychologists patiently conduct and analyze each year.

I said that a scientist is a man who goes and looks. Now I can explain what I meant. A scientist goes and looks, but his searching is not limited to material objects. He searches through ideas as well as through objects in order to find what he seeks. And he does not look indiscriminately—always he carries an image of what he seeks. What is he looking for? He is looking for what we all learned to look for in the first year of life. He is looking for something that matches up to his image of what the world must be, something that meets a test he himself imposes, something that has meaning only in terms of the standards he lives by. In that sense, the scientist is Everyman, looking just as you and I. We go and look for the things we want, and when we find them we find part of ourselves.

13 THE PSYCHOLOGY OF PERSONALITY

Robert H. Knapp

Robert H. Knapp, Professor of Psychology at Wesleyan University in Middletown, Connecticut, was born in Portland, Oregon, in 1915. After graduating from the University of Oregon, where he also received his Master of Arts degree, Dr. Knapp went to Harvard University in 1940 as a teaching fellow and assistant in the acoustical laboratory. During the war years, he was a technical consultant to the Office of Strategic Services and in 1946 joined the faculty of Wesleyan University, with which he has been associated since. From 1953 to 1954, Dr. Knapp served as Deputy Director of the Behavioral Sciences Program of the Ford Foundation.

Man, in all ages and in all climes, has shown a persistent and compelling interest in his fellows. In this sense, "the psychology of personality" is a concern as old as the species. But efforts to bring this interest under the aegis of scientific investigation are remarkably recent. If we except certain pseudoscientific endeavors such as phrenology, it is probably fair to say that this attempt has less than eighty years of history, and in America the principal efforts have been confined to the last quarter century.

Now, the psychology of personality is concerned with the individual as the final point of reference. In this respect it is to be distinguished from those psychological inquiries which are concerned primarily with some segmental function. Early studies of psychophysics, memory, conditioning, and similar processes, the beginning points of psychology, were pursued without reference to particular persons but rather in an effort to discover laws applying to "mind in general" or "behavior in general." Only thereafter did an individually oriented psychology emerge within scientific psychology in this country.

In many respects the late emergence of a psychological inquiry devoted to the understanding of the individual is not easy to explain. Certainly, as Boring has noted, American psychology from the outset was interested in individual differences as manifested in the work of Cattell or in the attitudinal studies of G. Stanley Hall, or in James' varieties of religious experience. Again, the traditions of American evangelical Protestantism provoked much self-examination and soul-searching and should have provided a strong impetus to personality study. And in certain departments such as the measurement of individual intelligence, we were, if not originators, surely pioneer developers of the field. Add to this the fact that Freud visited and was cordially received in America as early as 1909, and that a tradition of clinical inquiry was established at Harvard under Morton Prince in the first decade of this century. So, in looking back over the history of American psychology, we are confronted with this paradox: Numerous factors of inclination and precedent seem to have provided an auspicious ground for the early emergence of a "psychology of personality," yet it did not appear as a significant focus of intellectual effort until the 1930's. Such inquiry began in Europe, and especially in Germany, at least two decades earlier. But it was not until the year 1930, for example, that the first course in the psychology of personality was offered at Harvard. It was not until 1937, after much patient revision, that the first significant textbook in the field made its appearance. So, we must ask, "Why the delay?"

I think the answer is to be found in several historical considerations. First, the philosophical assumptions which guided the rise of American psychology were a fusion of British empiricism and American pragmatism. British empiricism first manifested itself in the school of Wundtian introspection and shortly after in behaviorism which, while eliminating "consciousness and mind" in the name of pragmatism, still approached psychology primarily in terms of learned association as defined by the conditioned reflex. As such it was atomistic in character and cognitive in orientation. Its doctrine of emotion was simple and arbitrary in the extreme, and its theory of purpose or conation virtually nonexistent. It was Watson, the chief spokesman for American behaviorism, who declared that personality, so far as it was a useful conception, consisted merely in the sum of one's habits and reflexes, native or conditioned. Consciousness, self, and conception of the unconscious, all were either denied or sternly ruled beyond the pale of psychology for systematic reasons. Again, as we shall presently see, any approach to personality must sooner or later involve considerable theorizing and abstraction. But the temper of the time, and especially of the ascendant American behaviorism, was hostile to such abstraction. In short, the climate of American psychological thought for the first three decades of the century was reductionistic in principle, cognitive in orientation, neglectful of conation, and hostile to untestable (or seemingly untestable) abstraction.

Precisely what broke the spell of behaviorism in America is not entirely clear. Partly it was that close experimental examination of some behavioristic tenets proved them to be false or inadequate, and partly that the gradual influx of European thought, Freudianism and Gestalt psychology notably, forced critical examination of the prevailing outlook. It may also be that social and economic events in America had a way of unhinging many established outlooks and making for a receptivity to new ideas. In any event, the decade of the 1930's saw the rise of the first clearly enunciated psychology of personality in America, and it took two distinct forms. The first was formulated by Gordon Allport, and the second by Henry Murray. Both drew heavily from European models and both survive as significant and shaping forces in contemporary thought. Let us consider these two men.

As we have noted, the first notable text in the field of personality and one of the first formal courses in this field in an American university were presented by Gordon Allport. It is important, therefore, that we look to the origins of his thought and to some of his basic doctrines. It is probably fair to say that Allport drew his inspiration from four primary sources, though much of his system remains peculiarly his own and as such has no attributable antecedents. First among his sources was William James, who had been peculiarly bypassed in many respects in the four decades following the publication of his *Principles of Psychology*. Allport also drew heavily from the outlook of three German psychologists and philosophers, namely Dilthey, Spranger, and William Stern. The result was a view of personality which was centered in the recognition of the peculiar uniqueness of the individual, an emphasis upon traits and attitudes as fundamental units, and the theory of the emergence of unique motives contained in the doctrine of functional autonomy. This doctrine declares that human motives, though originating perhaps in biologically rooted needs, can become separate and independent of their origins. Thus, with respect to traits, attitudes, and motives, the door is open for an almost infinite variety of combinations. Under such circumstances the psychology of personality becomes an attempt to comprehend the marvelous uniqueness of the individual, a task in which intuitive skills as well as rigorous scientific methodology are called into play. Allport remains hostile alike to the fragmented reductionism of American behaviorism, the obscurities of psychoanalysis, and the effort to comprehend the individual in terms of some universal set of dimensions which ignore the individual's uniqueness. All of this was set forth with great lucidity and erudition in his *Personality,* published in 1937.

The work of Henry Murray was in most respects significantly different from that of Gordon Allport. Thus, Murray was primarily a disciple of psychoanalysis, drawing upon both Freud and Jung, while Allport had tended to dismiss these European thinkers. And, unlike Allport, he sought to develop a system in which personalities were studied in terms of common motives and other personality structures. But they were alike in several respects. Both were firmly committed to the study of individuals as total operating systems, both recognized the importance of motivation as a prime concept in the field, both rejected the reductionist theories of behaviorism, and both drew heavily upon European thought, though from different quarters. The work of Murray and his students, which culminated in the publication of *Explorations in Personality* in 1938, is noteworthy for at least five reasons. It represented the first serious attempt to submit psychoanalytic hypotheses to experimental verification. Second, a population of superior normal individuals drawn from the Harvard student body were employed, in contrast to earlier studies of clinical defectives. Third, even more clearly than in the case of Allport, Murray was committed to the study of motivation and the elaborations of motivation, including unconscious process, symbolism, defense mechanisms, and similar phenomena. Fourth, it presented a model for that type of "corporate" research involving the execution of a number of simultaneous and interrelated studies which has since become so common and profitable. And finally, it eventuated in a theory of human needs which has proved to be persistent and valuable in personality research.

It would be a mistake to conclude that America produced only two notable figures in the field of personality research during the decade of the 1930's. A more complete roster would surely include figures such as Kurt Lewin, who attempted to apply the tenets of Gestalt psychology to the field of individual personality. Mention should surely be made of Kurt Goldstein, who had already begun to explore individual patterns in cognitive processes. Nor should we neglect William Sheldon, who, taking his departure from Kretschmer's work in Germany, moved toward a study of personality as a function of physical constitution. This latter theory is noteworthy as the first of a rising tide emphasizing hereditary and constitutional factors and discounting the environmental determination which had marked traditional American behaviorism as well as psychoanalysis.

And so by the end of the decade a number of central questions had come clearly in view. To what extent, for example, could Allport's insistence upon the preservation of individual uniqueness really be preserved in scientific inquiry? What of the nature-nurture problem? What was the proper assignment of importance to environment and heredity with respect to different functions and in different persons? How about the complexity of the individual? How many levels of organization should be recognized? Again, what is the relationship of personality and culture? And finally, what is the relative importance of conation, cognition, and affection in determining the main lines of personality structure? Had the recent fascination with the studies in motivation been a wise and ultimately valid excursion?

Let us now review the span of years from World War II to the present and divide the discussion into three sections: First, what has happened to our theory of personality? Second, what types of tools or methods have we evolved to assess personality? And finally, what general advances have we made in our understanding of the human individual?

If we were to take stock of the general theoretical view of personality as it stood at the end of World War II, we would find the following. The Freudian schema, together with its European elaborations, and the American adaptation made by Murray had come into full recognition. The tripartite division of the personality into Ego, Superego, and Id was widely accepted together with the recognition of the various defense mechanisms of the Freudians and the psychosexual theory of development. In addition, Allport's theory directed toward the analysis of personality in terms of traits and attitudes and his doctrine of functional autonomy to explain the elaboration of motives was widely known, if not entirely accepted. Constitutional psychology in the form of Sheldon's system of physical and temperamental types had obtained qualified acceptance. The efforts of Kurt Lewin and Kurt Goldstein, each in his own fashion, had been directed to the application of Gestalt theory to personality. It is now for us to ask what has happened to expand this picture since that time.

First, let us note two indigenous American theoretical formulations which, while deriving generally from psychoanalytical thought, show marked qualities of independence. The first of these is the view propounded by Harry Stack Sullivan, which was first made widely known as a formal system in his *Interpersonal Theory of Psychiatry*. As the title of his principal work suggests, he viewed the entire foundations of personality as an extension and elaboration of social relations of which the most primary and important was that between the infant and the mother. He further propounded a rather fixed developmental schedule which, if not universal, seemed particularly applicable at least to the evolution of personality within the American culture. Central, also, to his conceptions was the existence of what he called the "self system." While his views have not provoked extensive experimental research, they have at least obtained widespread adherence among psychiatrists and clinical psychologists in practice.

A second development is contained in the work of Carl Rogers, who has evolved both a theory of personality and a widely recognized psychotherapy. The basis of both theory and therapy is an insistence upon the importance of the self and of the possibilities of the growth of the self into a more coherent system under the guidance of a non-directive type of therapeutic interview. Rogers is, of course, not alone in his growing concern with the ego and self. One should also include here Goldstein, Maslow, and Murphy, as well as others. In fact, concern with the self and the self-image is one of the most striking features of recent theoretical developments.

At least two thinkers have been conspicuous in propounding the possibilities of "higher motives and structures" distinctive to the human species. The first of these is Maslow, who has developed the conception of a hierarchy of instincts, the most advanced of which is a motive for self-actualization. A somewhat similar view has recently been propounded by Gardner Murphy in his *Human Potentialities*. The importance of this line of thought lies in its repudiation of the proposition that human behavior can be understood as mere extension of biological drives and elaboration of animal behavior. It assigns once again significant importance to the unique intellectual endowments of man, to his motivational complexity, and to his capacities for creativity.

Still another attempt at theoretical conceptualizations of personality has emerged from a group of psychologists of whom R. B. Cattell and J. P. Guilford may be taken as typical. Using a mathematical method known as factor analysis, they have sought to identify the primary dimensions of personality, just as earlier intelligence was reduced to its principal components. The system evolved by Cattell is more complex than can fairly be presented here. Suffice it to say that, by using this technique on a large battery of personality tests and ratings, he has identified what he believes to be sixteen basic dimensions of character.

What has happened to constitutional psychology? It can hardly be said that any formal system has either supplanted or supplemented it. Still it would be an oversight not to note that physiological and constitutional factors continue to be the object of considerable attention. Experimental evidence, coming from a number of sources, is making increasingly clear the importance of individual body chemistry as a determinant of both personality and mental disorder. Some of the most recent work in hallucinogenic drugs has given dramatic confirmation of this fact. It has also been shown recently that identical twins who suffer mental aberrations develop remarkably similar symptomatology, and even do so at the same stage of life. Thus, the theoretical dependency of personality upon hereditary and physiological factors is gaining increasing recognition.

Finally, something should be said of learning theory. Learning theory is, of course, almost as old as psychology itself. All the same, it has had its contributions to make to personality theory, for all psychologists recognize that, in good part, personality structures are derived from experience. Thus, there have been abundant efforts to explain the effects of socialization in terms of mechanisms of learning. Some have sought to rely on classical conditioning, and others, like Dollard and Miller at Yale, on a theory of learning related to tension reduction and the avoidance of anxiety. Still others have sought to explain personality development in terms of two or more types of learning mechanisms, operative under different conditions or at different ages. It is probably too early to say how significant these contributions have been, but it is certain that any final theoretical view of personality will have to incorporate an adequate theory of how and when and under what conditions learning occurs.

I have not yet touched upon the actual techniques of personality research. It is high time I did so, lest I leave the reader with the impression that personality research is confined to speculation, opinion, and the uncertain impressions obtained from everyday observation, or even from clinical practice. The significance of personality research lies largely in its method and in its capacity to find firm or reasonably firm answers to the questions which are provoked by theory. Accordingly, I should like to devote a short section to some of the methods which have been evolved to obtain data capable of scientific evaluation.

Among the most important methods which have been developed are the projective tests. The theory of the projective test is relatively simple. Give a person a vague or ambiguous stimulus and ask him to make something intelligible of it. What he produces will be in the nature of a rather free sample of his thought—free, that is, to incorporate and express his sentiments, his intellectual and cognitive habits, and quite possibly his affections and repulsions. In proportion as the outer determinants of the stimulus are uncertain, coherence must be supplied from inner sources. It is commonly presumed that the material supplied from these inner sources reveals both conscious and unconscious determinants of personality. Two of these tests are in very common use today. The first is the Rorschach, an ink-blot test developed in Switzerland shortly after the First World War. The second is the Thematic Apperception Test, consisting of pictures of human figures, evolved by Murray and his associates in the late 1930's. Both are employed as standard instruments in virtually all American clinics, and in recent years have also been used as experimental instruments. These two may be taken merely as examples. There are perhaps a dozen in common use, and for experimental purposes many more have been devised.

A second class of instruments for the evaluation of personality consists essentially of questionnaires. The art of asking questions and of evaluating answers has attained a very sophisticated level, in which all of the resources of modern mathematical statistics come into play. An example or two of this sort of device will suffice here. One of the first to be evolved was the Allport-Vernon scale of values. This questionnaire seeks to identify the individual's commitment to six basic life values: the economic, social, political, religious, theoretical, and aesthetic. Although now a quarter of a century old, it is still commonly used in psychological research, though it was recently revised and improved. A more advanced type of questionnaire inventory is the Minnesota Multiphasic Personality Inventory, which attempts in ten constituent scales to evaluate neurotic and psychotic tendencies such as hysteria, depression, schizophrenia, paranoia, and so forth. In addition to these, there are literally hundreds of standardized questionnaires designed to measure among other things anxiety, vocational interest, introversion, dominance, and the like. If the understanding of personality can be obtained simply through asking direct questions, then surely such efforts would have won us already to our goal. Unfortunately, however, such devices, while admittedly of great help, probably have inherent limitations.

These two devices, the projective test and the questionnaire, have been and probably still are the mainstays of personality research. But to these we should certainly add several others. For example, intelligence tests in a variety of modern and improved forms as well as tests of cognitive processes and styles are very extensively used. Again, interviewing skills and techniques have been most patiently and carefully analyzed and cultivated. Then there is the growing use of what might be called situational manipulation as a device for experimental research. Here individuals and groups are placed under conditions calculated to arouse anxiety or achievement motivation or competition for leadership and the resulting behavior then observed and recorded by conventional means. Finally, of course, some physiological indices are frequently employed, for example, the psychogalvanic skin reflex as an index of emotionality.

Turning from methods of obtaining data to methods of processing, we should, of course, note at the outset the very extensive use of statistical method in a wide variety of forms. Particularly noteworthy, however, is the development of factor analysis, since this procedure not only permits the evaluation of data but also, in yielding factors and clusters, suggests the latent structure of personality itself, as in the work of Raymond B. Cattell. Still another procedural method of very great significance for the study of development is the so-called longitudinal study. This involves the observation of individuals successively over a considerable period of time, in some cases many years, in an effort to note patterns of change and growth.

And now we are naturally led to a consideration of what has come out of the development of personality theory and research using the techniques which we have just described. It would be impossible to cite the numerous particular experiments and studies that have been published of some main lines of research. In the recent *Annual Review of Psychology,* the authors in reviewing recent years have noted that three subjects have been of particular concern to researchers in the field of personality, namely, anxiety, achievement motivation, and authoritarianism. Now it is interesting to note that all of these tended to evolve around the development of a particular measurement technique. In the case of anxiety, although attention was attracted to the problem by psychoanalytic and neo-psychoanalytic theory, still at least two attitudinal scales for the measurement of anxiety have recently been evolved. They have been used extensively for measuring anxiety under different conditions and have been correlated widely with other independent measures of personality. The great interest in achievement motivation has tended to derive from the basic work of McClelland in evaluating the Thematic Apperception Test for different psychogenic needs. In this instance a clearly established measurement technique for rating achievement motivation has led to an extensive body of experiments. Again, the interest in authoritarianism has centered around the development of the so-called F scale at the University of California. This presumably identifies tendencies toward authoritarianism or "Fascist thinking." The value of this attitudinal questionnaire has been widely disputed and has provoked a substantial body of research in its attack or defense. I should like to mention two more examples of current psychological research that I think are highly significant. Klein and Holt at New York University, supported by the Ford Foundation, are currently seeking to establish some of the principles governing the organization of thought and perception on the unconscious level in pursuance of psychoanalytic postulates. It is noteworthy that this research involves a most promising convergence of physiologists, experimental psychologists, and clinical psychologists.

Finally, a word might be said of the studies of creativity being carried out at the University of California. This elusive yet most important problem is being explored through some of the techniques initiated by Murray and alluded to earlier. Here again we find this research conducted by a team of individuals of various specialties and talents. The main spirit of the inquiry is directed not so much toward the measurement of abilities per se as toward the analysis of character and motivation as it is related to the creative process.

In conclusion, I think it would be profitable to try to present a view of the convictions to which most psychologists in the field of personality research today would subscribe. (1) From Freudian psychology, the doctrine of the unconscious and of defense mechanisms is pretty firmly established. On the other hand, the fixed rigidity of the psychosexual schedule of development as well as the overwhelming importance of early childhood experience is in a much less secure position since careful studies have failed to confirm their central importance. (2) There is a growing amount of evidence to indicate that significant personality changes may occur in adolescence and even in maturity, and that, in part, the capacity for such changes may depend upon maturation. (3) There is a mounting tide of evidence that genetic factors are more important than had been previously believed, and while the particular system of Sheldon has not made notable progress, the principle of significant hereditary determination appears to be gaining ever wider acceptance. (4) In one form or another, so-called field theories of personality, declaring the intimate connection between personality and culture, are gaining almost universal acceptance. In fact, the line of distinction between certain aspects of cultural anthropology and personality research is rapidly vanishing. (5) It is now recognized that several types of learning may well contribute to the growth and evolution of the individual. (6) Psychologists have long known of the dependence of the mind and personality upon physiological processes, but the subtlety and complexity of this relationship have been recently highlighted by discoveries of, for example, the production of aberrant hormones, the devastating effects of hallucinogenic drugs, and the discovery of midbrain structures related to the arousal of pleasure and anger. Psychologists at the present time, therefore, are keenly alert to the possibilities inherent in the physiological determination of dimensions of personality. (7) Most noteworthy, there is growing recognition that the self is an indispensable theoretical component of the personality. This trend is manifest among the younger psychoanalytic theorists, in several departures of American neo-psychoanalytic thought, and among such thinkers as Murphy, Allport, Maslow, Rogers, and others who cannot be included within the psychoanalytic framework. The self, which perished as a psychological entity some time before the turn of the century, has been rediscovered as a vital and necessary conceptual referrant. I predict that it will not soon be lost again.

14 SMALL GROUPS

George C. Homans

George C. Homans, Professor of Sociology at Harvard University, was born in Boston, Massachusetts, in 1910. A graduate of Harvard University, Mr. Homans has been associated with the faculty of that institution throughout his professional career with the exception of the years 1941 to 1945, when he served in the U.S. Navy. On leave of absence from Harvard University, Dr. Homans has twice served on the faculties of universities in England, in 1953 as Simon Visiting Professor at Manchester University, and in 1955–1956 as Professor of Sociology at Cambridge University. A specialist in sociological theory and industrial relations, he is a member of the American Sociological Society, the American Anthropological Association, and the Society of Applied Anthropology. He is the author of An Introduction to Pareto, English Villagers of the Thirteenth Century, The Human Group, Social Behavior, *and* Sentiments and Activities.

The field of investigation in the social sciences that has come to be called the study of small groups is not, in my view, properly so called. Small groups are not *what* we study, but *where* we often study it, as I shall presently try to show.

If you will look at the behavior that students of small groups actually investigate, you will find that it has the following characteristics. First, at least two men are in face-to-face contact, each behaving toward the other in ways that reward or punish him and therefore influence his behavior. Second, the rewards or punishments that each gets from the behavior of the other are direct and immediate rather than indirect and deferred. And third, the behavior of the two men is determined in part by something besides their conformity to institutional rules or roles. Indeed it is in this non-institutional aspect that small-group research is most interested; and so I prefer to speak of what we study as informal, sub-institutional, or elementary social behavior.

Why then is it in fact called behavior in small groups? Consider two kinds of social network. In an *open* network, Person A is in contact with Person B, who is in turn in contact with C, but C is not in contact with A—that is why we call it an open network. In a *closed* network, A is in contact with B, who is in contact with C, but C is now also in contact with A—that is why we call it a closed network. Since elementary social behavior obviously occurs in networks of both kinds, while only the closed network makes a real group, it is wrong to speak of our subject as if it were limited to small-group behavior. On the other hand, it is often convenient in practice to study elementary social behavior through observations made on small groups, for in them a number of people are interacting with one another in the same place within the same span of time, so that a single observer can economically collect many of the data he requires. It is this practical advantage that has determined the name of our field.

Now let us look at an example of elementary social behavior. Two clerks are assigned to the same sort of job in an office. That is, both are expected to obey the same institutional rules. But one of them is not very competent at his work. Should he ask his supervisor for help, he would confess his incompetence and perhaps hurt his chances for promotion; so he goes instead to the other clerk, who is more competent than he is himself, and asks help from him. The other helps him and thus rewards him; and he in turn rewards the other by thanking him, by praising him, by rendering him what I shall call *esteem*. Accordingly, we may look on the behavior of the two clerks toward one another, indeed we may look on all social behavior, as an exchange of goods; and the causes, the nature, and the consequences of the exchange are examples of the sort of thing small-group research studies.

The boundary of a field of investigation is the line between its *explicanda*—the phenomenon it undertakes to explain and ultimately to predict—and the things it does not undertake to explain but simply accepts as given. The behavior of the two clerks cannot be understood without reference to the institution, the office, to which both belong. For one thing, the help the first clerk gets from the second would have no value to him unless he were assigned to a certain kind of job. Nor can it be understood without reference to much more general cultural rules, for instance, the expectation that a man should thank someone who does him a favor. But the student of elementary social behavior does not undertake to explain why the institutional and cultural rules should be what they are. There are other social scientists to do that. What he does undertake to answer are questions like the following: Given that both clerks have learned the institutional rules, what determines whether one gets help from the other? What determines how much help he asks for and how much he gets? What determines how much esteem he gives to the other? The student of elementary social behavior takes the institutional framework of exchange as given and constant, and studies the variables entering into the process of exchange itself. He may be interested secondarily in the effect of the informal exchange on the success of the institution—on how, for instance, the informal exchange of advice may make the office better able to accomplish its assigned task.

At this point the reader may say to himself: "In different groups, in different societies, men exchange very different things. In one group they may exchange help for social approval; in another group they may exchange jokes for laughter. How can such things as joking and clerical help be measured along the same dimensions and so explained by the same theory?" The answer is that, from one point of view, they cannot indeed be compared. But from another point of view—and this is the point of view of the student of elementary social behavior—the two are comparable because both are activities given by one man to another in variable *quantities* or frequencies and both have variable *values,* that is, are more or less rewarding, to the man who receives them. Since the quantity and value of activities given by one man to another affect the quantity and value of the activities the other returns, the study of interpersonal exchange is the study of interpersonal influence. Note that *quantity* and *value* are also the variables of elementary economics—but this is hardly surprising, since economics too is concerned with exchange.

It should be clear that, by this definition, much human behavior is elementary social behavior, or, better, that elementary social behavior is one aspect of all social behavior. Indeed their behavior in face-to-face contact with others is the thing men are most familiar with, which makes it hard for us social scientists to explain why we study it. Laymen will necessarily find that many of the true propositions about it are obvious; and exceptions to some of the propositions that are not obvious will necessarily occur to them, unaccompanied by the realization that an exception need not disprove a proposition though it certainly calls for adding new propositions to a theory. It is as if the particles whose social behavior in the atom the physicist describes were able to talk back and tell him his propositions were either obvious or too abstract.

In fact the interest in the study of small groups came from two different directions and from two different disciplines. Early in this century the psychologists, studying individual behavior, became interested in phenomena like social facilitation—the curious fact that men do some kinds of work better when they are in the presence of others, even when the others do not communicate with them in any way, than when they are alone. From there it was a short step for the subdiscipline of social psychology to study the effect on men's behavior of more direct and explicit social influences brought to bear on them, including the influence of their immediate companions. In this field the most important recent contribution has been that of Kurt Lewin, his students, and his students' students.

The sociologists' interest in small groups was a little different. Their tradition was more theoretical than the psychologists'. They were obsessed with imitating the more advanced sciences and formulating general propositions from which a variety of empirical ones might be logically deduced under specified conditions. But if a theory as it matures takes a more and more deductive form, men do not arrive at it deductively. They arrive at it by induction from the very empirical propositions that the theory will ultimately explain. Some sociologists despaired of developing such a theory for large social units like national states. But small social units, those whose members were few in number, were another matter. In such units an investigator could make the detailed and comprehensive observations of social behavior on which alone the empirical propositions could be reliably based. Moreover, a very great number of such units were available for comparison, control, and even experimentation. As some of these sociologists used to say, they wanted to work with a unit small enough so that they could see all the way around it. More than by anything else their eyes were opened to these possibilities by the small-group studies made by Elton Mayo and his associates in the Western Electric researches—even though these researches were designed as studies of American industry and not of elementary social behavior as such.

I emphasize that the interest in small groups has been, at least on the part of the sociologists, primarily intellectual. True, the field does have, or many turn out to have, practical applications—in making the committees and other discussion groups that proliferate in our society more effective, in helping industrial workers become both more productive and more interested, in improving the new practice of group psychotherapy. But it is not the applications that most intrigue the sociologist. On the contrary, what he says is this: "Better a good theory in an unimportant field than a bad theory in an important one. Theory comes first." He likes small groups because they will let him pull off the kind of stunt he most enjoys. I must be honest about his values, even if it leads you to question them.

Speaking for myself, I doubt that the intellectual interest has been misplaced. The study of elementary social behavior occupies a strategic central position among the social sciences. On one side, it links up with behavioral psychology, which has been concerned with the effects of reward and punishment in changing the behavior of the higher animals. On another, it links with elementary economics, which is concerned, like itself, with exchange—the special but important form of exchange that occurs in an organized market. And finally, it is obviously and closely linked with standard sociology, or the study of institutions, for sub-institutional behavior is always becoming institutional—we need only remember that institutional Christianity began with a small group—and sub-institutional behavior is always modifying in actual practice the behavior called for by institutional norms. If we are to attain any intellectual understanding of social behavior, it is a good bet to begin here.

True to their different traditions, the psychologists once tended to study elementary social behavior through laboratory experiments on groups artificially formed, while the sociologists concentrated on observational—or field—studies of what they were pleased to call real-life small groups in industry and elsewhere. There is no reason to believe that the findings reached under the two different conditions are inconsistent with one another, though the sociologists are perhaps better at discovering what needs study and the psychologists at studying it rigorously. As time has gone on, these distinctions between the two disciplines have become blurred, and today in the study of elementary social behavior it is hard to tell them apart.

So far I have spent my time defining the field of research in elementary social behavior and showing why social scientists are interested in it. I have made no survey of the substantive findings in the field, nor have I space to do so here. Instead I shall end with an illustration. I shall put before you a couple of characteristic empirical propositions, and then suggest how a student of elementary social behavior would undertake to explain them. I claim no greater practical importance for the illustration than I do for the field as a whole.

Suppose, then, that several persons are able to associate freely with one another, subject only to the limitations imposed by tasks they must carry out together. They may be fellow members of a class at school; or, as above, they may be clerks working together in the same office. In such circumstances, different investigators have observed in several different groups the two phenomena that will concern us. In the first place, in connection with the tasks performed in common, some members of the group receive from other members a larger number of expressions of esteem than others do. Thus, in the office I have used as an illustration, some of the clerks get more esteem than others do. Indeed they receive not only more expressions of esteem but more communications in general; and the clerks who stand highest in esteem are relatively few in number. In short, the members of the group become ranked in esteem or, if you like, in status, though the word *status* is perhaps best reserved for the rank a man has formally received in an institution.

In the second place, outside the sphere of common tasks and inside what I shall call for convenience leisure-time activities, the distribution of expressions of approval and other communications among the members is different from, though still related to, what it is in the sphere of work. In leisure, members of the group tend to express liking for, and to associate with, other members who are their equals in esteem more often than they do with either their social superiors or inferiors. In having lunch or coffee or in visiting after hours, our clerks are apt to associate with other clerks who are their social equals in the office. These two findings can be reproduced under laboratory conditions, and something like them is familiar in the social experience of many of us. The question now is how a student of elementary social behavior would explain them.

First to be explained are the differences in esteem in the work situation. A member who is both able and willing to provide others with a service that many of them want but few are able to supply can get from them in return a more valuable reward than another member can get from supplying a less rare and less valuable service. Naturally the service need not be morally admirable, nor one that the rest of us mortals would enjoy, so long as the other members do in fact find it both rare and rewarding. This principle, which applies to ordinary market exchange, such as the exchange of money for physical goods, applies to any social exchange. It applies, for instance, to the exchange of help for esteem in our office. The few clerks who are so experienced and skillful in their jobs that they are able and willing to give the other clerks help and advice that the others badly need in doing their own work—these are the clerks who get most esteem from their fellows. We need not expect them to bargain consciously over the terms of exchange of help for esteem; we need only point to the kinds of service they supply. The persons who provide for other members services both rare and rewarding are the persons who manage somehow or other, by conscious or unconscious processes, to enjoy high esteem in informal groups. In short, something much like the old law of supply and demand explains why the members of a group are differentiated in esteem and why the members held in highest esteem are few.

We must next explain why members equal in esteem tend to associate with one another in their leisure time, and this will take us a little longer. In the office, both parties to the exchange, besides getting rewards—esteem for the few, help for the many—also incur costs. In our economics as in ordinary economics, their costs are the alternative rewards they give up, or forego, while they are exchanging help for esteem. What does each party give up? The skillful clerk who helps the others gives up the time he could otherwise have spent on doing his own work. That is clear enough, but it is much less clear what cost is incurred by the unskillful clerk who gets the help. Students of elementary social behavior believe that his cost lies precisely in his confessing, as he does when he asks for help, that he is in this respect a social inferior.

How much cost he incurs is determined by another explanatory principle, which Aristotle enunciated long ago, and which we now call the principle of *status congruence*. If one man is equal to another in all respects but one, which is in doubt, he will feel bad if he is not equal in that one too: his inferiority in that one respect will be incongruent with his equality in the others. But if, on the other hand, he is inferior in all respects but one, he will not feel so bad if he is inferior in that one too: his inferiority in that will be congruent with his inferiority in the others. To go to another man and ask for help is to confess oneself his inferior in skill. If one clerk is equal to another in the outward trappings of status—if, for instance, he has the same pay and seniority— then going to the other to ask for help will tend to bring him down in his social world, and this will be a cost to him. But if he has less pay and seniority than the other to begin with, then asking for help will not bring him down in the world but only confirm him in his present position of social inferiority, and so it will not cost him much. In short, it will cost an equal more to ask another equal for a service, and to give him esteem in return, than it will for an inferior to ask a superior.

The costs of each party to the exchange also increase with the amounts of help and approval they exchange. The skillful clerk who gives help takes more and more time from his own work, and accordingly what time he has left becomes more and more valuable to him. And the clerk who asks for more and more help confesses his social inferiority to an ever greater degree. Therefore, the longer the exchange goes on, the more reason both parties have for breaking it off and for working alone or entering into a new kind of exchange with a different person.

Let us now ask what the unskillful clerk needs in the way of a new kind of exchange. By giving the skillful clerk esteem in return for the help he has himself received, he has made the other his social superior and has himself incurred social costs in so doing. The people with whom he can still enter into exchange without incurring further costs in inferiority are, in the nature of the case, the clerks who are still his social equals, clerks, that is, who provide no services at work superior to those he can provide himself. For this reason, he is little motivated to approach them for assistance in the work situation; indeed to do so would, as we have seen, put his equality with them in jeopardy. Therefore, he is more likely to seek them out in the non-work situation, the sphere of leisure or "social" life in the narrow sense of the word *social*. There he can exchange with them activities that are indeed rewarding, for now that the skillful clerk has helped him take care of the problems he encountered in his work, he will welcome companionship of another sort. But the activities he shares with his new companions must not be the kind in which he can be made inferior: they must be activities in which he can return the same sort of reward as he gets —activities that in fact run all the way from exchanging jokes to exchanging hospitality. In such exchanges he is apt to say that he feels able to "be himself"—which means precisely that in them he runs no risk of being judged inferior, since his partners are in no position so to judge him. It is for reasons like this that people tend, in the sphere of leisure, to associate with, and to express liking for, other people who are their equals in esteem in the sphere of work.

In this way, a theory of elementary social behavior as an exchange of rewarding and costly activities is able to explain the two merely empirical propositions that we started with. The theory would not be interesting if it explained only these two, but it will account for others as well, which I have not space to go into here. I do not claim that I have given the full explanation. For one thing, I have not asked why the superior should avoid the inferior on social occasions, as the inferior does *him*.

Nor do I argue that ordinary men or, better, the novelists of manners, whose domain we have invaded, could not have come up with an explanation much like ours. On the contrary, men have always explained their behavior by pointing to what it gets them and what it costs them. That ours is an explanation of the same sort I claim as one of its positive advantages. Modern social science has gone far out of its way to show that common-sense explanations are incorrect, and it has ended by painting a picture of man that men cannot recognize. We students of elementary social behavior are not out to destroy common sense but to make explicit and general the wisdom it embodies.

Nor, finally, are the phenomena we have dealt with of great importance by practical standards. But remember this: what men have come to value in science is not only the practical importance of its subject matter but also the intellectual power of its methods. As long as men value the explanation and ultimately the prediction of *any* phenomena by the methods called scientific, they must value the study of elementary social behavior, for within its own modest field it will explain and, at least crudely, predict. So far, indeed, it has been more successful in attaining these ends than has the study of larger social units. This is the claim that may be made for it—and it is a purely intellectual one.

15 POLITICAL BEHAVIOR AND PUBLIC OPINION

Paul F. Lazarsfeld

Paul Lazarsfeld, Chairman of the Department of Sociology at Columbia University, was born in Vienna, Austria, in 1901. Educated at the University of Vienna, where he received his doctorate in 1925, Dr. Lazarsfeld began his teaching career as an instructor in mathematics and psychology at that institution. Following a three-year stint as Director of the Office of Radio Research at Princeton University, Dr. Lazarsfeld joined the faculty of Columbia University in 1940 as Professor of Sociology and in 1950 was appointed Chairman of the Department. An authority on social research techniques, and particularly on problems of communication, Dr. Lazarsfeld has been the recipient of the Sigma Delta Chi research award in journalism and the first Julian Woodward Memorial Award of the American Association for Public Opinion Research. He has written and collaborated with other authorities in the preparation of numerous articles, books, and textbooks on a wide range of subjects in the field of sociology.

In the United States, as in every other country, political life is an intricate web of individual activities and collective enactments. For a first orientation it helps to think of a pyramid with three levels. The foundation is formed by the voter in national, state, and local elections. At the top we find the legislature and the government, which conduct the formal business regulating the life of the republic. In between are the organizations of active citizens who are more involved than the general voter and who wish to influence the governmental process either in defense of their interests or in the expression of their social convictions.

All three levels have been studied by behavioral scientists; but available knowledge decreases sharply as we ascend our imaginary pyramid. Much is known about voting behavior because we have voting statistics and public opinion polls. Least is known about the workings of the top decision-makers; they tend to resist detached inquiry and, because they act under such diversified conditions, general findings are less likely to emerge. Organizations of political relevance hold a middle position in both respects. It is easier to obtain access to their records and, because of their large number, we have a better chance of finding regularities than is the case with governmental performance. Still, we know much less about them than about the general electorate. In this paper I shall give you a bird's-eye view of what behavioral scientists in the United States know about these three cross-sections of our political scene.

Let me begin with some observations on American voting behavior. Parties in America differ from those in Europe. They do not have strong ideological positions but, rather, represent coalitions of various population groups which want to capture the governmental machinery. And yet, voters for the two main parties have shown for many decades rather stable differences. Democrats are more likely to be recruited from urban centers and low-income strata. They want the government to play a greater role in economic affairs and are especially in favor of extending social legislation. Republicans, by and large, represent a coalition of the business community with farmers. The groups which migrated to this country from eastern and southern Europe are more likely to lean toward the Democrats; people of northern European extraction are more often on the Republican side. For similar historical reasons there is also quite a strong relation between voting and religion; Protestants have Republican tendencies, while Catholics and Jews veer more to the Democrats. All these factors, such as income, urbanism, and religion, are interrelated with each other; but careful studies have shown that they play an independent role along the lines just indicated.

To this general picture a large number of special features

could be added; but we can touch on only a few of them. Most countries of Western Europe present a broad spectrum of political differences, varying from the Communist left to a reactionary right. In the United States this range is much narrower, and one can only talk of groups which are somewhat to the left or something to the right of center. The majority of the intellectuals, especially those connected with the thousand or more colleges we have in the United States, are left of center. They have strong feelings regarding civil liberties, respect minorities, and oppose racial discrimination. The labor population is less liberal in this respect. Most American workers are not class conscious in the sense the term is used in Europe. They do not feel a basic antagonism toward business groups, and are not in favor of a political labor movement. They support their unions strongly but think these should restrict themselves to improving conditions of work and play. Most unions back the Democrats during election periods because of their stand on labor-management issues.

Much general knowledge about the American social scene derives from voting studies. Thus, for instance, we know that overwhelming numbers of young people vote like their parents; this is one of many indicators that the younger generation in this country does not develop strong rebellious feelings toward the older one. Women almost always vote like their husbands, indicating that they still feel that concern with public affairs is mainly a man's responsibility. Altogether, political cleavages are not taken too seriously; during campaigns there is a great deal of commotion, and outsiders might think that the fight is a very bitter one. But soon after the election, voters report that it made little difference to them who was elected. Political placidity is shown in still another way: however much discussion preceded the enactment of a specific law, once it is the law public opinion polls reveal a marked increase in approval.

Studies of specific campaigns have contributed to our psychological knowledge on opinion formation. Practically everyone in this country reads a newspaper and watches television. But the large majority of these audiences pay little attention to the political content of the mass media. They form their opinions through the personal influence of a small minority—about 20 per cent of the population—who are really interested; it is these opinion leaders who do the political reading and listening and pass it on by word of mouth to the rest. There was a time when the banker, the minister, and others in formal leadership positions were supposed to be the most influential in the community; and certainly in cases where they can control financial resources, or work through channels which people are accustomed to respect, they are indeed of importance. But recent studies have shown the crucial role of horizontal opinion leadership: the personal influence going on *within* social strata and exercised by people who stand out by their desire and ability to be listened to. Thus voting very often becomes an expression of solidarity with a group of friends and co-workers. During campaign periods, when discussion increases, voters show a tendency toward a consistent set of opinions. From week to week both Democrats and Republicans tend to develop agreement with the positions expressed in the platform of their party. But soon after the election, when interest has subsided, many voters hold quite inconsistent opinions, without being much bothered by it.

On a broader scale, voting data can contribute to our understanding of the way slow social changes come about. In general we find great constancy of voting behavior. If one draws maps to show county by county which party has the majority, one will find in many states that the pattern of voting has remained stable for eighty years, since the Civil War. And yet, at various points in time, major historical events have made a difference. Thus, for instance, Negroes used to vote Republican, supporting the party of their liberator, Abraham Lincoln. But during the Depression, beginning in 1929, the economic destiny of the Negro population was closely tied to the social legislation enacted by the Democratic party. By now, the large majority of Negroes are Democrats. This makes for a rather strange coalition, because the Democratic party also dominates the South, where the majority of white citizens still believe in segregation of the black race. The net effect is an example of what the British political scientist, Harold Laski, has called the self-correcting power of the American social system. During a presidential election, the Negro vote in northern cities is of crucial importance for the Democratic party. As a result, northern Democrats exercise continuous pressure on the southern wing to relax discriminatory practices. And indeed, while we still have many difficulties in the South, the polls over the last twenty years have shown slow but steady improvement of race attitudes within the white population.

Another kind of shift is noticeable right now and derives from a change in city life. An increasing number of people move to the suburbs and form communities of homeowners. Their whole social setting gets reorganized and with it new voting habits develop. In general they benefit the Republicans, but the extent of, and the reasons for, these new political allegiances are still controversial. Within the cities at the same time big new housing projects develop; they too will undoubtedly affect the urban voting pattern. If we were to list more of these trends, one would notice that they don't work in favor of just one party. For the country as a whole their net political effects about cancel out, which helps to explain why we have only small oscillations in the proportions by which presidential elections are won or lost. Students of politics show an increasing interest in the analysis of local and regional situations.

Voters go to the polls only once every few years; but political life goes on continually. Between elections it mainly flourishes in voluntary associations to which many Americans belong. These have always been a very characteristic feature of the American scene. In the early history of this country there was virtually no central government. Even today, many spheres of public life are left to the initiative of private associations. Most colleges, hospitals, and libraries were organized by informal citizens' groups and, even today, many are still supported by voluntary contributions. The United States is probably the only country which has no ministry of education. Elementary and secondary schools are under the jurisdiction of local communities, while most colleges are governed by private boards. American law has many transitions from formal political bodies to voluntary organizations: the business corporation vested with public interest and therefore subject to regulation, like the railroads; the non-profit research corporation which is tax-exempt; the psychiatric training center which has a charter and therefore can give certain degrees. The voluntary association is one of them. About five thousand such organizations have national scope and many times this number can be found on the local or regional level. A mere classification would be impossible within the space of this review. I can mention only a few examples.

Many *professional* organizations play a political role. The American Medical Association tries actively to block legislation which would extend the role of the government in medical insurance or would provide inexpensive medical services by publicly employed doctors. Inversely, a large number of teachers' organizations exercise a strong influence toward increasing school budgets and improving educational facilities. Organizations of lawyers have considerable influence in the appointment of judges of the higher rank, and in the nomination of lower-level judges who are elected by popular vote. A large number of *civic* organizations put their weight behind what is usually called progressive legislation: better housing, elimination of corruption in municipal administration, richer recreational facilities, and so on. They mobilize the attention of people who otherwise would not be interested in local politics. There is always the hope that fear of a defeat in the next election will make legislators sensitive to public opinion thus aroused.

A third group of associations is organized around *specific issues.* An interesting example is found in the efforts to increase public concern with international collaboration, and especially with the work of the United Nations. Most Americans favor participation in activities of the United Nations because they hope this will help preserve peace. At the same time, people are uninterested in, and uninformed about, the details of foreign affairs; they are especially unwilling to approve more far-reaching experiments in international government. A number of studies have shown that, over a short period of time, it is extremely difficult to affect this mood of ambivalence toward foreign policy.

One other instance of a specialized association are the taxpayers' organizations which are formed in many communities to fight increased educational expenses. Sometimes they enter into strange coalitions. By themselves, the members of such an organization would add up to only a small minority. But often they can count on the support of low-income groups who help them defeat many worthwhile referenda. There seem to be two explanations of this support. Many low-income voters have not had the experience, and therefore do not have the belief, that extensive education could be of value to their children. At the same time, they feel frustrated and think that they were deprived of many opportunities; their answer is aggression against any effort to extend an educational system from which they might still be excluded.

Ostensibly most voluntary organizations in America have nothing to do with politics. Their goal is the reduction of illness or the fight against juvenile delinquency, for example; many of them exist only to provide occasions when people can meet together in good fellowship. Still, even these types of groups often have important political consequences. For one, they are the proving grounds for local leadership. Many a person makes his way into the political arena by coming to public attention in a non-political organization. More important are the contacts which are made in these associations through conversation, joint readings, and discussions; they heighten a member's sensitivity to political events. Statistically speaking, people either belong to no organization at all or to a large number ranging from the political to the non-political pole.

This multiple membership helps to explain what at first looks like a contradiction. While there exist very many organizations in this country, less than half the adult population participate in any. And the proportion of participants decreases rapidly as we go down the socio-economic ladder. It is customary in American social research to divide the population into an upper class of about 20 per cent, a middle class of 50 per cent, and a lower class of the remaining 30 per cent. Approximately two-thirds of the upper class belong to some association; one-third of the middle class do; but we find that fewer than one-fifth of the lowest level belong to an organization. This fact has rather important social implications. It indicates, for one thing, that the formal management of these organizations is in the hands of the more privileged half of the population. Inasmuch as these groups have informal political influence, they counterbalance the equalitarian political system, which is based upon one vote for each person. In many cultural matters, this is probably all to the good. At the same time, those essentially middle-class organizations drain off the most active elements of the working strata. How this is to be judged depends upon one's general point of view. One can applaud the chances for upward mobility which these organizations provide for many individuals. But if one regrets the lack of a political labor party in the United States, then one would have to point to the structure of these voluntary organizations as one of the reasons.

The activities of the voluntary organizations have been

less studied than voting behavior because data are more difficult to come by. Still, regarding certain of their features we have rather interesting information. One good example is the relation between the general memberships and their leaders; this turns out to be more complicated than one might expect. Thus, for instance, the League of Women Voters, one of the largest civic organizations, has a definite policy that its officers should not participate in party politics. It feels that in this way it can better serve its goal, which is to strengthen good causes as they come up and to enlist the masses of women in their support. But, once a woman is drawn into the orbit of the League, she may become really interested in her new public role and may not see why she should stop short of active politics. Surveys have shown that a large proportion of League members do not approve of the self-imposed political restrictions which by-laws of the League require.

An inverse example can be taken from a group of what are usually called patriotic organizations: war veterans organized in the American Legion or descendants of old families organized in the Daughters of the American Revolution have rather strong nationalistic programs; they disapprove of international activities, are very suspicious of social reform, and, whenever they can, stress the symbols of old American traditions. The leaders of these organizations have continuing contacts with the leaders of other groups and are therefore willing to make more concessions to new ideas than is the more isolated general membership. Problems of leadership are most often studied in connection with unions. Their negotiations with management require a strong bureaucratic organization; this often leads to a very undemocratic government within the union and a consequent loss of member participation in union affairs. The literature on this subject is vast and interesting but lack of space prevents further consideration of it here.

I have not yet mentioned one organizational feature

which has an especially strong influence on American political life. Trade organizations, labor unions, and many other groups organized mainly around economic interests support so-called lobbyists at the seats of the fifty state governments and in Washington. Their task is quite avowedly to influence the vote of the legislators. These lobbyists are registered and officially recognized in their jobs. For obvious reasons not much is known about their activities. Only an occasional congressional investigation or a monographic study by a political scientist brings their work to light and indicates that they are often quite successful. Again, it depends upon one's point of view whether this is considered a sinister fact or a normal part of a democratic system where one task of government is to find compromises between various interest groups. In any case the role of these lobbyists leads to the third level of analysis which I have sketched above.

What determines the vote of the legislators themselves? Many efforts have been made to answer this question, but few have been successful. Thus, for instance, we know that many men in Congress and in the state legislatures are strongly influenced by the mail they get from their constituents. At the same time, studies have shown that such mail, although quite profuse in the United States, is by no means representative of general public opinion. It very often is organized by special propaganda groups and it comes, of course, from individual writers, who often have peculiar personalities or unusual involvement in a special cause. Efforts have also been made to find out whether public opinion polls influence legislators. Again, the evidence is conflicting. When elections are near, the polls probably play a fairly important role; between elections, legislators may not pay so much attention to polls because there is a greater chance that an issue will be forgotten by the time they are up for election again. Undoubtedly legislators also weigh in their minds the importance which various groups may have on election day. It should not be forgotten, incidentally, that it is a moot question to what extent an elected official should follow public opinion at every step. Many political scientists object to polls just on the ground that they tend to curtail independent judgment on the part of the representatives.

There is one area in which we have more precise data on the political behavior of the legislator; these come from studies analyzing their votes in Congress or in the state legislatures. Quite intricate statistical procedures have been used to bring out the main dimensions along which elected officials can be located. In general they replicate what was said before about the electorate. Labor-management issues and urban-rural differences are very important determinants. Many topics are decided by considerations of whether or not they would benefit the power position of the two parties. Legislation regarding foreign policy and civil liberties cuts across party lines. Of special interest are the men whose constituencies have deviant characteristics: for example, Republicans from poor and Democrats from well-to-do districts. They are under cross-pressures and the record shows that they are the ones most likely to break party discipline. Some states in the union vote so overwhelmingly on one side or the other that they really have only one party in the legislature. Under such conditions pressure groups have especially great power. It is generally accepted that clear-cut party organizations are preferable to the unchanneled play of innumerable influences. American tradition distinguishes three governmental functions: the enacting of laws by the legislatures; the administration of laws by the President, his cabinet ministers, state governors, the mayors of large cities, and so forth. The courts in the United States are also part of the governmental system because they decide conflicts between various parts of the executive branch and they can invalidate acts of the legislators if these violate the basic constitution. Some research has attempted to relate personality characteristics of judges and other public officials to their political acts. But most of this is still in the realm of conjecture.

To round out the whole picture one must mention one area of research which received much attention some decades ago. It was called crowd behavior; riots and other more or less spontaneous outbreaks which did not fit into the normal stream of political life were made the object of study. In the United States these events have become so rare that studies investigating them have practically faded from the work done by behavioral scientists.

The readers of this review might well ask how all this is related to the work of the historian, the jurist, and the philosopher, who have studied politics for hundreds of years. The answer is very simple. We provide new data which make it possible to deal with age-old questions somewhat more precisely; sometimes our work even raises problems which had been previously overlooked. Science is often called an everlasting dialogue between theory and empirical research. The behavioral sciences have added a few new lines to the evolving script.

16 SOCIAL STRATIFICATION AND THE ANALYSIS OF AMERICAN SOCIETY

Seymour Martin Lipset

Seymour Martin Lipset, Professor of Sociology and Director of the Institute of International Studies at the University of California in Berkeley, was born in New York City in 1922. A graduate of the College of the City of New York, Dr. Lipset received his doctorate in sociology from Columbia University. He began his teaching career at the University of Toronto in 1946, taught for two years (1948–1950) at the University of California, and then joined the Columbia University graduate faculty. He served as Assistant Director of the Bureau of Applied Social Research from 1954 to 1956, and since 1956 has been at the University of California. Dr. Lipset has lectured at the Salzburg Seminar in American Studies and was Visiting Professor at the Free University of Berlin in 1953. He was a Fellow of the Center for Advanced Study in the Behavioral Sciences in 1955–1956, and in 1960–1961 was the Henry Ford Visiting Research Professor of Political Science at Yale University. A specialist in political sociology and social stratification, Dr. Lipset is a member of the American Sociological Association, the American Political Science Association, and the Pacific Coast Sociological Society, and a Fellow of the American Academy of Arts and Sciences. His books include Agrarian Socialism, Union Democracy, Social Mobility in Industrial Society, *and* Political Man, *which earned him the Robert MacIver Award of the American Sociological Association in 1962.*

The study of social stratification—the ranking of men in a social hierarchy according to some valued attribute—for example, wealth or ancestry or skill or power—is as old as man's analysis of society. Both Plato and Aristotle were concerned with the nature of class differences and the way these varied in different societies. Plato noted a necessary connection between the family system and the inheritance of privileged position; while Aristotle linked the class system to the conditions for democracy, tyranny, and oligarchy, suggesting that where the middle-class was relatively large, there stable democracy could flourish, but that where the poor predominated numerically, there one should find tyranny (dictatorship based on mass support), or oligarchy (domination by the wealthy). The interest of the intellectuals of the Enlightenment in the natural history of mankind led many of them to study variations in systems of social stratification because, in the words of the eighteenth-century Scottish philosopher, John Millar, such variations "must have a prodigious influence upon . . . habits, dispositions, and ways of thinking," And nineteenth-century intellectuals, in reaction to the political and industrial revolutions of their time, devoted much of their thought to class analysis. The European conservative was concerned with the breakdown of the integrated pre-industrial society. In a pecuniary society, in which the cash-nexus rather than moral ties bound together the members of the nation, the need, as he saw it, was to find new sources of social solidarity which would prevent society from being torn apart by the interest struggle among the various classes. For the radical intellectual, such concern with moral breakdown was misplaced. To him the new stratification of society was part of an evolutionary process replacing the old code with a new one, one where freedom and civil rights would flourish generally.

But apart from the moral lesson which any of the figures drew, all those who studied class differentiation did so in a context wherein aristocracies, inherited social position, and differential rights and privileges for different classes in the society were taken for granted. America, however, has been different. America was a continent newly born. It was the society of the Social Contract, where men came to establish a new world. Only in America could it be written that "all men are created equal." Thomas Jefferson, the third president of the United States, once insisted that his cabinet sit at a round rather than a square table, so that there be no question of relative rank or status. In the 1820's the first political parties which ever called themselves Workingmen's Parties were formed in the United States, and one of their major concerns was to reduce the advantages which the well-to-do pass on to their children. They demanded the extension of state-supported education to all and, quite seriously, proposed that at the age of six all children be taken away from their parents and sent to state boarding schools so that everyone would have an equal start in life's competition. These early American exponents of egalitarianism seemed to believe, with Plato, that the help which parents necessarily feel they must give to their children has been the principal cause of inherited privilege; hence they sought this radical solution to inequality. While the extremist proposal obviously found little support, the demand for the extension of education to all was waged so successfully that in 1849 New York City established a free, publicly-supported college of higher education.

The lack of aristocracy, the strength of egalitarian norms in America, has meant that almost every study of American society, whether or not it dealt explicitly with social stratification, has been preoccupied with the meaning of equalitarianism. The first such analysts, the celebrated book-writing foreign travelers of the nineteenth century, almost without exception were struck by this phenomenon. Thus a summary by an historian, Max Berger, of the reports of hundreds of British travelers in America before the Civil War, states that "most prominent of the many impressions that the Britons took back with them was the aggressive equalitarianism of the people." Frances Trollope, who came to America in 1830, complained about that "coarse familiarity, untempered by any shadow of respect, which is assumed by the grossest and the lowest in their intercourse with the highest and most refined," while her equally conservative son Anthony, visiting thirty years later, objected that "the man to whose service one is entitled answers one with determined insolence." As would be expected, liberal sympathizers with democratic institutions evaluated the same phenomenon quite differently. So Harriet Martineau, another British visitor of the 1830's, reported that "the English insolence of class to class is not even conceived of. . . . Nothing in American civilization struck me so forcibly and so pleasureably as the invariable respect paid to man, as man." And similar comments were made by the two most noted foreign travelers to the United States in the nineteenth century, Alexis de Tocqueville and James Bryce. A more recent effort by Robert Smuts to compare the published judgments of European visitors in America at the turn of the present century with those written by members of British Productivity Teams in the 1950's states that almost all reports surveyed from both periods, whether written by socialists or conservatives, by representatives of management or labor, have commented on "the absence of sharp class differences. Even hostile visitors confirmed this judgment. Some foreign visitors found the arrogance of American workers intolerable."

The American system of social stratification which so interested the foreign travelers of the nineteenth century has been of equal fascination to the American sociologists of the present era. They differ from the earlier commentators in at least two major respects: first, the sociologists have been concerned with differentiating *among* Americans rather than with analyzing *the* American, and they, therefore, have tended to emphasize the way in which class differentiation accounts for widespread differences in values and behavior within the society. Consequently, they often seem to stress inequality rather than equality. Second, they have been able to use recently created quantitative methods of investigation, which means that they can often report on the distributions of sentiments and behavior in total populations, as contrasted with the travelers whose general observations were based on contact with limited segments of the population.

Perhaps the most interesting result of the myriad of sociological inquiries is the demonstration of the variety of ways in which social stratification in America is not too different from its manifestation in Europe. Early American studies of occupational prestige, some begun in the 1920's, revealed a status hierarchy in which positions of political power, intellectual eminence, and economic authority were ranked at the top. Subsequent studies made in the 1940's and 1950's revealed very little change in the relative position of different occupations. And most interesting of all, comparable studies completed in the last decade in various European and Asian countries such as Germany, Great Britain, Japan, Brazil, the Philippines, the Netherlands, and among a large sample of post-World War II Russian emigres, suggest that in each country similar occupations have comparable status. Another subject which has interested modern sociology has been social mobility, the extent to which men are able to move up and down the social hierarchy, both as between fathers and sons, and also within one's own lifetime. Two common popular beliefs about this subject have been that in the nineteenth century many men were able to make great fortunes, and that then and now, Americans have had an easier chance to improve their social and economic position than have Europeans. These assumptions have been subjected to close statistical scrutiny and have been found to be in error. For example, two American sociologists, Reinhard Bendix and Frank Howton, who investigated the backgrounds of business leaders in the early nineteenth century, found that few of them were actually of low-status back ground. At a time when only 5 per cent of Americans attended a high school, almost one-third of the business leaders had been to college, and another 51 per cent had studied in high school. The consensus of the various studies which have been made of the social origins of the business elite is that in the United States few individuals have *ever* been able to make the jump from the lower strata to the top in one generation, and that the small proportion who have done so, somewhere between 5 and 10 per cent of the existing elite, has *not* declined over time. But while we lack comparable historical data for Europe, recent studies of the contemporary business elite which have been made in a number of countries, Great Britain, Switzerland, the Netherlands, and Sweden, point to similar origins among high-level businessmen in these countries as well. The area of statistical comparisons has been extended to social mobility in national populations, not simply in the business elites. There have been a half-dozen studies of the extent of mobility within the entire American population since World War II based on systematic samples of the national population. It is difficult to report briefly on their main findings, particularly since one never knows how to interpret a given statistic: does it mean as few as, or as many as? These studies agree that about 30 per cent of Americans of non-rural background have moved across the line between the manual working class and the non-manual "middle class" as compared with their father's position. (Two-thirds of these have moved up, and one-third down.) However, if instead of limiting the definition of mobility to movement between two classes, it is extended to movement among seven classes, as did Joseph Kahl of Washington University at St. Louis, we find that 67 per cent of the population have moved up or down the class structure. And studies in different American cities which have painstakingly compared social mobility over forty years through examining documentary records have concluded that social mobility has "increased steadily from 1910–1920 to 1940–1950," a result which is in part a function of the upgrading of the occupational structure, i.e., the proportion of low-status manual jobs has been declining. These findings also can be paralleled in other countries. Thus when we compare the results of national investigations in countries as different as Great Britain, France, Japan, Germany, Denmark, and Sweden with the United States, we find comparable rates of movement across the manual–non-manual line. Only Italy among the countries surveyed seems to have a lower rate of mobility. And the surveys of changes in rates of mobility in some of these countries, such as Great Britain and Germany, suggest that the social structure there, as in America, has become more fluid.

The belief often voiced by political commentators that the social bases of political party conflict in America has differed sharply from those of Europe in not being linked to class cleavage has also been subject to sharp challenge by sociological inquiries based on interviews with samples of the electorate, or on the correlation of the social traits of different areas with their voting habits. A very large number of surveys agree that the Democratic party is based on the lower status occupational, religious, and ethnic groups in the population, while Republicans are much more commonly found among those with socially superior traits. The Democrats have the workers, the Jews, the Negroes, and other minority religious and ethnic groups, while the ideal-typical Republican is most likely to be a middle-class white Protestant. In one recent election, that of 1948, the Democrats received a larger proportion of the working-class vote, over 80 per cent, than is usually obtained by European left parties. Conversely, studies of the politics of the business elite show that they are overwhelmingly Republican. Perhaps no better example may be given of the pervasiveness of stratification as a factor in American life than the results of one survey, made in 1955, of the opinions of the leaders of large corporations, which reported that among those heading corporations with more than 10,000 employees only 6 per cent were Democrats, that among those heading corporations employing between 1,000 and 9,999, the Democratic percentage was 8 per cent, while among the presidents of companies with between 100 and 999 workers, as many as 12 per cent gave their party affiliation as Democratic. These figures parallel findings in Great Britain. These differences in the social base of the two parties are not recent developments flowing from controversies over the New Deal or the rise of the trade-union movement. Recent quantitative studies by sociologists and political scientists of presidential elections in 1800, in 1828, and in 1860, to mention just a few crucial election years, have found that in these elections as well the Democrats secured their votes disproportionately from the poorer strata, both rural and urban, and from the groups of more recent immigrant origin, and hence lower status, such as the Catholics, the Irish, the Germans, and so forth. The Federalists of Hamilton, the Whigs of Clay, and the Republicans of Lincoln, each in turn, like the contemporary Republicans, had greater strength among the more well-to-do and the native-born Anglo-Saxon Protestants. The evidence clearly suggests that American political party conflict has always been closely tied to stratification differences. And sociological survey studies of the social and political opinions of Americans show the way in which position in the class structure influences a wide variety of opinions. Thus, as might be expected, the lower strata are more likely to support trade unions, welfare-state measures, government economic planning, progressive income taxes, and to describe their class status as "working class" rather than "middle class" when asked which class they are in. On non-economic issues, however, which involve toleration for diversity, the lower strata are much less liberal than the more well-to-do. On questions dealing with belief in civil liberties for unpopular minorities, on civil rights for Negroes, on immigration, on internationalism, on corporal punishment for criminals, the poorer, in large part because they are less educated and more insecure, are less likely to favor the more liberal position. Hence we find that on economic reform measures, low class position is associated with the more liberal position, while on non-economic policies the correlation is reversed. These patterns also are comparable to the results of recent European investigations dealing with comparable issues. There are, of course, great differences between the various European and American political parties, but the fact of explicit class appeals in European party programs clearly does not mean that European party diversity is more closely linked to class differentiation than is the American.

Perhaps the best known and most costly studies made of social class in America are the various surveys of W. Lloyd Warner and others which have applied modern methods of survey analysis to document the nature of prestige or status classes which affect the extent of social intercourse among people of various backgrounds. In the first major study of this kind, completed during the 1930's, Warner asked the residents of a small New England city to name those with whom they associated at home gatherings, parties, social clubs, and the like. And by exhaustively interviewing most of the community, and cross-classifying the social ties of its residents, he reported the existence of six distinct status classes. Subsequent studies of other communities have reported comparable findings, although some of them suggest that there are five rather than six major status divisions in the typical American small city. These status classes in large part reflect the combination of ascribed (inherited) characteristics and economic position as criteria for social rank. Thus in each community surveyed, the upper class has characteristically been composed of old wealthy families; the next highest class includes the nouveaux riches and well-to-do families who belong to minority ethnic groups with lower status, such as Jews, Catholics, and others of a non-Anglo-Saxon and non-northern European ethnic origin. Below the "upper classes" social prestige is largely determined by economic position, although within the middle classes also ethnic background may contribute to raising or lowering the position of a family in the social hierarchy. Research on the status position of members of minority ethnic groups suggests that many such groups exist as more or less separate communities within which status differentiation occurs. A large Jewish or Irish population in a given city will usually have a status structure that more or less parallels the structure of those of Anglo-Saxon Protestant background.

The students of the social class or prestige structure have been criticized by some sociologists for drawing generalizations which are applicable only to relatively small cities and towns. It has been argued that the status criterion of "who associates with whom" cannot really function in a large metropolitan city since people do not know the background of those whom they meet as intimately as do residents of smaller communities. But while this criticism is undoubtedly valid, a recent survey of the upper class of one major American city, Philadelphia, by Digby Baltzell, has shown the way in which the same pattern develops among those at the very top of the system. In Philadelphia and in most large American cities, the Social Register Association exists as a formal body to determine who belongs to "high society." One is admitted only after three families already listed in the *Register* certify that they associate with you regularly on an intimate basis. And Baltzell has shown that although membership in *The Social Register* is based on criteria of family background, it includes, on the whole, the wealthiest individuals, with the significant exception of wealthy members of minority ethnic groups. And as in Great Britain, the scions of the upper-class families attend high-status private schools and study at a limited number of socially prestigeful universities, at which they tend to associate with others of comparable backgrounds to themselves.

The findings which have been briefly touched on here are but a limited sample of the extensive findings concerning the nature of class differentiation in American society. Other studies have dealt with the way in which family, sex, and demographic patterns are linked to class with findings such as these—the lower the class position, the higher the divorce rate, the greater the amount of family instability, the more use of authoritarian methods of parental discipline, the higher the birth rate (although the differential is declining rapidly), the greater the probability of pre- and extra-marital sexual intercourse and the less interest in the career goals and educational achievements of children. Leisure habits differ greatly according to class. The more well-to-do are more likely to be involved in different forms of organized activity, and to make more use of the artistic culture of the society. The classes read different newspapers and magazines, and listen to different radio and television programs. Working-class people are much less likely to have friends outside of their families than those in the middle classes. Lower-class persons are more likely to be oriented towards securing immediate perceivable rewards, and to show an inability to delay gratifications for subsequent rewards than do those of higher position. Many studies have also documented the close link between religion and class in American life. Among the Christian denominations, one can rank the relative socio-economic status of each ranging from the Episcopalians and Congregationalists at the top to the Baptists, Catholics, and the various fundamentalist sects at the bottom. In large measure, also, the practice within specific denominations varies considerably to accommodate to the varying religious needs of persons at different social levels. And research on social mobility has shown that men tend to change their church affiliation when they move up the class structure, a phenomenon which helps perpetuate the relative status rankings of the different denominations.

The thousands of studies of different aspects of social stratification in the United States clearly demonstrate that in America, as in other parts of the world, there are many social environments, the world of the well-to-do, of the middle class, and of the poor, even if the American poor do have a higher standard of living than the middle classes of many nations of the world. Yet, surprising as it may sound, these contemporary findings would not have surprised the European travelers who have been so struck by American egalitarianism, and are not viewed by most American sociologists as negating the image of America as a society which stresses equality and achievement. Many of the nineteenth-century travelers called attention to patterns of class differentiation much like those discussed here, in the same books in which they commented on American egalitarianism. In fact, those travelers who were so impressed with the pervasive equalitarianism of American society, also suggested that, *precisely as a result of the emphasis on equality and opportunity,* Americans were *more* status-conscious than those who lived in the more aristocratic systems of Europe. They believed, for example, that it was easier for a nouveau riche individual to be accepted in European high society than in American. British travelers *before the Civil War* noted that Americans seemed to love titles even more than Englishmen. Writing in the 1830's, Harriet Martineau pointed to the existence of status discrimination in Philadelphia in terms which sound like Warner's report on New England in the 1930's: status lines are drawn according to *which* generation made the money; one group will not associate with another because "the fathers of the Arch Street ladies . . . made their fortunes, while the Chestnut Street ladies owed theirs to their grandfathers.*

* *And Frances Trollope in the same period reports an anecdote about a girl excluded from a ball in New York City, although all her schoolmates from no more prosperous families attend, because her father "is a mechanic artisan; he assists in making the articles he sells: the others call themselves merchants." Upper-class families in New York City in the 1840's paid to have their names published in an early version of the social register, a book listing the members of high society. One British visitor in this decade, J. S. Buckingham, reported that Americans described their status structure in terms of four classes: (1) aristocracy of family; (2) aristocracy of wealth, not so high; (3) middle class—merchants, traders, clergy, and professionals; (4) laborers.*

In the 1880's James Bryce, who stressed the fact that "there is no rank in America," nothing which entitled a man to "deference or respect from others," also noted "a passion among Americans for genealogical researches," as a means of establishing objective sources of status differentiation. And Max Weber, the justly celebrated German sociologist, who visited America in 1904, reported that "only the resident of a certain street ('the street') is considered as belonging to 'society,' is qualified for social intercourse, and is visited. . . ." And like Bryce he called attention to the way in which wealthy Americans use the fact of descent from early settlers to "usurp 'status' honor."

Thus the seeming contradiction between the strong emphasis on egalitarianism and on status striving was no contradiction to many of the foreign travelers or the Americans with whom they talked. As Robert Smuts points out in his summary of the attitudes of the travelers at the beginning of the twentieth century, they agreed that "social and economic democracy in America, far from mitigating competition for social status, intensified it." The very emphasis on equalitarianism in America, that is, the lack of a well-defined deference structure linked to a legitimate aristocratic tradition in which there is no question about the propriety of social rankings, forces well-to-do Americans to emphasize status background and symbolism. As James Bryce noted in the 1880's, "it may seem a paradox to observe that a millionaire has a better and easier social career open to him in England than in America. . . . The existence of a system of artificial rank enables a stamp to be given to base metal in Europe which cannot be given in a thoroughly republican country."*

The very emphasis on the value that everyone is expected to be able to get ahead in the United States has also been seen by some observers as a source of status striving, of the propensity toward conspicuous consumption, of "keeping up with the Joneses." To spend money so that others can see you have money is a way of showing you have succeeded in a society which emphasizes success. Hugo Münsterberg, a well-

* Later commentators on differences between British and American society, such as the British historian Denis Brogan in the 1940's, or the American sociologist Howard Brotz in 1959, have independently called attention to the greater efforts at snobbery among upper-class Americans as compared to upper-class Britons. Brotz has observed that "in a democracy snobbishness can be far more vicious than in an aristocracy. Lacking that natural confirmation of superiority which political authority alone can give, the rich and particularly the new rich, feel threatened by mere contact with their inferiors . . . whereas in an aristocratic society such as Britain an upper-class individual is at ease in the presence of members of the lower classes and in associating with them in recreation. . . . It is this 'democratic' attitude which, in the first instance, makes for an openness to social relation with Jews. One cannot be declassed, so to speak, by play activities."

known German psychologist of the turn of the century, noted that given the pressure in America to succeed, conspicuous consumption naturally followed, since "the ability to spend was the only public sign of success at earning." His compatriot, the economist and sociologist Werner Sombart, whose great book, *Why Is There No Socialism in the United States?*, stressed the role of egalitarianism in values and manners in mitigating working-class resentments, also noted that America was a nation of status strivers. "Since all are seeking success . . . everyone is forced into a struggle to beat every other individual; and a steeplechase begins . . . that differs from all other races in that the goal is not fixed, but constantly moves even further away from the runners."

The emphasis on egalitarianism in American society has never meant, as Tocqueville and others noted, that there were not major differences in status, wealth, and authority. Even the pioneer settlements, in their first decade of existence, were often quite differentiated on the basis of economic position. In a recent book, *The Making of an American Community*, the historian Merle Curti has applied quantitative techniques to the study of the first twenty-five years of a pioneer mid-nineteenth-century Wisconsin community, and found that there was as much economic difference among these these new settlers after one decade as existed in a New England community of comparable size which had almost two hundred years of history behind it.

The American value system has never denied the existence of or the need for status differences; in fact, as the travelers noted, more than any other society it called upon all men to seek to climb the hierarchical ladder. Where America has differed from other societies is in its belief that such social differences are accidental, not essential attributes of men, that as one summary of foreign comments states, though "different occupations, of course, brought differences in prestige . . . neither the occupation nor the prestige implied any fundamental difference in the value of individuals." It has simply not been good taste in America to insist on publicly emphasizing status differences. Hence in every relationship between those higher and lower in the status pyramid, the social conventions require men to emphasize the similarities rather than the differences among them. For example, one important way of so de-emphasizing the actual difference is the custom of people calling each other by their first names, whether employer and employee, professor and research assistant, lawyer and client, and so forth. There are, of course, ways in which those of high-status background may more readily recognize each other (the sociologist Bernard Barber has pointed out the minute differences in style used by tailors patronized by the well-to-do which make it possible to recognize that type of suit); but the essence of such methods is that only the superiors know about them.

To return to the differences or lack of differences between American and European society discussed earlier, the evidence clearly suggests that many patterns of class differentiation are comparable. The difference between the two considered in the grossest of terms essentially still lies in the fact that inherited social position and inequality retain more legitimacy, are considered more proper, by various strata in Europe than has ever been true in the United States. The American value system's emphasis on equality and basic similarity among those in different classes has been reinforced by the fact that distribution of consumers' goods, one of the main components of what we mean by style of life, tends to become more equitable as the size of the national income increases. Today as in the nineteenth century there is greater variation in the styles of life of the different classes in Europe than in America. To a European, different classes mean distinct ways of life, even though in many European countries the rates of social mobility or the relative position of an occupation in the social hierarchy are the same as in the United States. As Europe becomes more wealthy, as the masses begin to enter the market for goods and services which once were limited to the well-to-do, Europe will become increasingly "American" in its social structure. And American research on social stratification has shown that to become increasingly American, to become more egalitarian, does not mean the end of social stratification. A close reading of studies of the American class structure is recommended to any European who wants to know the direction in which the triumph of the welfare state, increased productivity, and the political power of the masses to enforce egalitarian reforms, are leading the more industrialized nations of Europe.

17 SOCIAL DEMOGRAPHY

Kingsley Davis

Kingsley Davis, Professor of Sociology at the University of California in Berkeley, was born in Tuxedo, Texas, in 1908. A graduate of the University of Texas, Dr. Davis pursued advanced studies in sociology at Harvard University, where he received his doctorate. Before he joined the University of California faculty in 1955, Dr. Davis taught sociology at Clark, Pennsylvania State, Princeton, and Columbia universities. He was Head of the Department of Sociology at the Pennsylvania State University from 1937 to 1942, a research associate at the Office of Population Research at Princeton from 1942 to 1948, and Director of the Columbia University Bureau of Applied Social Research from 1949 to 1952. A specialist in population, urbanization, and the family, Dr. Davis is the author of Human Society, The Population of India and Pakistan, *and co-author of* Modern American Society. *He has served as President of the American Sociological Association, United States Representative on the Population Commission of the United Nations, and President of the Population Association of America.*

Is demography a "behavioral science"? Some people would say "no," because demography considers the *results* of behavior rather than behavior itself, or because the term "behavior" implies motivation, the province of psychology and sociology. But a new science of population is emerging, distinguished precisely by its interest in behavior and motives. It does not claim that the *sole* approach to population study is by way of attitudes and goals—for demographic behavior is not always motivated or, when motivated, free from influence by external conditions; but it does maintain the importance of investigating the motivational linkages between changing conditions on the one hand and demographic behavior and population trends on the other.

This new science—technically, sociological demography

—has so far had its main impetus in America. The United States, being the country with the greatest volume and variety of immigration ever known and with a resulting plethora of religious and ethnic groups and problems, has taken up empirical sociology more than any other nation. As a result, most of the teaching and research in population is done by people who are trained in sociology. It is understandable, therefore, that they should give a sociological emphasis to their work.

The European country which has placed most emphasis on social demography is France. There the reason is not so much an affiliation between sociology and demography (the two disciplines are pursued separately), but rather a strong official interest in applying the science of demography to national problems. The French government has a National Institute of Demographic Studies which, with a staff of experts, investigates such diverse subjects as alcoholism, married women in the labor force, Algerians in France, instruction in primary schools, attitudes toward the family, etc. The Institute publishes the world's most distinguished and versatile demographic journal, *Population.*

In Great Britain, too, considerable emphasis is being placed on direct investigation of motives and behavior. This trend has had to overcome the traditional linkage in Britain between demography and economics, a tradition that dates from the days of Malthus. Insofar as population is thought of mainly in terms of the food supply, there seems to be little reason for studying attitudes and motives; but, beginning with the constitution of the Royal Commission on Population in 1944, there has been an ever growing focus in Britain on the sociology, as distinct from the economics, of population. This interest has arisen partly from the concern of Britain with her birth rate and her problems of migration, but also partly from the transformation of her society since World War I.

In Japan and in less developed countries, notably India,

field studies of demographic attitudes and behavior are becoming frequent. Clearly, in much of the world, demography is no longer confined to the analysis of census data and vital statistics. The new science of social demography is illuminating complexities of population which once were ignored or else settled by armchair theorizing. To understand how, let us begin by facing the crucial truth that population trends are almost entirely unintended, that they are neither foreseen nor desired by the very people whose behavior brings them about.

This hiatus between personal intent and collective consequence arises at two levels: first, the demographic behavior itself may not be intended at all; second, if intended, it is for individual purposes which do not envision the collective consequences of similar behavior by many individuals. Thus, of the three types of behavior that directly affect population —childbearing, migrating, and dying—the last is not self-motivated except in the case of suicide, whereas the other two may or may not be. A child who is moved by his parents from one country to another, or a citizen sent by his government to another country in an "exchange of minorities," is a migrant though he did not intend to be. Similarly, a woman may give birth to a child as an unintended and undesired by-product of intercourse indulged in for other reasons. A recent study in America, for example, found that 16 per cent of the most recent pregnancies of married women were not wanted by the wife or husband. The percentage rose rapidly with the number of children the couple had borne—from 6 per cent being unwanted when the most recent pregnancy was the first one, to 62 per cent when it was the ninth or more.* Contraception being widely practiced in the United States, the proportion of unwanted pregnancies is relatively low, but in countries where con-

* Ronald Freedman, Pascal K. Whelpton, and Arthur A. Campbell, *Family Planning, Sterility and Population Growth* (New York: McGraw-Hill, 1959), p. 75.

traception is hardly used at all, the proportion is much higher. A sociological investigation in Jamaica, for example, found that 38 per cent of the women in a sample drawn from the lower ranks of society said they had more offspring than they considered ideal. Fewer than 3 per cent of the women who had two or less surviving children said they had more than their ideal, whereas 65 per cent said so among those who had three or more surviving.*

Even when demographic behavior is intended—that is, when the result is consciously sought, as when a wife *plans* to have a child—the motivation refers to the individual and his situation, not to the society at large. People do not normally migrate or refrain from migrating, reproduce or refrain from reproducing, in order to achieve a given population size for a nation. Instead, they have in mind such goals as improving their own economic prospects, being respectable in the eyes of their friends, enjoying children but not being overburdened with them, etc. In their demographic behavior they not only fail to consider the future of the population, but are often too unaware of the facts to do so. Even in well-educated countries, opinion polls have revealed much ignorance and misconception concerning demographic conditions. In 1943, for instance, the Gallup poll asked the following question in the United States: "The population of the U.S. is about 134,000,000. What would you guess is the population of Canada? Only 8 per cent of the respondents came within one million of the right answer, and about half could hazard no guess at all.† Similarly, a *Fortune* poll in 1944 revealed that 35 per cent of the United States respondents had no idea, or else a fantastically erroneous idea, of the proportion of the American people living on farms.‡

We thus see how it happens that demographic trends, although a product of human behavior, are for the most part

---

* Judith Blake, *Family Structure in Jamaica* (Glencoe, Ill.: Free Press, 1961).
† Reported in *Public Opinion Quarterly*, Vol. 8 (Spring, 1944), p. 148.
‡ *Fortune*, August, 1944.

unintended or undesired by the people concerned. Not only is some demographic behavior not motivated at all, but even when it is, the goals are personal rather than collective. This fact makes it seem, to many at least, that there is something automatic or inevitable about population trends, that they are beyond human control. Actually, however, they are potentially subject to human control in the same way that business cycles or bureaucracies are; the lack of control up to now is largely a result of ignorance and indifference concerning the demographic consequences of behavior.

The most significant and far-reaching modern population trend is the worldwide decline in the death rate. This was not only the *first* major change to be observed in the evolution of the modern demographic cycle, but also the one that has triggered most of the other changes, for it was upon mortality that the technological and economic revolution of modern times had its first and main demographic impact. Yet the amazing decline in human mortality, a monument to human ingenuity, was not itself foreseen in either its degree or its timing.

As early as the eighteenth century in northwestern Europe the death rate was noticeably undergoing a gradual though fluctuating retreat. The drop became faster and steadier in the nineteenth century, but did not reach its most precipitous fall until early in the present century (see Table 1). A notion of how drastic the reduction was is seen in the fact that in five western European countries, the number of people surviving *to age 60* out of each thousand born was greater in the 1940's than the number surviving *to age 15* in the 1840's (763 as against 674). Or, to put it another way, in the 1940's in these five countries, on the average half the population was dead by age 44½, whereas in the 1940's, half had not died until age 73½.* Among eleven Western coun-

* Derived from George J. Stolnitz, "A Century of International Mortality Trends: I," *Population Studies*, Vol. 9 (July 1955), p. 29. The countries are Belgium, England and Wales, France, Netherlands, and Sweden.

Table 1

Average Crude Death Rate in Four
Scandinavian Countries, 1740 to 1958[1]

PERIOD	AVERAGE ANNUAL DEATHS PER 1000 INHABITANTS[2]	PER CENT DROP FROM PRIOR PERIOD[3]
1740–59	29.1	——
1760–79	28.1	3.6
1780–99	26.2	7.2
1800–19	25.8	1.6
1820–39	23.0	12.1
1840–59	21.4	7.4
1860–79	20.9	2.3
1880–99	18.0	15.6
1900–19	15.4	17.2
1920–39	11.7	31.3
1940–59	10.2	13.3

[1] The countries are Denmark, Finland, Norway, Sweden.
[2] Average rates for the eighteenth century calculated from H. Gille, "Demographic History of the Northern European Countries in the Eighteenth Century," *Population Studies*, Vol. 3 (June 1949), p. 65.
[3] Crude death rates do not afford an accurate basis for comparing the force of mortality from one time to another, because they are influenced by the age structure independently of mortality. The effect of changes in the age structure is particularly important when birth rates are declining rapidly. However, since the alterations in the crude rate from one twenty-year period to the next are not markedly distorted in this way, the percentage changes give a fair index of the rate of change with time.

tries for which long series of life-tables are available, seven had their most rapid short-run gains in life expectancy after 1915, three had their most rapid gains between 1900 and

1915, and one fell into the first period with respect to males and into the second period with respect to females. None of the eleven countries had its most rapid extension of life expectancy prior to 1900.

The gains in life expectancy in the Western industrial nations, though unprecedented at the time, are now being eclipsed by faster improvement in the underdeveloped countries. Most of these enjoyed a gradual lowering of mortality prior to World War I, but the fall was not generally remarkable until after that conflict. Since then the drop in the death rate has accelerated in a spectacular way until it has become faster than anything ever experienced by the industrial nations. For seventeen underdeveloped countries for which fairly reliable death rates are obtainable, for example, the decline in the average crude death rate in 1940–59, as against 1920–39, was 37 per cent.* This is nearly three times the drop found in the four Scandinavian countries between the same periods (Table 1), and it is greater than any preceding drop in those four countries as between two successive twenty-year periods.

The more gradual drop in death rates in the industrializing Western nations arose from a basically different set of causes from those currently operating in backward lands. In northwestern Europe and among the northwest European peoples overseas, the mortality gains were comparatively slow because they depended on self-generated economic and scientific advance. Until late in the nineteenth century the main factor was economic—improvements in commerce, agriculture, and manufacturing—which provided a higher level of living, better housing, education, sanitation, etc. The quickening of the pace of death control around 1900 was due to the fact that, along with continued economic im-

* The countries used in the analysis were Barbados, Ceylon, Costa Rica, Cyprus, El Salvador, Fiji Islands, Jamaica, Malaya, Mauritius, Mexico, Panama, Philippines, Puerto Rico, Surinam, Taiwan, Thailand, and Trinidad-Tobago. These countries are still, for the most part, very underdeveloped economically.

provement, discoveries in scientific medicine and public health were at last beginning to yield fruit in the massive saving of lives. However, the scientific discoveries had to be slowly invented and applied.

In today's underdeveloped countries, on the other hand, the spectacular declines of mortality are being made by importing the latest medical discoveries from the most industrialized countries, usually with the help of medical personnel and funds from the latter nations. Modern techniques, applied on a mass basis under government sponsorship, have achieved almost miraculous results in the control of infectious diseases and other ailments among backward peoples. These results do not depend on economic development within the areas in question, because funds and personnel can be brought in from outside. They do not depend on scientific discoveries within the areas in question, because the research is done in the laboratories of America, Australia, and Europe. This is why the extremely fast drop in the death rate in the world's backward areas is occurring at a more primitive stage of economic development than it did in the Western industrial nations. As noted above, the most rapid death-rate declines in the latter countries came after 1900, a time when these countries were already industrialized and when their birth rates had already started down. In the backward lands today, death rates are being brought down at a faster clip among peoples who in some cases are scarcely removed from savagery and in other cases are overwhelmingly agrarian.

The speed of the drop in the death rate of non-industrial countries can be seen by comparison with Japan, the latest country to industrialize. One would expect that, owing to the recency of Japan's industrialization, the rapid economic improvement *plus* twentieth-century medical advance would enable her to reduce her mortality faster than the older industrial nations did at a similar stage of development. And this is true. Her average death rate in 1940–59 (despite her war losses) was 37 per cent lower than her average rate in 1920–39. This, it will be recalled, is exactly the percentage reduction made by our seventeen underdeveloped countries between the two twenty-year periods! The fact that countries like El Salvador, Fiji, and Mauritius can make gains in lengthening life as fast as a rapidly industrializing country, shows that such gains are now independent of local economic development.

The first, most obvious result of the dramatic lowering of mortality was rapid population growth. Again, however, the story in the underdeveloped countries of today differs from what it was earlier in the currently advanced nations. Since the death rate fell first among the industrializing west European peoples, these peoples experienced a remarkable colonization of new regions and continents. The same social and economic advances that were giving them control over deaths were giving them dominance over more backward races. But another consequence of their falling mortality was a drop in their birth rates. The latter began to turn down noticeably in the 1870's, long before the death rate had reached its present low level and before it had exhibited its fastest drop. The reason was that since the gains in saving lives were made primarily in infancy and early childhood, parents were having to contend with larger numbers of living children than they had ever had to contend with before, precisely at a time when, with industrialization and urbanization, large broods were more of a handicap. Accordingly, people reduced their procreation, partly by postponing marriage and partly by practicing abortion or contraception within marriage. Eventually, from about 1900 to 1932 (depending on the particular country) the birth rate in industrial nations fell even faster than the death rate, thus decreasing the speed of population growth.

In the 1930's, then, it looked as though the industrial nations had passed through a cycle of rapid population growth and were heading for a normal condition of virtual demographic stability. It was naively believed that this might be the transition through which the whole world would move in an orderly fashion.

But two things happened to change this outlook: first, the birth rate went up again in the industrial nations themselves; second, the death rate went down faster in the underdeveloped nations than it had done previously among the advanced European peoples and at a more primitive stage of economic and social development. As a consequence of the way death control was being brought to backward regions, their birth rates were not dropping; and this, with the extremely rapid fall in mortality, gave them the fastest rates of population growth ever experienced by whole nations. The total result, since 1940, has been an increase in the world's population so unprecedented and unpredicted that it has been appropriately called a "population explosion." With more than 2.9 billion today, humanity is multiplying at better than 2 per cent per year. This rate, if continued, will double the population every thirty-five years.

Most of the world's increase is occurring in precisely the areas least able to accommodate increased numbers— the poorer and more underdeveloped regions. Between 1920 and 1960, for example, the increase in the world's underdeveloped regions amounts to 70.5 per cent as compared to 41.1 per cent in the industrialized regions.

Rapid population growth is impeding economic development in the underdeveloped regions by causing the gains in national income to be used to maintain swelling numbers of people at the old level of living rather than to improve the level of living itself. Furthermore, when mortality is reduced rapidly without any reduction in the high birth rate, the resulting population is abnormally young. Costa Rica, whose death rate dropped 50 per cent during the last thirty years, has one hundred and five children aged 0–14 for each hundred adults aged 20–59; whereas Belgium has only forty-one (see Table 2). Such young populations mean a heavy

Table 2

Indices of the Age Structure in Selected Countries

	CHILD-DEPENDENCY RATIO (Children under 15 per 100 adults 20–59)	YOUTH-ADULT RATIO (Youths 15–19 per 100 adults 20–59)	OLD-AGE DEPENDENCY RATIO (Oldsters 60–plus per 100 adults 20–59)
UNDERDEVELOPED COUNTRIES			
Libya, 1954	87	20	22
Algeria (Moslems), 1954	101	24	12
Ceylon, 1956	90	19	12
INDUSTRIAL COUNTRIES, OLD WORLD			
Belgium, 1956	41	11	31
Denmark, 1956	51	14	28
France, 1957	47	12	33
NEW WORLD			
U.S.A., 1958	62	15	26
New Zealand, 1956	65	15	26
LIFE-TABLE POPULATIONS			
U.S.A. White-Female West-North-Central Region (1949–51), with life expectancy of 73	39	13	44
Hypothetical future U.S.A., with life expectancy of 83	38	13	60

child-dependency ratio added to the burden of total population increase. An underdeveloped country tends to compensate by starting children to work at an early age, a practice that lowers the productivity of labor because education is cut short. The entry of large numbers of youth into the labor market each year tends to bring large-scale unemployment and political instability. Costa Rica, for example, has one-fourth as many youths in the five-year age span, 15–19, as she has adults in the forty-year age span, 20–59; whereas Belgium has a little more than one-tenth as many (see Table 2).

It seems that the agrarian nations must make a choice between rapid population growth and rapid economic progress. If they decide to cut their population growth, it will presumably be by way of reducing the birth rate. However, as noted already, reproductive behavior is not motivated by views as to the national interest. An Indian peasant does not decide to have two children instead of ten because he is told that population growth is hindering India's economic development, but only because he feels it is to *his* interest. He may feel it is to his economic interest and yet do nothing to limit his offspring, because other goals (for example, subordination of the wife, desire for male offspring, avoidance of ridicule) take precedence. There is every indication from field studies that peasant women do not like having a large number of children, especially when most of the children remain alive. All such studies show that on the average women prefer only two, three, or four children, not five to fifteen. Peasant men, however, since the burden of children does not fall directly on them, are less resistant to having large numbers of children except when hard-pressed economically. Actually, as long as the costs of children impinge directly on the parents, the economic incentive to limit offspring is mounting, because the aspirations of the people in the peasant lands are running ahead of the actual economic growth. Insofar as the costs fall on the joint family (as in certain traditional social systems) or on the government (as in the welfare state), the potential parent can reproduce without economic penalty. No state has yet seen fit, however, to relieve parents of all the economic costs of reproduction, much less the non-economic costs in terms of energy and inconvenience.

As the aspirations of the agrarian peoples rise while their economic growth falters, the burden of unusually large families will tend to force parents to reduce their reproduction. If they are encouraged in this by educational measures, by the availability of birth control devices, and by a system that holds parents responsible for their children, the lag of the birth rate behind the declining death rate will be less than otherwise, and the alternative of increasing the death rate will more likely be avoided.

But even if the birth rate around the world is reduced, the question still remains, "Will it be reduced enough to match the low mortality?" Such a depressed birth rate would entail a heavy sacrifice. The sacrifice is commonly thought to consist in the abandonment of traditional values extolling large families; yet it must be emphasized that under conditions of high mortality—the normal situation during nearly all of human history—families were *not* large despite the high birth rate. There were, to be sure, large *households* in many societies, but this was due to living arrangements of kinsmen, not to the high birth rate. There was also a wider *range* in the number of living children than there is today, since couples varied sharply in their biological fecundity and in their capacity to keep their infants alive. The price of adjusting fertility to low mortality is therefore not small numbers of living children, for this has been the normal situation of mankind. Rather, what would be sacrificed is the *chance* of having a sizable family and the *proportion of life* spent with children. If the incidence of death falls so low that most couples need have only two children to replace the population, and if the average lifetime is extended to eighty-three years, each parent will spend only about a fourth of his adulthood with a child of his own under age fifteen in the household, and only about a tenth of it with a child under five. In view of the love for children, which cannot be unquestionably attributed to culture, one can question whether people will make such a sacrifice.

Perhaps an even greater cost of really low fertility is its effect on the age structure. Although lessening the child-dependency burden, it would enormously expand the old-age-dependency problem. Already, in countries where the birth rate has long been rather low, the population has become top-heavy with oldsters. France, for example, now has thirty-three persons aged 60 or over for each hundred aged 20–59. In the future, as life expectancy is continually lengthened, a rate of reproduction low enough just to replace the population will yield a higher ratio of elderly. For instance, the life expectancy of white females in the north central region of the United States is now seventy-three years. If the whole population reached this figure and maintained it indefinitely, and if the birth rate constantly matched the death rate, the United States would have forty-five persons over 60, and forty-eight under 15, for each hundred aged 20 through 59. If we imagine future mortality improving by an orderly continuance of the fall in age-specific rates observed between 1900 and 1950, until the life expectancy at birth reaches eighty-three years, a birth rate that just sustained the population would produce an age structure with sixty persons aged 60-plus, and thirty-eight children under 15, for each hundred aged 20–59. This would be nearly double the old-age-dependency ratio in France, which thinks it has too old a population now.

Partly because the price is so high, no nation has as yet reduced its reproductive effort sufficiently to match regularly a low modern death rate. Although such a reduction is not inconceivable (especially under radically new institutional arrangements), it should not be complacently assumed to be inevitable or probable or to entail no cost.

The number of citizens is too important a matter to be ignored by governments. It cannot be safely left as an accidental by-product of behavior undertaken for other purposes such as saving lives, enjoying children, and conforming to old customs. Numerous governments have therefore tried to influence demographic behavior, but the particular nations concerned and the nature of their efforts have shifted markedly. During the 1930's the industrial nations became worried about their low birth rates, and some of them—notably Sweden, Germany, Italy, and France—adopted policies designed to stimulate reproduction. Although the more radical measures for this purpose have now been abandoned, family-allowance legislation and other measures favorable to reproduction are now common, being found in nations as diverse as Russia, Canada, Belgium, and Britain.

This governmental effort to raise the birth rate was based on fallacious reasoning. The birth rates of the 1930's were low, to be sure, but it was a mistake to assume that they would stay that way unless measures were taken. The subsequent baby boom in industrial countries, especially after World War II, was not the result of the depression-born pronatalist policies, for it occurred in countries that had no such policies. It was mainly a result of prosperity and full employment permitting couples to get married and to have children. Although in most European countries the baby boom has subsided in recent years, it has remained at such a high level in the new-world industrial countries (Canada, the United States, Australia, New Zealand) that, with a continued influx of immigrants, they are still experiencing very fast rates of population growth, their combined population being expected to increase by 22 per cent from 1960 to 1975. In both the old-world and the new-world industrial countries, rising levels of living are added to population growth to create ever more congestion. Escape from the nuisances created by crowding—noise, smog, traffic—cannot be found, because there is not enough space. In the United Kingdom, for example, there are sixty-two motor vehicles per square mile of land; in the United States there are twenty-two, and in France twenty-five. For this reason, even in the most prosperous countries, voices are beginning to be heard which urge the official encouragement of birth control.

So far, however, the only industrial country that has really carried out an anti-natalist policy is Japan. There the government's permissiveness with respect to abortion and its sponsorship of birth control clinics and family-planning education have helped reduce the crude birth rate 26 per cent below its lowest war-time bottom (1945) and 50 per cent below its postwar peak (1947). This is probably the sharpest birth-rate decline ever experienced by a large nation.

Some of the underdeveloped countries, worried by rapid population growth in the face of poverty and chronic overcrowding, have adopted policies designed to diminish births. The most successful of these has been Puerto Rico, where the birth rate, though still high, has steadily declined since the postwar peak in 1947. Red China vigorously pursued such a policy for a while, and still takes certain measures that lessen reproduction, such as the de-emphasis on the family and the use of women in the labor force. India is strengthening her nationwide anti-natalist policy, and countries such as Mauritius, Bermuda, El Salvador, Haiti, and the Federation of the West Indies are considering a similar policy.

The limitation of population growth, however, is not easy. The reduction of mortality in underdeveloped countries has been so fast, and so unconnected with fundamental economic and social change in those countries, that parents cannot be expected yet to limit their offspring by their own efforts. In trying to hasten such an adjustment, no government can succeed by appealing to patriotism or to enlightened awareness of the population problem. It has to influence behavior by altering the conditions. In general, the alterations consist in increasing the effectiveness and availability of contraceptives and/or abortion and sterilization, increasing the participation of women in the labor force (making them not only personally ambitious but also economically independent), allowing the costs of children to fall on the parents themselves rather than upon the joint family or the state, and raising the parents' aspirations for their children's future. These are conservative measures. If they do not succeed, some governments may eventually consider radical means.

There is, of course, the possibility that the world's present climactic population increase will be stopped by a rise in mortality rather than a drop in fertility. The death rate can rise faster and higher than the birth rate, wiping out whole populations in a matter of days or weeks.

Nations and individuals are thus caught in the dilemmas created by the unanticipated and unintended consequences of demographic behavior. The marvelous success achieved in banishing disease and prolonging life has given rise to an unfortunate by-product, unprecedented population growth. In the early history of the currently industrial nations, this by-product was not so overwhelming. Not only were these countries relatively few in the world, but their rates of population growth were modest, because the death rate came down so slowly that the birth rate eventually had time to adjust partially to it. Now, however, the two-thirds of the world that lives in agrarian countries is reducing deaths so rapidly, with international help, that its wave of population growth exceeds anything ever seen before. It is slowing the rate of economic development in these countries, widening the gap between them and the industrial nations, and creating popular unrest and political instability.

The humane way out is presumably to reduce the birth rate. Yet the costs are so great, in national as well as individual terms, that it is doubtful this will be done in sufficient degree to solve the population problem. Presented with such dilemmas, human beings tend to work out novel solutions that are extremely difficult to foresee. One direction that such a novel solution might take would be to alter the basic institutional structure of the family. On the other hand, a sudden rise in mortality may wipe out much of the world's population, a result which increased crowding (liability to infection) and advancing technology (capacity for war) tends to make more probable. The one thing certain is that, in the demographic as in the other spheres of life, human beings are not free from the consequences their own behavior sets in motion. If the world wishes to enjoy permanently a low mortality, it must accept a low fertility as a necessary condition. If the costs seem too great, then a selective increase in mortality may be preferred to a blind, cataclysmic increase. With respect to future population there is thus no easy, conservative road. For more than a century we have been in the midst of a demographic revolution, and we are now in a critical stage of it. Like other revolutions, the important thing about this one is not how it starts but how it ends.

18 BEHAVIORAL SCIENCE APPLICATION IN THE PROFESSIONS

Donald R. Young

Donald R. Young, President of Russell Sage Foundation in New York City, was born in Macungie, Pennsylvania, in 1898. A graduate of Lafayette College, Dr. Young pursued advanced studies in sociology at the University of Pennsylvania. From 1919 to 1945 he was a member of the faculty at Pennsylvania, serving as Chairman of the Department of Sociology from 1943 to 1945. Dr. Young joined the staff of Russell Sage Foundation in 1948 as General Director and was appointed President in 1955. A specialist in intergroup relations and population, Dr. Young was President of the International Social Science Council from 1952 to 1961. He was President of the Sociological Research Association in 1937, Executive Director and President of the Social Science Research Council from 1945 to 1948, and President of the American Sociological Association in 1955. He is the author of numerous articles and books, including American Minority Peoples *and* Minority Peoples in Depression.

The immediate purpose of basic research in the behavioral sciences, as in all fields of learning, is the discovery of relationships inherent in the nature of the phenomena under study. Few scientists, devoted as they may be to research for its own sake, would deny that ultimately their work should be of use to others.

The questions to be considered here concern the professional utility of the behavioral sciences: sociology, anthropology, social psychology, and a number of closely related disciplines. What good are they? Who uses them? For what purposes? Why is their value not more widely recognized? Are they not a source of danger to society as tools capable of being used to manipulate the public? Do the realized and potential gains from their use outweigh the dangers?

The behavioral scientist has two prime duties. His first duty is to advance the understanding and generalization of the regularities in the behavior of people. That this purpose is being accomplished with increasing success has been made evident in the preceding papers. It has been amply demonstrated that human behavior is not capricious, that it is subject to humanly inherent and external influences, and that accurate observation and measurement well within practical limits of tolerance are possible.

The second duty of the behavioral scientist is to transmit his techniques and findings to others. His scientific experience naturally must be made available to his colleagues as an aid in their research and to the oncoming generation in training for research careers. Furthermore, the results of his research must be made available to the public for the improvement of public understanding both of the self and of society. Members of the practicing professions constitute a third group needing access to behavioral research results, the group with which we are here most concerned.

Recent years have witnessed increasing cooperation between behavioral scientists and practitioners in the several applied professions. To many persons this seems strange, for the relationship is concealed by popular conceptions of the nature of these professions: medicine, public health, law, social work, education, government, the ministry, engineering, architecture, and the professionalized aspects of business and agriculture. All of these nevertheless are professions in which behavioral science is now recognized as having an important role to play. The potential relationship between the behavioral sciences and these professions becomes clear when it is observed that their function is to provide skilled assistance in attaining human objectives. Both the objectives and the means of attainment always involve behavior: the objectives can be expressed only in terms of people's actions and values; the means, in terms of what has to be done by someone if the objectives are to be achieved.

The concept of the professions as groups of people with similar training, skills, and interests that exist solely to help other people in the accomplishment of some purpose correctly suggests that there are two ways in which the behavioral sciences may be helpful. First, the professions themselves may be and have been studied as social institutions, as complex organized means for accomplishing ends considered desirable by society. Second, the behavioral sciences may add and have added to the skills of the practitioner in the performance of his professional tasks.

Social institutions, the accepted patterned ways of providing for human needs, are man's inventions and are never perfect. This has been true in relatively static societies; in modern societies now undergoing rapid social change the problems of institutional adaptation have been multiplied manifold. Consequently there is always a question of how well any social institution is serving its purposes, to what extent it may be said to be anachronistic or otherwise inappropriate. All social institutions, including the professions, tend to be conservative. Yet changes must be made to keep reasonably in step with changing circumstances.

Necessary adaptive changes in the professions require institutional analysis for which members of the professions have little or no formal preparation. Indeed, they are usually ill prepared even to recognize the need for change. This is a kind of problem best suited for attack with the concepts, research methods, and accumulated knowledge of the behavioral sciences. It requires study of the many factors involved in the activities and interrelations of the practitioner, his colleagues, his supporting subprofessional personnel, the client (or patient, patron, employer, or customer, as the case may be), and the community. Of course, the adequacy of physical facilities in relation to current and anticipated need must also be taken into account. These are not matters to which professional schools devote much attention, if only because of lack of time; they are subjects that behavioral scientists are trained to study.

The contribution of the behavioral sciences to the technical skills of the professional practitioner are harder to appreciate. To take the health services as an example, it is not difficult to realize that the factors involved in the efficient cooperation of physician, nurse, and patient are proper subjects for study by the social psychologist, sociologist, or social anthropologist. Also, the hospital obviously presents management problems that are not medical. On the other hand, a high degree of sophistication is required to appreciate the significance of behavioral factors in the prevention of illness, in therapeutic procedures, and in rehabilitation and adjustment to chronic illness and physical handicap. Medicine long has been popularly regarded as the art of treating specific illnesses with chemicals or knife; treatment of the patient as a person and not just the disease as an entity is a concept fully understood by few. Furthermore, the behavioral sciences, young in themselves, have only recently undertaken major collaboration with the health services. The need for their collaboration is plain to students of the problem, but their contributions have been so far outweighed by those of the physical and biological sciences as to be visible only to the expert; hence they are not now in the public consciousness.

Yet the Health Information Foundation 1958 publication, *An Inventory of Social and Economic Research in Health,* was able to list more than seven hundred ongoing social science studies related to health levels, mental health, sociological factors in health, health facilities and services, and health service personnel. The individual social scientists engaged in these studies were associated with medical schools, schools of nursing, schools of public health and the non-professional faculties of liberal arts colleges and universities; with government agencies such as the National Institutes of Health and the health departments of cities and states; with hospitals and other publicly and privately supported agencies concerned with medical care both on the national and local levels. Behavioral scientists and the materials resulting from their studies are now being used widely and increasingly in medical schools in such fields as mental health, environmental and preventive medicine, rehabilitation, and, less frequently, the core areas of medicine and surgery. The curricula of schools of nursing and of public health also have a surprising amount of behavioral science content. The nature and extent of such developments as these make clearly evident the breadth of opportunity for behavioral science careers in the health fields.

Space does not permit me to offer even the most brief illustration of similar but in general quantitatively lesser behavioral science utilization in the other major professions. I might, however, cite engineering as an example of an applied profession seemingly related to human behavior in rather trivial ways in comparison with its dependence on the physical sciences. Nevertheless, insofar as engineering is not a trade involving merely the routine application of handbook formulae to physical materials, the objectives of client or employer and their achievement can be materially advanced by knowledge of people and their ways, as is now recognized in the curricula of leading technological institutions. Further, the engineer must make certain that his instruments, machines, and other constructs are compatible with the behavior potential of those who are to use them. Even though some professions, such as architecture, have virtually ignored the potential contributions of behavioral research, the fact remains that they could perform their functions of helping and working with people more effectively if they placed less confidence in casual inference from personal experience and more in rigorous behavioral research.

The question may be asked whether behavioral scientists should be expected to take sufficient interest in the applied professions to serve the indicated needs. The answer is that such interest is certain to be developed in response to the growing demand. Help is needed from behavioral scientists working as such on behavior problems of concern to the various professions. There is also need for specialists well trained in the behavioral sciences and familiar with some area of an applied profession who will devote themselves to the task of making accumulated behavioral knowledge available to that profession. This involves both applied research and the reworking of existing research results so that they apply to selected human problems with specificity and in a form usable by the practitioner. Such middlemen already are engaged in the medical, business, and welfare fields in appreciable numbers, and to a lesser extent in other areas of professional activity.

This improving liaison between behavioral science and the applied professions is advantageous to behavioral research in several ways. It provides excellent sources of data for basic as well as for applied research. There is no limit to the variety of truly scientific research questions that may be asked of data obtainable in the fields of professional activity. Studies of cultural differences, of interpersonal relations, or of group conflict and cooperation have neither more nor less scientific value if the subjects are primitive tribesmen, captive college students, or randomly available fellow citizens than if they happen to be obtained through the cooperation of a practitioner colleague. The essence of the matter is the significance of the research question asked and the adequacy of the research design, not the source of data per se.

Behavioral scientists have been handicapped by the difficulty of establishing experimental conditions and of testing their findings. The nature of the applied professions—the fact that they work with and for people with whom there is good rapport—is such that they offer exceptional opportunities for controlled experiment and for verification of findings in use, and thus can serve as a substitute for the laboratory. It may also be that research can benefit from being conducted in a setting where the critical eyes of interested practitioners are kept on procedures and results. Certainly the spirit of behavioral scientists is lifted by the added rewards in prestige and self-satisfaction, to say nothing of money, which come to academicians whose findings are scientifically verified and also proved of practical value by professional application. There are those who fear that the growth of applied behavioral science may interfere with the advance of basic research; the fact is that rationalized utilization of research results by the several professions frees those primarily concerned with basic research from the presently common necessity for choosing between allowing their findings of obvious practical import to gather dust on library shelves or engaging directly in application to the neglect of fundamental investigation.

The case for close cooperation between behavioral scientists and the practicing professions is convincing when viewed either theoretically or in the light of experience. Why, then, is there not more of such cooperation throughout the professions? Much of the answer lies in the fact that time is required for the integration of new concepts with those of long acceptance in social institutions such as the professions. Time is also required to develop essential personnel. There are further difficulties that may be anticipated even when personnel is available for collaborative work in a receptive environment. Cooperation assumes agreement on an objective, mutual understanding of the specific roles to be played, personal satisfaction in those roles, and adequate means of communication between those engaged in the task. These conditions are not easily fulfilled when relative strangers first attempt to work together.

Broad objectives, such as saving lives, improved housing, better interpersonal relations, and the like, cause little disagreement. However, the necessarily more immediate and specific objective or expectation of the practitioner turning to behavioral science for help often is in conflict with the understanding of the behavioral scientist whose help is asked.

The practitioner may hope for a behavioral generalization applicable with certainty to a specific case or client when only the actuarial approach is possible. The behavioral scientist may agree to cooperate because of a research object in conflict with some inviolable professional obligation to client or patient. There is a common tendency in the early stages of cooperation both to ask for and to promise far more than can possibly be delivered. Conflicting and unrealistic expectations are a product of interspecialty ignorance, and happily are reduced as interspecialty liaison improves.

Although behavioral scientists working in applied settings frequently find themselves in ambiguous situations at the start, it has proved possible for most such individuals to establish suitable roles for themselves. This has been most easily accomplished in the health services and in government, including the military services. Even in these professions, however, the relationship is tentatively and precariously structured, with all conceivable varieties of research, consulting, and administrative interrelationships advocated and in use. Trial and error is a wasteful method of establishing satisfactory patterns of interprofessional relations, but it is perhaps the only method presently available. Its wastefulness, however, may be materially reduced by early clarification of the nature of two major sources of initial difficulty in interprofessional collaboration, namely, concern with social status and conflicting habitual patterns of professional behavior.

The acceptance of a social role may be facilitated or retarded by the degree of status ascribed to it. Members of the applied professions probably neither gain nor lose status by collaboration with behavioral scientists; in general, their status is already too firmly established to be materially affected by such association. Behavioral scientists, on the other hand, commonly fear a loss of prestige among their disciplinary colleagues by such collaboration. Also, it is the fashion in academic circles to express more regard for basic than for applied research. There is consequently considerable resistance to engaging in the kind of research most obviously needed by the professions, and some embarrassment for many who have overcome such resistance. Further, basic research in any field rarely is ready for practical use as originally reported or in isolation from other relevant research and experience. This means that there is need for the multiple rewriting of accumulated behavioral research focused on specific applied problems. Such "translation" of existing knowledge can be costly in terms of prestige, for rewriting, like the preparation of a textbook, can be regarded as hack work even when well done.

Every profession necessarily has a technical language of its own, a system of values, and its preferred ways of working. These professional subcultures facilitate the accomplishment of professional tasks, but they are a handicap to interprofessional communication. Words change in their meaning from one profession to another, and, of course, each has terms that are exclusively its own. The word "case," for example, has distinctly different meanings for medical, legal, social welfare, and both statistical and clinical research specialists. The sociologist and the social worker have differing usages of the term "social organization." Disciplines differ in the degree to which they are structured on a hierarchical as compared with a partnership pattern. With regard to values, the difference in emphasis between practitioners and research specialists on doing something *for* the client (or his equivalent in the various professions) as compared with learning *from* subjects is a serious matter in collaboration. The practitioner's conviction that primary responsibility is to the individual seeking help is not always compatible with the scientist's sense of obligation to add to knowledge. Because the man of direct action and the scientist differ in motivation, education, and experience, complete harmony seems unlikely; it is not necessary if there is forbearance and a willingness to compromise while mutual appreciation is in process of growth.

The problems of behavioral science application in the professions should be considered not only from the respective points of view of behavioral scientists and of specialists in practice. The interests of society as a whole must be taken into account; they are, in fact, paramount. Scientists have developed a tendency to accept uncritically the dictum that what is good for science is good for humanity. This may be true, but it is no more than an assumption based on personal interpretation of relatively recent human history. Similarly, practitioners in the professions all too frequently are unable to resist the impulse to decide what the client should want as well as how best to accomplish his objective. At what cost in pain or self-denial a few months or years of extra life should be bought is more a matter of decision for the patient than for his physician. The decision to build or not to build a bridge or house, to plead guilty or innocent to a criminal charge, to begin or not to begin a civil suit, to accept or not to accept a caseworker's counseling, is neither the obligation nor the general privilege of the relevant professions. Professional aid is always sought with one or more contemplated objectives already in mind; advice and service regarding the advantages and costs of objectives and means for their accomplishment is what the professions offer with propriety. In the long run, of course, it is neither the professions nor their individual clients who decide on objectives and the acceptability of the means available for their achievement. Society as a whole is the ultimate judge.

There are elements in society today very much concerned about the growing utilization of behavioral science by the professions. The fear is expressed that the rapidly growing understanding of factors influencing human behavior will be used unscrupulously for purposes of personal advantage by individuals avid for money or power and by corrupt and demagogic political groups. Attacks on the use of social research in merchandising, in the military services, in labor-management relations, and in the gauging of public opinion, particularly on political matters, are common expressions of this fear of social manipulation and control.

Society could not survive without its many forms of social control, ranging from legislation and the policeman on the street to informal praise and mass ridicule, all capable of misuse. Improved understanding of human behavior does no more than make possible improved utilization of the existing forms of social control for socially approved purposes, and, unfortunately, also for unconscionable human manipulation. This does not mean that the freedoms of democracy are incompatible with the utilization of behavioral knowledge, but that democracy must be watchful for its misuse. Knowledge of any kind is power that has neither virtue nor evil except in use by people.

Society apparently is convinced that the dangers of misuse are fewer than the potential advantages of behavioral research, for it is flourishing to a degree today that would not be tolerated by the public if this were not the case. The behavioral as well as the physical and biological fields are receiving generous public financial support, both directly from national treasuries generally and indirectly in the form of tax relief for philanthropic grants by foundations and individuals in countries where private benevolence is encouraged. In the United States and a few other countries, business organizations also are contributing to the behavioral sciences to some extent by outright gift and heavily by direct utilization for commercial purposes. The practicing professions consequently are in accord with public sentiment in their endeavors to increase their understanding of human motivation and behavior.

The overriding public and professional concerns of today are with the problems of people living and working with other people. The struggle for survival and the good life is not just one of man with his material environment but also of man with his fellow man. The professions have contributed immeasurably to human welfare through their skillful application of physical and biological science in meeting man's more tangible needs and wants. It now takes little imagination to realize that their next broad advance will come through the further integration of the behavioral with the other sciences already serving as the foundation of their arts.

19 SOME CONTRIBUTIONS OF BEHAVIORAL SCIENCE TO CONTEMPORARY LIFE

John W. Riley, Jr.

John W. Riley, Jr., Second Vice President and Director of Social Research of the Equitable Life Assurance Society of the United States, was born in Brunswick, Maine, in 1908. After completing his undergraduate education at Bowdoin College, Dr. Riley received his doctorate in sociology from Harvard University in 1936. Before joining The Equitable in 1960, he taught at several colleges—Marietta, Wellesley, Douglas—and for many years was Chairman of the Department of Sociology at Rutgers University. Dr. Riley has served as consultant to such organizations as the Market Research Company of America, the Columbia Broadcasting System, Holt, Rinehart and Winston, and many agencies of the federal government. He was Vice-Chairman of the Advisory Panel on Special Operations, Department of Defense. He has held office in a number of professional organizations and has collaborated in the writing of several books, including The Student Looks at His Teacher, The Reds Take a City, Sociological Studies in Scale Analysis, *and* The Modern Corporation and Its Publics.

Before proceeding to my subject, I should like to remind you of a most interesting recent change in the American scene. Not very many years ago—certainly not more than a generation ago—professors of sociology, psychology, or anthropology were employed almost exclusively within the traditional academic setting. Here they held their classes, conducted their studies and experiments, and occasionally, to be sure, went into the field (as in the case of the anthropologists) but above all else they comported themselves as scholars and teachers. Two decades ago the professor who was deeply involved in the world of affairs in his capacity as an academic man was indeed rare.

Today, however, the situation is quite different. Behavioral scientists are employed as such, and in increasing numbers, by governments, by business and industry, by hospitals and other agencies devoted to problems of health, by correctional institutions, by welfare agencies, by city commissions, by school systems, and by many, many other types of organizations and enterprises in which some systematic knowledge of human behavior is required. My own occupational history will serve as an illustration. After nearly thirty years as a teacher, I recently joined a large insurance company, with the unprecedented mission of forging a *basic* research link between that large and complex world of affairs, on the one hand, and the world of sociological ideas and scholarship, on the other. While this innovation, in encouraging a basic and continuing relationship between men of affairs and men of ideas, itself constitutes a chapter in the sociology of behavioral science knowledge, my immediate task is to illustrate some of the ways in which behavioral science knowledge and techniques are being applied in contemporary American society.

Because of its immediate relevance to this topic, one of Dr. Young's points in the preceding paper bears re-emphasis. I refer to his observation that "human behavior is not capricious," and that, despite the complexities, it is just as susceptible to scientific study as any other aspect of nature.

Now to my mind, this is a point of great importance because the layman—quite understandably overlooking the theoretical and methodological problems involved in the scientific study of social phenomena—tends to consider himself a qualified expert. *All* of us have had far more personal experience with the phenomena of family life or with the problem of learning than with chemical colloids or atomic particles, and we do not hesitate to make everyday use of our homemade social science. Yet, due to the increasing sophistication of both their theory and their techniques, behavioral scientists are in a position to cast grave doubts upon such apparently good common-sense generalizations as that agreement within the family produces stable and happy families, or that learning is more effectively produced under conditions of minimum anxiety. In both cases, of course, there is a kernel of common-sense validity, but it is such a small kernel as to be almost meaningless. The behavioral scientist points out that expressed disagreement or anxiety often serve useful functions, and he is now able to use such phenomena as independent variables and to throw new light on an impressively wide range of human behavior.

What we are talking about, then, is a body of behavioral science knowledge and method drawn largely from psychology, sociology, and anthropology, which is coming to be increasingly useful in its applied forms to such areas of American life as education, welfare, medicine, public policy, business and industry, and many others. And what I propose to do is simply to suggest some of these fields of application by citing some concrete examples.

Permit me, however, one caveat. Lest my examples give the impression of an uninterrupted series of successes, let me assure you that this most recent chapter in the history of the behavioral sciences is, in fact, strewn with failures and misunderstandings. As Dr. Young has pointed out, the role of the behavioral scientist is far from clear and his efforts to apply his knowledge have frequently resulted in naught. Certainly the operational problems of the behavioral sciences will continue to vex us for many years to come.

Now to my examples: Almost every young adult today has taken a number of tests during his lifetime. He has taken intelligence and achievement tests in school, aptitude and personality tests when he entered the armed forces or applied for a job, and perhaps has even been subjected to some of the so-called "projective" tests designed to get at his innermost ideas and feelings about himself and others. All this testing, common as it is today, began only about fifty years ago. To be sure, there has been some current reaction against the widespread use of such tests, on the grounds that they are not infallible and that they sometimes constitute an invasion of privacy. On the other hand, there can be but little doubt that these tests are highly useful and free of abuse in the hands of qualified experts.

One of the most important figures in the development of such testing was a French psychologist, Henri Binet. Binet had been experimenting before the turn of the century with certain tests designed to measure the differences between people. He used a number of simple tests, including tests of reaction time and memory, but was dissatisfied with them as measures of general mental ability or intelligence. Then, in 1904, the French government wanted to set up a program to educate mentally retarded children and set Binet the practical problem of selecting the children who should receive such help.

In response to this need, Binet developed a series of items designed to cover the mental abilities which normal children of different ages ought to possess. Many of these original items would look very familiar to the teacher and student of today. Binet's ideas of what should go into a test of intelligence proved to be so good that most of our modern tests are based on his concepts.

The chief contribution to intelligence testing since the time of Binet has been in the area of what is called test "standardization." It is said that although they grew out of his experience with children, some of Binet's figures on what the average child of a certain age could be expected to do were based on as few as ten children. Today, ideas of what the average child will do on an intelligence test are based on months of research with many hundreds and often many thousands of children. Binet's own test was revised and standardized at Stanford University in the United States and thus acquired the name by which it is now well known—the Stanford-Binet.

About the time when intelligence testing began to appear to be a real possibility, the first World War broke out, and with it came the need to screen draftees. One of the most challenging problems was to test in a very short time large groups of people many of whom could neither read nor write. The fact that the psychologists met this challenge successfully was an important factor in the great surge of interest in all kinds of testing which began after the war ended.

Today, testing has reached such a level of sophistication that many important decisions about people are made on the basis of test results, and thousands of psychologists are exclusively engaged in the business of administering and interpreting standard tests relevant to an enormous range of attitudes, aptitudes, performances, and behaviors. Only a few years ago, such a state of affairs would have seemed incredible.

Let me give you another example of the application of the behavioral sciences. The history of man's efforts to cope with the problem of mental disorder has, as we all know, been full of cruelty, magical belief, and dark superstition. And while this story is far from complete, one of the brightest chapters, in addition to the great advances in modern psychiatry, has only in recent times been contributed by the psychological and social sciences. Here the contributions to a more adequate understanding of human behavior have been codified and applied through an approach which is usually called psychotherapy, of which there are two main types: individual therapy and group therapy. In its simplest aspect, the task of psychotherapy is to give the mental patient a close working relationship with the therapist. Thus the patient is placed in a secure and reassuring position where he can explore his problems and come to new understandings. The recent development of tranquilizing drugs has enhanced the possibility of psychotherapy by making many seriously disturbed patients available for this sort of treatment. The drugs enable the therapists to "get through" to such patients.

Furthermore, it has long been suspected that a complex relationship existed, for those who were so mentally ill as to require hospitalization, between the type of institutional setting and their recovery rates—regardless of the skill of the psychotherapist—but only relatively recently have some of the details of this relationship been clearly specified. Perhaps one of the most influential recent findings indicates that mental patients tend to become upset whenever there is either a manifest or latent tension or discord within the hospital's administration and that, conversely, whenever such conflicts or problems are resolved, the symptoms of patient-disturbance tend to disappear. Certainly this type of insight into the relationship between the social structures of hospitals and the well-being of patients is being increasingly applied, and there are probably but few large mental hospitals in the United States today which do not have access, either directly or indirectly, to *research* experts from the behavioral sciences. The situation is well summed up by a recent medical-behavioral science experiment which involved three types of mental hospitals: a large state institution, a Veterans Administration hospital, and a smaller public hospital used for teaching and research. In each case, important research findings from the behavioral sciences were found to be applicable, and the title of this report, *From Custodial to Therapeutic Patient Care in Mental Hospitals,* is suggestive of the present state of affairs.

At this point, another quite different type of application in the field of health comes to mind. In 1942 the Taos County Cooperative Health Association began to offer modern medical services to about one thousand rural, predominantly Spanish-American families in an area, located in the southwestern part of the United States, characterized by appallingly bad health conditions. For example, in 1941 no death certificates had been issued for 62 per cent of those who had died and between 1937 and 1939 almost two-thirds of the reported deaths indicated "cause unknown," which meant that there was no attending physician. During the same period, over two-thirds of the births were attended by midwives with little or no formal training. The infant mortality rate was one of the highest in the country.

The backing for the new Cooperative Health Association came from the local medical society, the University of New Mexico, the Farm Security Administration, and the Carnegie Corporation. Here, as the report on the project puts it, "was an enterprise that could not fail. Here was a serious medical need that an organization had been set up to meet." And yet, despite tremendous efforts to win local family support, the project served only a few patients and was finally abandoned within ten years. While we obviously cannot begin to tell the full story of Taos, the subsequent research reports indicate clearly that it was a failure to apply the basic behavioral science implications of the concept of culture which led to the collapse of the Association.

Let us consider two instances.

Common sense frequently equates culture with human nature. Thus, for example, if "it is human nature for the sick person to want to get well," why should not any good medical program be equally acceptable in any cultural setting? With such a view the behavioral scientist, of course, takes sharp issue. He is not too surprised when Pedro, a Taos resident and a tuberculosis patient, sneaks out of the hospital to attend his brother's wedding, or when a young Indian mother delays in bringing her critically sick child to "the new doctor." How a person responds to the problem of illness, the behavioral scientist insists, will be largely reflective of his cultural conditioning rather than of some trait of human nature. A brother's wedding or a family rite can be far more important in one scheme of values than the demands of a new and but little understood hospital or clinic.

Similarly, consider the common-sense reliance upon reason—or what has sometimes been called the rationalistic bias—in cross-cultural affairs. In such a view, man is thought to be a reasonable creature and any non-rational indications or behaviors are all too simply disregarded as ignorance and superstition. To the behavioral scientist, on the other hand, these non-rational beliefs, whether they refer to folk medical practices or to family arrangements, are all part of a culture pattern which must be seen and dealt with as a whole. He is quite ready to understand and to be tolerant of the keys which pregnant Taos women wear about their waists because he knows that this is believed to be a prophylactic precaution "lest the baby be deformed by the effect of the moon's shadow falling on the mother."

In short, the 1942 attempt to superimpose a technical medical program from one culture upon the folkways and beliefs of people from quite a different culture was doomed from the start. Today, however, behavioral scientists are successfully at work on most major public health programs, and they are also beginning to play important roles in the fields of medical education and research.

Similarly, other problem areas are attracting attention. Consider, for example, the problems of crime and delinquency.

Although the behavioral sciences have contributed heavily to the solution of various problems in the field of criminology and penology (for example, parole selection, prison management, etc.,) one of the great dilemmas in the United States is posed by the high recidivism rates which continue for most types of correctional institutions. Not only do we seem to be better at custody than at rehabilitation, but many recent studies suggest the remarkable efficiency of the prison or reformatory in assimilating the inmate into the "prison culture" or in bringing about what one authority has called "prisonization." Certainly in most correctional institutions there exists a wide gap of distrust and suspicion between prison administrators and inmates, and one major attack on this problem makes use of the techniques of group therapy. The theory has been that such "programs seek to help the inmate redefine himself in conventional terms and to bring about a shift of value orientations." Unhappily, however, the research record does violence to the theory, and such has been the case until some recently reported studies in New Jersey suggested how these group therapeutic sessions might be structured in such a way as to take into account the inmate's position in the larger social system of the prison. The shift in emphasis is away from the individual case and in the direction of the network of interpersonal relationships. Very briefly, this is accomplished by organizing the sessions around the already existing informal social structure of the prison or, in the case of small experimental institutions, by involving the entire inmate population. At Highfields in New Jersey, for example, we find young delinquent boys in an institutional setting without guards or bars working out their problems and learning new values with a remarkable degree of success. Although this approach is still controversial, the application, under controlled conditions, of such abstract behavioral science concepts as "guided interaction" and "resocialization" holds much promise for the future.

Perhaps the largest and one of the most impressive programs of applied behavioral science research was conducted during World War II by the Research Branch of the Information and Education Division of the War Department. Organized late in 1941 "to provide the Army command quickly and accurately with facts about the attitudes of soldiers which, along with other facts and inferences, might be helpful in policy formation," this group of behavioral scientists carried out over three hundred separate studies on the so-called "civilian army" ranging all the way from clothing preferences to combat motivation to psychoneurotic inventories.

One of the best-known studies of the Research Branch had to do with the problem of demobilization. Shortly after Normandy it came to be generally expected that the war in Europe would end before the war in the Pacific. It would then be possible to discharge a certain proportion of the men, but very substantial numbers of those serving in Europe would have to be transferred to the Pacific. An important group in the Army command, on perfectly good *military* grounds, quite understandably wanted to use the most seasoned veterans for the final phases of the war against Japan, since they were militarily the most effective troops. This policy was, however, questioned on the ground of its possible deleterious effect on morale.

Consequently, a series of studies was made of soldiers' opinions as to what priority of discharge was thought to be fair. With remarkable consistency throughout the army the factors of length of service, overseas duty, combat duty, and parenthood were given the highest ratings. The first three were, of course, highly correlated with each other. Even the troops in the United States shared the view that the combat veterans had "done their bit" and should be discharged if anyone was to be.

The implications of these findings were adopted by the army in the so-called "point system" of demobilization, and the case is frequently cited as an illustration of the utilization of relatively simple social science research in the formation of relatively important policy.

Another application of the basic techniques of social research which occurred early in World War II is not without interest to this brief review. Whereas prior to the middle of 1943 shortages in consumer goods had not been a particularly serious problem, the spread of the war thereafter was such that consumers began to feel the pinch and the agency which has been set up to protect consumer needs—the Office of Civilian Requirements—was faced with the problem of sifting reports of critical shortages which ranged from insecticides to bobby pins to spare parts for washing-machines to garbage cans. The general governmental mandate was that "the level of civilian supply in fields of scarcity should be the minimum necessary to maintain health and morale and working efficiency," but even the most basic facts were lacking.

No one knew to what extent scarce goods had been hoarded nor to what extent the mounting consumer complaints were real or were reflective of special interest groups, and the problem was subsequently turned over to a panel of social scientists employed by the agency.

For the social scientists this was a problem in question-naire construction and interviewing—but perhaps more basically it was a problem in sampling made more complex by the high degree of geographical mobility of the popula-tion during the war years.

To make a long story very short, these studies of consumer shortages were, in fact, carried out with a remarkable degree of accuracy but only after a demanding series of field experi-ments in the design of survey research had been conducted. To give one small illustration, it was found in the washing-machine studies that the data on families who were at home at the first interview differed enormously from those who could be reached only after repeated call-backs. This was obviously reflective of the differing family composition of working wives and meant that the interviewer must keep calling back to reach all of his sample families in order to have a complete picture. Had not this and hundreds of other predictable social regularities been taken into account in these studies, some very bad errors in the wartime allocation of scarce goods would certainly have been made.

Since the war, of course, the sample survey has been in wide use not only by the government but also by business, industry, the mass media, and a wide variety of agencies dedi-cated to the health and welfare of the population.

Finally, I should like to draw attention to communica-tions as a field of application, since it touches upon such well-known operations as market research, public opinion surveys, content analysis, motivation research, small group studies, mass media audience research, and many others. Like rapid transportation, communication is one of the most central and pervasive aspects of the modern age, yet we are only just beginning to be able to specify some of the details of communication as a *social* process. The older, oversimple, and purely technological concern with communication as a transfer of information from one point to another has been discarded in favor of a complex series of interrelated questions about the communicator, the nature of the message, the significance of the channels, the social situation of the audience, and the like. Not only has an elaborate research technology been marshaled in an attempt to answer such questions, but a substantial body of theory has been brought to bear. Perhaps, however, some illustrative findings—since this is my own special field of research interest—will better serve to suggest the scope and complexity of this important area of application. We have found, for example:

that messages are typically more effective when there is discussion among the audience

that one-way communication in the small group tends to lower morale

that mass communications are passed on in patterned ways through opinion leaders

that voters or buyers or readers who are under social cross-pressures tend to vacillate and often to withdraw from decision-making

that audiences for the mass media tend to be self-selective

that the informal channels of communication in such organizations as industrial plants, armies, and business are typically more effective than the formal channels

that individuals tend to purchase or to vote or to look at television programs *with* other people rather than *for* a particular brand or candidate or program that high credibility sources have greater immediate effects on audiences but the differences tend to disappear after a few weeks

that the use of strong fear-appeals in messages tends to interfere with the effectiveness of the communication

that mass communications tend to be mediated through the values of the groups which are important to the audience, and these are called reference groups

that under certain conditions the effects of communicated messages do not become manifest for some time after exposure, and this is called the "sleeper effect"

that recipients of messages do not hear or see the total message, rather they perceive what they want or need, and this is known as selective perception.

And perhaps this is a good point at which to conclude my examples. Keeping in mind my earlier caveat that many failures frequently constitute the price of one success, we have ranged from psychological tests to mental hospitals, to public health programs, to correctional institutions, to military demobilization and wartime shortages, and finally to communications. We have tried to suggest that what is being applied in these various cases is a special kind of science, and our central message has been that when such basic concepts as culture, social structure, socialization, and reference groups are put to work via such technologies as sampling, statistical validation, content analysis, and questionnaire construction, the result may be taken as an important chapter in man's age-old search to find out who he is and where and how he fits into the larger scheme of things.

20 THE MOSAIC OF THE BEHAVIORAL SCIENCES

Robert K. Merton

Robert K. Merton, Professor of Sociology at Columbia University, was born in Philadelphia, Pennsylvania, in 1910. After graduating from Temple University, Dr. Merton pursued advanced studies in sociology at Harvard University, where he received his doctorate in 1936. He remained at Harvard until 1940 as an instructor in sociology and then went to Tulane University as Professor and Chairman of the Department of Sociology. He became a member of the Columbia University faculty in 1941, at which time he was also appointed Associate Director of the Bureau of Applied Social Research. A specialist in the sociology of professions and science, and in sociological theory, Dr. Merton has collaborated with other authorities in the writing of many published books and is the author of Social Theory and Social Structure, Science, Technology and Society in Seventeenth Century England, *and* Mass Persuasion. *He is a member of the Board of Trustees of the Center for Advanced Study in the Behavioral Sciences and was President, in 1957, of the American Sociological Association.*

The preceding nineteen papers on the behavioral sciences have mapped out the scope and purposes of the behavioral sciences and have sketched the outlines of three of them—anthropology, psychology, and sociology—with shorter reference to the other three, economics, history, and political science. More specialized papers have examined the major methods of inquiry now employed by behavioral scientists and have reported current investigations into such matters as the evolution of behavior; neuropsychology; animal behavior; language and linguistics; thinking, cognition, and learning; the psychology of personality and the sociology of small groups; political behavior and public opinion; social classes and population. Finally, the two papers preceding this one have given us a glimpse into the current uses of be-havioral science for man and society.

I have been asked to gather up these many strands of thought and to tie them together as neatly as I can. Many loose ends will remain untouched, of course, but what is written here may be enough to recall to the reader the many details I must omit.

In this review, I have found it useful to examine the great array of information that has been presented to you under three main heads: First, how have the behavioral sciences come about? Second, what is now going on in them? And third, what does it all amount to?

I. HOW HAVE THE BEHAVIORAL SCIENCES COME ABOUT?

History does not really furnish us with dates that mark the strict beginnings of cultural developments. As with evolution in general, the dominating fact is that every part of culture evolves as a continuing process, with only occa-sional discontinuities that can be vaguely identified as the beginning of a new phase. To adopt a date as the decisive beginning of any of the behavioral sciences, then, would be to impose an arbitrary fiction on the cultural reality, in the unexamined belief that all things, including a science, must have a determinable and datable beginning. But this would be a most a-historical view. Each alleged beginning has ante-cedents which have themselves been anticipated. This is true except when men ritually fix the beginning of an organiza-tion, as they do when opening a new laboratory or in-corporating a new business. It is not so with the origins of a science. To date the start of sociology, for example, from 1838, when Auguste Comte first coined the word "sociology" (in order to distinguish what he was doing from what his contemporary, Adolphe Quetelet, was doing under the title of "social physics")—to adopt this date as the beginning of sociology would be historically naive. It would only serve the purpose of providing students with a rote answer to a pat question that might be raised in an examination. Forgetting the conventional practice of establishing an exact chronology for these things, we can say that the modern beginnings of the several behavioral sciences are largely found in the nineteenth century. Even so, we should note that many specialized interests in the behavioral sciences—psychosurgery, for example, or the structural analysis of language—have emerged only in recent years. Perhaps we would do best to give up the quest for a datable beginning altogether and, paraphrasing Galileo, conclude only that the behavioral sciences comprise "a very new science of a very ancient subject."

Whatever their origins, the behavioral sciences are the distinct possession of our own time. That this statement is true rather than merely provincial can be shown by a single fact: some 90 to 95 per cent of all behavioral scientists who have ever lived are now alive. Though crude, the estimate is reasonably correct. It follows the observation made by the historian of science, Derek Price, that "some 80 to 90 per cent of all physical and biological scientists that have ever been" are with us still. Since behavioral science has burgeoned even more recently, the estimate of 90 to 95 per cent of contemporaneous ancestors in this field does not seem extravagant. The fact, not the calculation, is the result of the increasing rate at which behavioral science grows. As Ernest Hilgard has noted for psychology and as Derek Price has demonstrated for other sciences, this growth has proceeded "exponentially rather than linearly; that is to say, it has increased at compound interest rather than simple interest." Only the constant varies: in some fields, such as psychology, the number of personnel has been doubling in about eight years; in other behavioral sciences, in about fifteen years.

This matter of the numbers engaged in the behavioral sciences should be seen comparatively. There are, for example, about six thousand sociologists in the United States.

This is a large number when compared with that of a generation or so ago, or when compared with the number of sociologists now found in Britain, France, Germany, Japan, or Italy. But it is a small number when compared with the sixty thousand physicists or the eighty thousand chemists currently engaged in research in the United States. This temporary emphasis upon numbers naturally does not imply the importance of numbers above all. Nevertheless, it remains true that today many thousands of men working methodically with improved methods are required to advance knowledge in a discipline rapidly, rather than slowly by almost imperceptible increments. Advances in the behavioral sciences have been substantially dependent upon growth in the number of men and women willing and through trained capacity able to do their job.

Although exact figures fail us, it is also the case that the great majority of behavioral scientists are now found in the United States. But contrary to what has sometimes been alleged, both by American chauvinists and by critics of these sciences elsewhere, it is *not* the case that the behavioral sciences are a distinctively American product. As the preceding papers have made plain, it is quite otherwise (just as we know it to be otherwise in the physical and biological sciences). Time and again, attention has been called to the indisputable and largely undisputed fact that the roots of contemporary social and psychological science first took hold chiefly in Europe, not in the United States. As the anthropologist Cora du Bois noted, for example, the principal ideas about social organization now employed by American anthropologists were set forth by the French sociologists Durkheim and Mauss and by the German, Max Weber. Psychology, as Ernest Hilgard observed, has benefited from the influence of Fechner, who did much to originate psychophysics; of Pavlov, on conditioning and learning; of Galton and Binet, on the study of psychological differences between individuals; and, of course, of Freud, who revolutionized the dynamic conception of personality. The list of minds that proved seminal for today's sociology as it is developing in the United States would include Weber, Simmel, Durkheim, Pareto, Hobhouse, Sorokin, and Znaniecki. Or again, Harry Harlow has reminded us of the great debt that American students of animal behavior owe to the unsurpassed work of Karl von Frisch on communication among bees.

As European ideas were transplanted in the American scientific culture, they were often transformed. Characteristically, these ideas were converted into an array of hypotheses requiring systematic investigation rather than remaining intact as final truths. One question has typically been put in each of these instructive ideas: Is it really so? And to answer this question, it was judged necessary to look and see. All this, presumably, is caught up in what is often described as the strongly "empirical temper" of behavioral science in the United States.

As the number of behavioral scientists increased and the diversity of their ideas was compounded, there has come about, in accord with the Spencerian thesis, a growing differentiation in their scientific work. The continuing multiplication of specialties has resulted at times in reshaping the intellectual jurisdiction of particular disciplines. Anthropology, for example, was once regarded, possibly by etymological fiat, as *the* science of man. It has since divided and subdivided into a variety of specialties: physical anthropology, social and cultural anthropology, archeology, and linguistics, with each of these, in turn, spawning even more restricted specialties. As Professor Greenberg remarked about linguistics, some of the newer specialties have emancipated themselves from the mother discipline—sometimes too much so—to become fairly independent sciences. Or, to take another fact that expresses this tendency toward differentiation, the American learned society of psychologists now has twenty-two divisions and many of these are even now proliferating into new specialties.

In part, the process of differentiation has forced behavioral scientists to a toleration of diversity, and in part has led them to put a premium on diversity, this, in turn, inviting further specialization. But with all its conspicuous benefits for increasingly precise and focused inquiry, this growing differentiation has its dangers, too. Chief among these is the danger of an excessive fragmentation of inquiry. Important problems can drop out of sight into the interstices between the specialties. This can be seen, for example, in the fact that there is now comparatively little research designed to investigate the processes of social change. American sociologists, insufficiently tutored in historical knowledge and method, have given slight attention to the study of long-term change in social structure, and American historians, unequipped with a knowledge of the substance and procedures of sociological inquiry, often continue with their largely descriptive rather than analytical historiography.

Yet, in the main, the danger that important classes of problems will be lost to view as a result of great specialization seems not to have materialized as often as might be supposed. Perhaps this is because the danger, once recognized, has brought about its own counterpoise. One such offset is the growing collaboration among specialists. As was reported in the paper on language and linguistics, for example, exacting formulations of semiotic problems have led linguists to collaborate with logicians, communication engineers, and mathematicians. Again, studies of the structure and operation of authority are now pursued jointly by sociologists, anthropologists, and social psychologists, the social fact of authority being no longer considered the separate preserve of the political scientist. Economists have joined with social anthropologists to see how far their theory holds for economies of the most varied kind. And, to take a last instance from an indefinitely large store, representatives from practically all the behavioral sciences now collaborate in research on "national character structure," a subject once considered the almost exclusive possession of culturally minded historians and romantic novelists.

With the multiple convergence of behavioral scientists upon the same subjects, problems and methods become sustained and this gives rise to new interdisciplines. Just as biochemistry, biophysics, and chemical embryology emerged from the repeated crisscrossing of separate physical and life sciences, so have new mergers appeared in the behavioral disciplines (and not because they were playing the sedulous ape to their elder siblings among the sciences). Here, too, collaborations fused into intellectual unity have been registered by descriptive tags for interdisciplinary specialties. Psycholinguistics, social biology and psychobiology, political sociology and social psychiatry, human ecology, ethology, and sociological history, or, at the edges, such a composite as paleopathology, are only a few of the many new specialties testifying to this process of intellectual affiliation. In this way, the interstices between the specialties become gradually filled with new cross-disciplinary specialties. What caustic literary historians once liked to describe as the "imperialism" of the social and psychological sciences, in which each field lays claim to intellectual domains preempted by others, including some of the humanistic ones, no longer prevails (if indeed, it ever did). Instead, there continues an unpublicized and undramatized merging where this seems required by the nature of newly identified problems. Rather than one department of behavioral science trying to annex another, they usually agree to meet on the neutral ground between them in order to get on with their work.

The filling in of empty interdisciplinary spaces with new specialties has not always proceeded smoothly. There have been and there continue to be squabbles between behavioral scientists of differing provenience about the proper nature of the new field. Occasionally there is a babel of alien technical tongues before they evolve a common language. And some problems, important in their own right, are no doubt neglected when they do not fit clearly into one bailiwick or another. But, for the most part, growing specialization has narrowed rather than widened the separatism of the behavioral sciences.

Now it is important to note that all this does not result from the cultish belief that it is good to "interdisciplinize," that a togetherness of men with diverse intellectual antecedents is simply a good thing. Instead, these consolidations have come about because different but related bodies of knowledge have been found indispensable to investigate effectively new-found or long-unsolved problems of animal and human behavior. In these collaborations, men from the several sciences continue to focus on a problem common to them all from the perspectives of their own disciplines. They do not abdicate their competences but merge them. This becomes the easier to do as each of the behavioral sciences has successfully found its distinctive place in the academic scheme of things. Its practitioners are then quite ready to abandon the defensive posture of intellectual isolation they may once have held. And so, when the occasion seems to require it, they enter into an *entente cordiale,* not for the sake of academic diplomacy but for the sake of getting on with their job.

In this quick and incomplete sketch of recent formations in the behavioral sciences, I have been able only to touch upon the scale of their growth, both in numbers of personnel and in the work they are turning out, just as I have only mentioned rather than closely examined the intellectual roots of these disciplines, which are largely to be found in European soil. Because the process of differentiation in the behavioral sciences—principally caught up in the growth of specialties—is so widely misunderstood, I have taken time to examine this a bit more thoroughly and to suggest that under favorable conditions the specialization of knowledge in behavioral science, as in science generally, goes hand in hand with the consolidation of knowledge.

In all this, as I intimated, there have of course been growing pains. Since the behavioral sciences are still growing, some of these pains are with us still. The new popularity of the behavioral sciences in some quarters has brought with it an occasional tendency toward popularization of the worst sort, toward vulgarization that, in the guise of acquainting the public with current developments, distorts both the accomplishments and the limitations of behavioral science. But these and related difficulties can more advantageously be considered later, after we have reviewed what behavioral science today is all about, by sampling some of its content and some of its methods of inquiry. Therefore, let us proceed by reviewing the first of these—some new questions, problems, and findings of behavioral science—and with this in mind, we can then consider the second—the tools and methods that bring some answers to these questions into being.

II. WHAT IS GOING ON IN THE BEHAVIORAL SCIENCES?

We might best begin by noting one thing that is *not* now going on in behavioral science or that has *almost* disappeared. This is an active concern with the question: Are the behavioral sciences really science? In a popular alternative form that bears the mark of its philosophic origins, this question reads: Is a science of behavior really possible?

Not too long ago—endemically in the nineteenth century but still sporadically in the twentieth—this question, in either of its forms, usurped the attention of many men engaged in reflecting upon the social and psychological studies. John Stuart Mill was only one among many to be thoroughly preoccupied with this question. There were many thick tomes, especially but not exclusively originating in Germany, and many thin books, especially but not exclusively in England, as well as books of middling size in the United States, all directed to the task of providing logical and therefore abstract answers to the questions: Is social science really possible?

The behavioral scientists of today have not so much answered this question in the abstract as they have allowed it to commit suicide after a period during which it suffered seriously from severe neglect. They have dealt with the question, not by continued debate, but by proceeding, through their investigations, to produce scientific results. They have, in effect, adopted the doctrine unforgettably expressed by Thomas Love Peacock: "Whatever is, is possible."

This does not mean that behavioral scientists have converted themselves into philistines of philosophy, that they have blandly given up all interest in exploring the philosophical foundations of behavioral science. The important work of the psychologists Egon Brunswik, Gustav Bergmann, and Kenneth Spence, or that of the sociologist Paul Lazarsfeld in collaboration with the logician Ernest Nagel, or that of the political scientist Harold Lasswell in collaboration with the philosopher Abraham Kaplan—and I halt the long list here—testifies to the contrary. But this rejection of the old question does mean that they have refused to substitute an interest in the philosophic bases of behavioral science for the actual work of investigating substantive and procedural problems of behavioral science.

This work, you will have noticed, runs a wide gamut of subjects, questions, and procedures. It ranges from investigation of the brain cortex of the individual man to investigation of the structure of a complex society, say that of Soviet Russia or of England. It tries to cope with age-old questions —for example, the relation of population growth to human welfare; and it attends to new questions about man, his behavior, and his works that could not have been raised before or, if raised, could not have been answered: the question, for example, of how the pacing of activity in a social organization affects the system of social control in that organization. It deals with practical problems of social life, such as the conditions making for crime, mental disease, or the domestic casualties of divorce and desertion, and with problems that are, or seem to be, so remote from the practical that some would deny the behavioral scientist any right to concern himself with them: for example, such ostensibly trivial matters as regularities in the sound-changes taking place in the development of a language. In these and other respects, the behavioral sciences move, in their way, across a wide, varied, and, to the layman, often bewildering range of topics, problems, and methods, much as those other families of science, the physical and life sciences, move in their complex and only apparently mysterious ways.

A quick, unsystematic sampling will recall to mind that this is so in the behavioral sciences and will raise the question whether it should be otherwise. Anthropologists are hard at work trying to discover the degree to which societies are integrated, with the several parts of their social structure and culture hanging together with reasonable consistency. They try to find out how far a culture can be riddled with internal contradictions of precept and values and still maintain itself. In this, they are extending inquiry into the process that William Graham Sumner, the late nineteenth-century sociologist, described as the "strain toward consistency"—in values, in the mores, and in the structure of society. At an extreme from this sort of problem, other anthropologists, notably Spuhler and Washburn, are examining the old dogma that "the human organism has been essentially static since the development of culture," are asking whether this is really so, and are finding that it is not.

Psychology covers as wide a gamut of questions new and old and of subjects microcosmic, macrocosmic, and, of course, in between. What Karl Pribram has described as "the hitherto silent areas of the brain cortex" have recently "yielded up some of their mystery" as a result of researches on the effects of brain lesion that have begun to answer the "age-old" question whether the brain is or is not a *tabula rasa.* (As we might suspect, these prove to be false alternatives: the brain being quiescent under one set of identifiable conditions and spontaneously active under others.) Or to move far afield, social psychologists have found it possible to introduce experimental designs of inquiry, not only in the contrived situations of the academic laboratory but out in open society, thus settling by trial, rather than by argument, the old dogma propounded by John Stuart Mill, among others, that experiment is in principle impossible in the study of social behavior. Aiming to advance a theory of social conformity and nonconformity, for example, R. R. Blake has systematically observed the frequency with which ordinary citizens on the streets of a Texas city violate laws regulating pedestrian traffic. He has done this under experimentally varied conditions by alternately introducing and withholding the precedent of violations initiated by a member of his research group. (I must be quick to add that this adaptation of the techniques of the *agent provocateur* to the purposes of research in social psychology does not really raise a moral issue; not one of the many pedestrians emulating the violation of the law by the experimental agent was penalized for his misdemeanor.) Although the particular instance may seem trivial—almost as trivial as the practice among seventeenth-century scientists of measuring the pressure of gases or of assiduously watching balls rolling down an inclined plane—it is, nevertheless, a fact of some consequence. For experiments such as these may open the door to the experimental study of all sorts of social behavior in the ordinary situations of everyday life, an objective that not long ago seemed unattainable. Once the method becomes more crisply defined and established, it can be adapted to the study of problems having much wider import.

Sociology, also, has a wide range of research in progress. Popular assumptions, such as the unauthenticated belief that the rate of social mobility has greatly declined among the peoples of the West, have been put in question by systematically assembled data; the alleged breakdown of the family, with obsequies read regularly over the remains by those who should know better, has been found to be specious rather than real, as thorough analyses of data on divorce and death find American marriages remaining intact more often now than they once did. In collaboration with colleagues in other behavioral sciences, sociologists have been systematically investigating so vast a subject as the social structure of the U.S.S.R., and through the work of such men as Alex Inkeles, Raymond Bauer, and Clyde Kluckhohn we have come to know more about the workings of Soviet society than even the most perceptive of political jouralists can authentically tell us.

Even a swift review of what is now going on in the behavioral sciences must be put in the context of its relatively recent past. Like many other disciplines in this age of science, the behavioral sciences have been growing at a comparatively rapid rate, in recent generations doubling the numbers of their practitioners every eight to fifteen years and multiplying published work at an even greater rate, since those that come after can build on what has gone before. That behavioral science, in composite, is a world science, rather than provincially centered in this or that country, is part of its history as well as its current condition, with chiefly European scholars having provided much of its effective beginnings and with the United States having turned, during the last generation or two, to its particularly intensive development. As part and consequence of this rapid growth, there have developed a great number of specialties, both within each of the core behavioral sciences of anthropology, economics, history, political science, psychology, and sociology, and in their interdisciplinary spaces, as with such newly developed specialties as pscholinguistics, historical sociology, and social biology. The core disciplines and the specialties springing up in the interstices between them comprise the diversified mosaic of the behavioral sciences.

259

The scope of work now going forward in these sciences can be variously described: in the scale of the objects under study, from investigations of the brain cortex to those of entire societies; in the familiarity of the questions under study, from those of ancient lineage, such as the passive or active role of the brain in behavior, to those which have only lately become identifiable, such as the operation of feed-back systems of control in social organizations; and, to stop at a third aspect, in the degree of uncertainty about the findings in hand, ranging from those that are reasonably plausible but still far from demonstrated to those that are fairly well established as matters of new fact.

All this has been set forth in the previous papers. In this there is involved the question of how behavioral scientists go about the business of finding out. It is, therefore, to this matter of tools and methods of inquiry that we now turn.

Just as the physical and biological sciences found it necessary to develop new instruments for investigating problems both old and new, this becoming marked in the seventeenth century and proceeding at a more rapid pace ever since, so, on a far more limited scale, has this been the case for the behavioral sciences principally in the last two generations or so. In many ways, the development of the behavioral sciences took a critical turn when their advocates slowly and belatedly recognized that they too must fashion tools of inquiry adequate to the problems they would study if they were seriously to get on with their job. It is, after all, only a truism rather than a radical or peculiar idea to decide that if you want to find out the conditions and consequences of various forms of behavior, you had better devise effective ways of doing so. Yet, to the present moment, there are people who genuinely believe that, unlike all other disciplines, the behavioral sciences should somehow get along without tools and methods. They believe this, evidently, even though such a discipline as historiography, that hybrid of science and art, long ago found it essential to devise methods of paleography, epigraphy, numismatics, heraldics, philology, genealogy, and geography, to mention only a few, in order to work up its historical materials from manuscripts, monuments, coins and medals, inscriptions, drawings, paintings, buildings in ruin, and dead men's bones.

Earlier essays in this book, those of Samuel Stouffer and Carl Hovland, took inventory of the tools and methods now stocked by behavioral scientists. To a less extent, practically all the other writers here have found it necessary to refer to some of these. Again, I can only summarize rather than reproduce what was said.

Each behavioral discipline and each set of problems has required its own array of tools and methods. First are the devices that tell us something about the intra-organismic makeup of man and of other animals. At one end, these encompass what Professor Karl Pribram has described as the "electrical techniques designed to amplify and measure potential changes that can be recorded from brain and nerve," these being the tools that in some measure enable us to find out how the brain regulates particular aspects of behavior. Toward the other end of this range of intra-organismic tools are the psychological tests of almost infinite variety, designed to search out differences in aptitudes, abilities, attitudes, and configurations of personality. Some, like the Rorschach ink-blot test and the systematic use of free association have become widely known among laymen; others, like the Thematic Apperception Test, the F-scale, and the semantic differential, are less widely known outside the behavioral sciences though often used within them. These tools of intra-organismic assessment and measurement vary greatly, of course, in their precision, reliability, and demonstrated validity. If they should follow the pattern laid down in the history of science, most will no doubt be modified and improved, others will give way to superior alternatives, and some will be scrapped altogether as brave but mistaken attempts. But the point is that all are designed to make it possible to investigate some aspects of behavior which were before matters of impression only. All are subject to repeated scrutiny and are, sooner or later, put to severe test before they are finally adopted as acknowledged tools of the trade.

Although the distinction cannot be made sharply and strictly maintained, as you will see, we can identify other sets of tools and methods that center not on what presumably goes on within the organism but on its outward behavior. These largely deal with what is called "molar behavior," those units of behavior that have a distinct character deriving from the ends they serve or from the effects they produce in the external world. For example, there is steady improvement in much of the apparatus devised to study complex processes of learning, in man and other animals, these including new types of test mazes, that device for the measurement of learning rates known eponymously as the Skinner box, polygraphs used to record outward behavior as well as physiological reactions almost instantaneously, and, to turn to quite another type of problem, the newly invented sound spectograph that makes possible exact study of the acoustic properties of speech sounds. Not least significant is the change that has displaced the rat from his previous eminence as the experimental animal in psychology par excellence, an eminence long maintained because of his composite virtues of being cheap, small, adaptive, and easily available. Professor Harry F. Harlow has reported to you "the growing percentage of investigations using as subjects, not rats, but other animals, including chimpanzees, monkeys, cats, dogs, raccoons, mice, pigeons, chickens, ducks, fish, worms, and even more primitive forms," as well as men and women outside the confines of the academic classroom. In the modern study of behavior, few species of animals are in principle now regarded as alien to study.

Turning now from tools aimed principally at the study of individual behavior, we find others developed chiefly to investigate the behavior of men and other animals in small groups, ranging from the smallest group of a pair to something of the order of ten or fifteen. For this purpose, behavioral scientists use all manner of sociometrics, systematic measures of what the members of a reasonably small group perceive, think, and feel about one another. The Harvard sociologist, Robert F. Bales, has devised a much-used system for observing and recording the sequence of social interactions, that is, the mutual exchange in conversation and other behavior between members of a small group assembled in a particular place. These and comparable methods have made it possible to identify patterns of social relations that, to a significant degree, are not recognized by the members of these groups themselves.

Proceeding from small groups, through larger oganizations, to social aggregations on the truly large scale, we meet still other methods that have transformed the study of society. In behavioral science, it is no longer regarded as satisfactory to describe the behavior, attitudes, values, and social relations obtaining in a complex society simply on the basis of impressions, however well informed, about what is going on in it, impressions based on a large but scattered array of written documents, both public and private, and on educated guesses about what people are thinking and feeling as they do what they do. This type of inquiry still goes on and for a long time to come it will probably be indispensable. After all, studies of the historical past have no alternative. But in the study of present-day societies, these methods are giving way to systematic, though far from perfected, methods of assessing the behavior and correlated attitudes and values of large numbers of men in different regions and in the various social strata of a complex society. Of particular importance for this purpose is the "sample interview survey" which sounds out the practices and attitudes of a sample of people who we have reason to suppose are representative of the larger population from which the sample is drawn. The interview survey is of course now part of the intellectual landscape: we all know of it and some of us deplore it, when it appears in the form of the "opinion poll." In political season and out, these polls report in the press the spread of opinion and of intended action, in the realm of voting, buying, conversing, appraising, and reacting to public events. But the versions that appear in the popular press are not necessarily a true sample of the uses to which the sample survey are put by academic scholars. Yet these limited pratical uses of the survey, with all their faults, some of which we shall consider in a moment, have had the indispensable value of providing ample experience on the basis of which the survey as a tool can be continuously improved, as in fact it has been. Not least among these improvements, as Professor Stouffer has indicated, is the invention of the panel survey, the periodic reinterviewing of the same sample of people so that *changes* in their behavior, experience, attitudes, and values can be gauged.

The reading of what goes on in particular societies of course leads to comparisons between societies, to what is sometimes called, by behavioral scientists, "cross-cultural comparisons." Here, the effort is to understand better than we have before the reasons for the great diversity of cultures, a fact which was known, of course, to the ancients. ("Other times, other manners" is a proverb that still rings in our ears.) This ancient but once indecipherable fact, the diversity of cultures, has now become a problem for investigation. The resource of the cross-cultural survey, a library of systematically classified and roughly comparable facts about a great number of cultures, both living and dead, now provides at least part of the basis for our beginning to understand how the diversities, as well as the similarities, between cultures come to be and to persist or change.

In this swift tour through the domain of current methods and tools now used by behavioral scientists, we have touched upon those that are more or less geared to studies of behavior varying in scope from the reconstructed processes that take place within the single organism to the reconstructed processes that take place within and between complex societies. But there are, of course, tools and methods that are not confined to studies on the one scale or the other; these cut across the various fields of behavioral science. Of these, there is seemingly no end: the mathematics, new and old, that are now being utilized to cope with distinctive problems of behavioral science; the logic and practice of sampling; the use of statistical procedures such as factor analysis and, as a special case, latent-structure analysis; or, to open the gates wide enough to follow Professor Hilgard in his listing of recently applied instruments, the use of vacuum tubes, photographic recording, electromagnetic tape, and, above all, the electronic computer.

The reader will have noticed, I am sure, that at least half the accounts of the several behavioral sciences and of programs of investigation within them have referred, in one way or another, to the actual and coming use of the electronic computer. Whether it is in the experimental study of the nervous system, as detailed by Karl Pribram, or studies of the process of developing the skills of recognizing objects, as reported by George Miller, or, to take a long leap, the simulation of behavior and social relations in large social systems, as described by Samuel Stouffer and Carl Hovland, the electronic computer emerges time and again as a new-found resource of the behavioral scientist. Within roughly definable limits, this is as it should be. For this massive and complicated tool is rapidly becoming the universal mind of our time. The tool refuses, however, to have a mind of its own, as Professor Hovland has made plain. It must be told what to do. Only then and with complete obedience (at least, within the wide range of its competence), it promptly does what it is told. It does so more rigorously, more accurately, and, beyond all easy measure, more rapidly, than can be done by the minds that created it. But it will go through its rapid paces only upon instruction and only after it is fed basic information and is firmly instructed, that is, programmed, to do certain things and not others. In short, it computes in a most extended sense.

As with most technical creations of man's mind, the electronic computer, in behavioral science as elsewhere, has become an object of man's ambivalence. For some, and not entirely among those who have no close acquaintance with it, the electronic computer is a monster. If left to its own devices, it is a monster that threatens to reduce thinking to an automatic calculus, that tempts its tenders, in this case the behavioral scientists who minister to its needs, to cast all manner of raw data into its maw and to wait for the thoroughly digested product that will itself be senseless if the thought of its managers is without much sense. As Professor Stouffer has emphasized to a degree that does not allow us to forget, the electronic computer provides a temptation to the behavioral scientist to return once again to raw and ready empiricism. Since thousands of correlation coefficients, for example, can be computed by this machine in the time craft work would have taken to compute a mere handful, it is a great temptation to run data through the computer almost at random and then swiftly to take possession of the so-called results. Nor can it be denied that, here and there, behavioral scientists find this mechanized temptation to thoughtless efficiency irresistible, turning from laborious though thoughtful work to mere busywork. But then, every new technology has its capacity for deflecting men from the pursuit of purposes they genuinely respect, and the electronic computer is no exception. But since the danger is recognized by most of its potential victims, many of them succeed easily in extricating themselves from it.

It is with this instrument as with most of the rest: the most devastating criticisms of its misplaced use have come, not from the laymen who know about it only through hearsay, but from the professionals who are prepared to study their sometimes drab and disappointing experience with it. For example, in the use of the interview or questionnaire or other devices for collecting data about the behavior of large numbers of people, it is the professionals who, by experimental and other means, have put the method to rigorous test. For they, at least the best of them, know that whatever the instrumental worth of the tool, it is the questions put to it that determine the significance of the results. If the questions are trivial, that is, inconsequential for our understanding of behavior, then the answers will of course be trivial. That is why, with the development of each new tool of inquiry, a greater premium than ever before is put upon creative thought. For only significant questions, suitably programmed for solution, can, through the almost unmatched skills of the machine, produce significant answers. That is why, also, the undeniable mistakes that behavioral scientists, like other men, occasionally make in overrating the significance of a new technology of investigation, are sooner or later caught up with and thrown into the discard.

III. WHAT DOES IT ALL AMOUNT TO?

This leads us, then, to our final set of questions: what are some of the accomplishments, limitations, and consequences of present-day behavioral science? What, in most general terms, is its present condition? What does it all amount to?

The questions are misleading, if they imply that they can be seriously and responsibly answered in a few short paragraphs. Yet there is space for a few generalities that sum up part of the answer.

The behavioral sciences have made detectable, even considerable, strides toward their distant and never fully attainable objective. We now know more, appreciably more, about the conditions and processes leading to one or another kind of behavior, chiefly among men, who continue to interest us strangely, but also among other animals. We know, too, something of the limits of our knowledge. A competent behavioral scientist is, at least in his professional capacity, a humble man; he has no choice; he must be. For he knows how little he knows and how much is yet to be known. Yet in his brighter moods, he is anything but humble, he may on occasion even seem arrogant, for at least he knows a little more than his predecessors about the nature of his ignorance and is persuaded that he is, part of the time, on the right track to reduce, however slightly, the vast scope of that ignorance. The behavioral scientist is in a mood of subdued exuberance, of restrained optimism, of modest confidence.

In part, this mood results from the fact that the world about him has gradually, though grudgingly, begun to take notice of the behavioral scientist. Undisturbed humanists like Gilbert Murray, confident of the worth of what they themselves are doing, have become ready to say that the behavioral sciences—Murray employed the restrictive term, sociology, but what he has to say may hold for the family of which it is a part—are "destined to bear abundant and ever-increasing fruit." In like fashion, a political journalist of the first rank, Richard Rovere, acknowledges that "those of us who have been educated in the twentieth century habitually think in sociological terms, whether or not we have had any training in sociology." And a charismatic though not un-disputed figure such as T. S. Eliot can cast himself in the role of social scientist when he reflects on the social world around him and writes *Notes toward the Definition of Culture.*

What these men are saying—and their voices are echoed by a less imposing array of businessmen, politicians, clergy-men, physicians, lawyers, social workers, and occasional men-in-the-street—is that this is an Age of Behavioral Science just as it is, of course, an Age of the Atom and an Age of Automation. For better or worse, and there is a division of opinion on which is the case, behavioral science is with us to stay. If we don't live comfortably with it, the fact remains that we can't do without it—not, at least, if we are to preserve and to extend the values that matter to us.

This new popularity of the behavioral sciences is of course only part of their current story. More than ever before, they are subjected to violent attack. Yet this notoriety is ultimately of a piece with their popularity. Both tribute and attack testify that they can no longer be ignored. Behavioral science, with all its limitations, is now, and, in its degree, for the first time, an integral part of our culture.

This ambivalent popularity carries its own complement of excesses and dangers. First is the danger of vulgarization, in which the successful hack writer coarsens what small knowledge we have. Take only the most conspicuous recent instance of this danger become reality: for months, Vance Packard's *The Status Seekers*, a book ostensibly summarizing in palatable form the findings of sociologists about class structure and class behavior, headed the list of non-fiction bestsellers in the United States. In the opinion of many behavioral scientists who have read it, this exceedingly popular book, with its frequent distortions of the facts, could more aptly have been transferred to the head of fictional bestsellers. For some of us, Vance Packard is as much a sociologist as was Scopes a Darwin (Scopes being, you may remember, the secondary school teacher who insisted on teaching evolution in spite of the archaic laws of Tennessee which forbade it.)

Popularity carries with it also a second danger, this one being the excessive claims to knowledge by professional behavioral scientists responding to demands by the public that this knowledge be promptly put to effective use. Dr. Young, in his paper, spoke of how the profession tries to restrain any such tendencies toward professional megalomania. Instead, as he points out, behavioral science of a responsible sort has moved beyond its secure and narrowly academic haven to be utilized by medicine, public health, law, social work, education, government, the ministry, engineering, architecture, business, and agriculture.

We can here only touch upon a third danger of an effective and popular behavioral science: the danger that it will be put to use in ways that rightly do not enjoy the respect of man. As all of us have been saying ever since Francis Bacon put the words into our mouths, knowledge is power. It remained for Lord Acton to supply the second premise of the historically evolving syllogism, power corrupts (or, less elegantly and more accurately, power can corrupt). To the extent that behavioral science achieves sound knowledge and so creates a potential for power, it too may corrupt. In short, the same dilemma confronts the new behavioral sciences as has long confronted the older physical and biological sciences. The power of knowledge lends itself to use for purposes which many of us regard either as good or as evil. (Being human, we luckily find it hard to remain wholly indifferent.) Yet no more than the older sciences can the new ones throw out the good with the bad. Each case of the use of behavioral knowledge must be judged on its merits. It is essential, above all, to avoid the hysteria that rates the knowledge achieved by behavioral science too highly and so sees in it a powerful device for manipulating man for wholly self-interested or disgusting purposes. Behavioral science has really not achieved this degree of effectiveness. And in the long interim before it does, it rests upon all of us to work out ways in which widespread publicity for decisions about the use of behavioral science for what are called practical purposes and clearly assigned responsibility for those decisions will provide a reasonably though not wholly adequate restraint upon its misuse. (Did space allow, this seemingly pious opinion could be defended.)

There is, finally, another danger created by a developing behavioral science that has often been called to our attention. This is the danger that it will join in the attempt to substitute science for ethics and aesthetics, to displace humanism with scientism. Here in particular, there is nothing really distinctive about the behavioral sciences. As C. P. Snow has reminded us, in his Rede Lecture on *The Two Cultures and the Scientific Revolution,* the sword cuts two ways. Humanists ignorant of the character and intent of science have been quite as effective in creating a gulf between themselves and the scientists as have many scientists, especially those who have become almost arrogant in their dedicated and purposeful grip on one part of reality which they are inclined to regard as the whole of reality.

Every responsible behavioral scientist, and there are not a few of them, knows that his knowledge is no substitute for artistic thought. Even when, as in studies of the psychology and sociology of art or of the sociology of knowledge, a behavioral scientist elects to understand, so far as he can, the processes through which creativity and cultural growth come about, he does not rob that creativity and growth of its own character. No more so does the sociologist of science, engaged in finding out the social conditions of scientific productivity, suppose that an understanding of these conditions substitutes for the still unknown qualities that make some men scientifically creative and others not.

We have before our eyes the occasion and the hope of a rapprochement between the more relaxed and understanding minds in each camp—in the humanities and in the behavioral sciences. Each of these groups refuses to force the other into a mould that has no sufficient resemblance to the reality. The thinking humanist recognizes that the behavioral scientist who knows his business seeks only to provide a disciplined understanding of certain, not all, aspects of the behavior of the creative mind; the thinking behavioral scientist recognizes that his science is not and never can be a substitute for poetry. Yet humanist imagery and creativity can be stimulated by the new and exciting developments in the behavioral sciences today, just as they have been stimulated by the exciting developments in many of the sciences, from astronomy to zoology, since at least the days of the Scientific Renaissance in the seventeenth century. Moreover, behavioral scientists can and sometimes do learn from their humanist colleagues about the values that make the life of man more than the life of other animals and so direct part of their inquiries, at least, to subjects that, in the end, really matter.

Altogether, if the behavioral scientists have no adequate basis for complacency, for simply resting on their oars, neither do they have need for severe self-reproaches. The mosaic of the behavioral sciences is uneven and unfinished, but it is one which many generations of informed men hard at work on an unending run of problems will gradually smooth out, and never fully complete.

Index

hARPER 🔥 ⲧORCҺBOOҞS

HUMANITIES AND SOCIAL SCIENCES

American Studies: General

LOUIS D. BRANDEIS: Other People's Money, *and How the Bankers Use It.* ‡ *Ed. with an Intro. by Richard M. Abrams* TB/3081

THOMAS C. COCHRAN: The Inner Revolution. *Essays on the Social Sciences in History* TB/1140

HENRY STEELE COMMAGER, Ed.: The Struggle for Racial Equality TB/1300

EDWARD S. CORWIN: American Constitutional History. *Essays edited by Alpheus T. Mason and Gerald Garvey* △ TB/1136

CARL N. DEGLER, Ed.: Pivotal Interpretations of American History Vol. I TB/1240; Vol. II TB/1241

A. HUNTER DUPREE: Science in the Federal Government: *A History of Policies and Activities to 1940* TB/573

A. S. EISENSTADT, Ed.: The Craft of American History: *Recent Essays in American Historical Writing* Vol. I TB/1255; Vol. II TB/1256

CHARLOTTE P. GILMAN: Women and Economics: *A Study of the Economic Relation between Men and Women as a Factor in Social Evolution.* ‡ *Ed. with an Introduction by Carl N. Degler* TB/3073

OSCAR HANDLIN, Ed.: This Was America: *As Recorded by European Travelers in the Eighteenth, Nineteenth and Twentieth Centuries. Illus.* TB/1119

MARCUS LEE HANSEN: The Atlantic Migration: 1607-1860. *Edited by Arthur M. Schlesinger* TB/1052

MARCUS LEE HANSEN: The Immigrant in American History. TB/1120

JOHN HIGHAM, Ed.: The Reconstruction of American History △ TB/1068

ROBERT H. JACKSON: The Supreme Court in the American System of Government TB/1106

JOHN F. KENNEDY: A Nation of Immigrants. △ *Illus.* TB/1118

LEONARD W. LEVY, Ed.: American Constitutional Law: *Historical Essays* TB/1285

LEONARD W. LEVY, Ed.: Judicial Review and the Supreme Court TB/1296

LEONARD W. LEVY: The Law of the Commonwealth and Chief Justice Shaw TB/1309

HENRY F. MAY: Protestant Churches and Industrial America. *New Intro. by the Author* TB/1334

RALPH BARTON PERRY: Puritanism and Democracy TB/1138

ARNOLD ROSE: The Negro in America TB/3048

MAURICE R. STEIN: The Eclipse of Community. *An Interpretation of American Studies* TB/1128

W. LLOYD WARNER and Associates: Democracy in Jonesville: *A Study in Quality and Inequality* ¶ TB/1129

W. LLOYD WARNER: Social Class in America: The Evaluation of Status TB/1013

American Studies: Colonial

BERNARD BAILYN, Ed.: Apologia of Robert Keayne: *Self-Portrait of a Puritan Merchant* TB/1201

BERNARD BAILYN: The New England Merchants in the Seventeenth Century TB/1149

JOSEPH CHARLES: The Origins of the American Party System TB/1049

HENRY STEELE COMMAGER & ELMO GIORDANETTI, Eds.: Was America a Mistake? *An Eighteenth Century Controversy* TB/1329

CHARLES GIBSON: Spain in America † TB/3077

LAWRENCE HENRY GIPSON: The Coming of the Revolution: 1763-1775. † *Illus.* TB/3007

LEONARD W. LEVY: Freedom of Speech and Press in Early American History: *Legacy of Suppression* TB/1109

PERRY MILLER: Errand Into the Wilderness TB/1139

PERRY MILLER & T. H. JOHNSON, Eds.: The Puritans: *A Sourcebook of Their Writings* Vol. I TB/1093; Vol. II TB/1094

EDMUND S. MORGAN, Ed.: The Diary of Michael Wigglesworth, 1653-1657: *The Conscience of a Puritan* TB/1228

EDMUND S. MORGAN: The Puritan Family: *Religion and Domestic Relations in Seventeenth-Century New England* TB/1227

RICHARD B. MORRIS: Government and Labor in Early America TB/1244

KENNETH B. MURDOCK: Literature and Theology in Colonial New England TB/99

WALLACE NOTESTEIN: The English People on the Eve of Colonization: 1603-1630. † *Illus.* TB/3006

JOHN P. ROCHE: Origins of American Political Thought: *Selected Readings* TB/1301

JOHN SMITH: Captain John Smith's America: *Selections from His Writings. Ed. with Intro. by John Lankford* TB/3078

LOUIS B. WRIGHT: The Cultural Life of the American Colonies: 1607-1763. † *Illus.* TB/3005

American Studies: From the Revolution to 1860

JOHN R. ALDEN: The American Revolution: 1775-1783. † *Illus.* TB/3011

MAX BELOFF, Ed.: The Debate on the American Revolution, 1761-1783: *A Sourcebook* △ TB/1225

RAY A. BILLINGTON: The Far Western Frontier: 1830-1860. † *Illus.* TB/3012

EDMUND BURKE: On the American Revolution: *Selected Speeches and Letters.* ‡ *Edited by Elliott Robert Barkan* TB/3068

WHITNEY R. CROSS: The Burned-Over District: *The Social and Intellectual History of Enthusiastic Religion in Western New York, 1800-1850* △ TB/1242

GEORGE DANGERFIELD: The Awakening of American Nationalism: 1815-1828. † *Illus.* TB/3061

CLEMENT EATON: The Freedom-of-Thought Struggle in the Old South. *Revised and Enlarged. Illus.* TB/1150

CLEMENT EATON: The Growth of Southern Civilization: 1790-1860. † *Illus.* TB/3040

LOUIS FILLER: The Crusade Against Slavery: 1830-1860. † *Illus.* TB/3029

DIXON RYAN FOX: The Decline of Aristocracy in the Politics of New York: 1801-1840. ‡ *Edited by Robert V. Remini* TB/3064

WILLIAM W. FREEHLING, Ed.: The Nullification Era: *A Documentary Record* ‡ TB/3079

FELIX GILBERT: The Beginnings of American Foreign Policy: *To the Farewell Address* TB/1200

FRANCIS GRIERSON: The Valley of Shadows: *The Coming of the Civil War in Lincoln's Midwest: A Contemporary Account* TB/1246

FRANCIS J. GRUND: Aristocracy in America: *Social Class in the Formative Years of the New Nation* TB/1001

ALEXANDER HAMILTON: The Reports of Alexander Hamilton. ‡ *Edited by Jacob E. Cooke* TB/3060

THOMAS JEFFERSON: Notes on the State of Virginia. ‡ *Edited by Thomas P. Abernethy* TB/3052

JAMES MADISON: The Forging of American Federalism: *Selected Writings of James Madison. Edited by K. Padover* TB/1226

BERNARD MAYO: Myths and Men: *Patrick Henry, George Washington, Thomas Jefferson* TB/1108

JOHN C. MILLER: Alexander Hamilton and the Growth of the New Nation TB/3057

RICHARD B. MORRIS, Ed.: The Era of the American Revolution TB/1180

R. B. NYE: The Cultural Life of the New Nation: 1776-1801. † *Illus.* TB/3026

JAMES PARTON: The Presidency of Andrew Jackson. *From Vol. III of the Life of Andrew Jackson. ‡ Ed. with an Intro. by Robert V. Remini* TB/3080

FRANCIS S. PHILBRICK: The Rise of the West, 1754-1830. † *Illus.* TB/3067

TIMOTHY L. SMITH: Revivalism and Social Reform: *American Protestantism on the Eve of the Civil War* TB/1229

ALBION W. TOURGÉE: A Fool's Errand. ‡ *Ed. by George Fredrickson* TB/3074

A. F. TYLER: Freedom's Ferment: *Phases of American Social History from the Revolution to the Outbreak of the Civil War. 31 illus.* TB/1074

GLYNDON G. VAN DEUSEN: The Jacksonian Era: 1828-1848. † *Illus.* TB/3028

LOUIS B. WRIGHT: Culture on the Moving Frontier TB/1053

American Studies: The Civil War to 1900

W. R. BROCK: An American Crisis: Congress and Reconstruction, 1865-67 ° △ TB/1283

THOMAS C. COCHRAN & WILLIAM MILLER: The Age of Enterprise: *A Social History of Industrial America* TB/1054

W. A. DUNNING: Essays on the Civil War and Reconstruction. *Introduction by David Donald* TB/1181

W. A. DUNNING: Reconstruction, Political and Economic: 1865-1877 TB/1073

HAROLD U. FAULKNER: Politics, Reform and Expansion: 1890-1900. † *Illus.* TB/3020

HELEN HUNT JACKSON: A Century of Dishonor: *The Early Crusade for Indian Reform. ‡ Edited by Andrew F. Rolle* TB/3063

ALBERT D. KIRWAN: Revolt of the Rednecks: *Mississippi Politics, 1876-1925* TB/1199

ROBERT GREEN MC CLOSKEY: American Conservatism in the Age of Enterprise: 1865-1910 TB/1137

ARTHUR MANN: Yankee Reformers in the Urban Age: *Social Reform in Boston, 1880-1900* TB/1247

WHITELAW REID: After the War: *A Tour of the Southern States, 1865-1866. ‡ Edited by C. Vann Woodward* TB/3066

CHARLES H. SHINN: Mining Camps: *A Study in American Frontier Government. ‡ Edited by Rodman W. Paul* TB/3062

VERNON LANE WHARTON: The Negro in Mississippi: 1865-1890 TB/1178

American Studies: 1900 to the Present

RAY STANNARD BAKER: Following the Color Line: *American Negro Citizenship in Progressive Era. ‡ Illus. Edited by Dewey W. Grantham, Jr.* TB/3053

RANDOLPH S. BOURNE: War and the Intellectuals: *Collected Essays, 1915-1919. ‡ Edited by Carl Resek* TB/3043

A. RUSSELL BUCHANAN: The United States and World War II. † *Illus.* Vol. I TB/3044; Vol. II TB/3045

ABRAHAM CAHAN: The Rise of David Levinsky: *a documentary novel of social mobility in early twentieth century America. Intro. by John Higham* TB/1028

THOMAS C. COCHRAN: The American Business System: *A Historical Perspective, 1900-1955* TB/1080

FOSTER RHEA DULLES: America's Rise to World Power: 1898-1954. † *Illus.* TB/3021

JOHN D. HICKS: Republican Ascendancy: 1921-1933. † *Illus.* TB/3041

SIDNEY HOOK: Reason, Social Myths, and Democracy TB/1237

ROBERT HUNTER: Poverty: *Social Conscience in the Progressive Era. ‡ Edited by Peter d'A. Jones* TB/3065

WILLIAM L. LANGER & S. EVERETT GLEASON: The Challenge to Isolation: *The World Crisis of 1937-1940 and American Foreign Policy* Vol. I TB/3054; Vol. II TB/3055

WILLIAM E. LEUCHTENBURG: Franklin D. Roosevelt and the New Deal: 1932-1940. † *Illus.* TB/3025

ARTHUR S. LINK: Woodrow Wilson and the Progressive Era: 1910-1917. † *Illus.* TB/3023

GEORGE E. MOWRY: The Era of Theodore Roosevelt and the Birth of Modern America: 1900-1912. † *Illus.* TB/3022

RUSSEL B. NYE: Midwestern Progressive Politics: *A Historical Study of Its Origins and Development, 1870-1958* TB/1202

WILLIAM PRESTON, JR.: Aliens and Dissenters: *Federal Suppression of Radicals, 1903-1933* TB/1287

WALTER RAUSCHENBUSCH: Christianity and the Social Crisis. ‡ *Edited by Robert D. Cross* TB/3059

JACOB RIIS: The Making of an American. ‡ *Edited by Roy Lubove* TB/3070

PHILIP SELZNICK: TVA and the Grass Roots: *A Study in the Sociology of Formal Organization* TB/1230

IDA M. TARBELL: The History of the Standard Oil Company: *Briefer Version. ‡ Edited by David M. Chalmers* TB/3071

GEORGE B. TINDALL, Ed.: A Populist Reader ‡ TB/3069

TWELVE SOUTHERNERS: I'll Take My Stand: *The South and the Agrarian Tradition. Intro. by Louis D. Rubin, Jr., Biographical Essays by Virginia Rock* TB/1072

Anthropology

JACQUES BARZUN: Race: *A Study in Superstition. Revised Edition* TB/1172

JOSEPH B. CASAGRANDE, Ed.: In the Company of Man: *Twenty Portraits of Anthropological Informants. Illus.* TB/3047

W. E. LE GROS CLARK: The Antecedents of Man: *Intro. to Evolution of the Primates.* ° △ *Illus.* TB/559

CORA DU BOIS: The People of Alor. *New Preface by the author. Illus.* Vol. I TB/1042; Vol. II TB/1043

RAYMOND FIRTH, Ed.: Man and Culture: *An Evaluation of the Work of Bronislaw Malinowski* ¶ ° △ TB/1133

DAVID LANDY: Tropical Childhood: *Cultural Transmission and Learning in a Puerto Rican Village* ¶ TB/1235

L. S. B. LEAKEY: Adam's Ancestors: *The Evolution of Man and His Culture.* △ *Illus.* TB/1019

EDWARD BURNETT TYLOR: Religion in Primitive Culture. *Part II of "Primitive Culture."* § *Intro. by Paul Radin* TB/34

W. LLOYD WARNER: A Black Civilization: *A Study of an Australian Tribe.* ¶ *Illus.* TB/3056

Art and Art History

WALTER LOWRIE: Art in the Early Church. *Revised Edition.* 452 *illus.* TB/124

EMILE MÂLE: The Gothic Image: *Religious Art in France of the Thirteenth Century.* § △ *190 illus.* TB/44

MILLARD MEISS: Painting in Florence and Siena after the Black Death: *The Arts, Religion and Society in the Mid-Fourteenth Century.* 169 *illus.* TB/1148

ERICH NEUMANN: The Archetypal World of Henry Moore. △ *107 illus.* TB/2020

DORA & ERWIN PANOFSKY: Pandora's Box: *The Changing Aspects of a Mythical Symbol. Revised Edition. Illus.* TB/2021

ERWIN PANOFSKY: Studies in Iconology: *Humanistic Themes in the Art of the Renaissance.* △ *180 illustrations* TB/1077

ALEXANDRE PIANKOFF: The Shrines of Tut-Ankh-Amon. *Edited by N. Rambova.* 117 *illus.* TB/2011

JEAN SEZNEC: The Survival of the Pagan Gods: *The Mythological Tradition and Its Place in Renaissance Humanism and Art.* 108 *illustrations* TB/2004

OTTO VON SIMSON: The Gothic Cathedral: *Origins of Gothic Architecture and the Medieval Concept of Order.* △ *58 illus.* TB/2018

HEINRICH ZIMMER: Myth and Symbols in Indian Art and Civilization. *70 illustrations* TB/2005

Business, Economics & Economic History

REINHARD BENDIX: Work and Authority in Industry: *Ideologies of Management in the Course of Industrialization* TB/3035

GILBERT BURCK & EDITORS OF FORTUNE: The Computer Age: *And Its Potential for Management* TB/1179

THOMAS C. COCHRAN: The American Business System: *A Historical Perspective, 1900-1955* TB/1080

THOMAS C. COCHRAN: The Inner Revolution: *Essays on the Social Sciences in History* △ TB/1140

THOMAS C. COCHRAN & WILLIAM MILLER: The Age of Enterprise: *A Social History of Industrial America* TB/1054

ROBERT DAHL & CHARLES E. LINDBLOM: Politics, Economics, and Welfare: *Planning and Politico-Economic Systems Resolved into Basic Social Processes* TB/3037

PETER F. DRUCKER: The New Society: *The Anatomy of Industrial Order* △ TB/1082

EDITORS OF FORTUNE: America in the Sixties: *The Economy and the Society* TB/1015

ROBERT L. HEILBRONER: The Great Ascent: *The Struggle for Economic Development in Our Time* TB/3030

ROBERT L. HEILBRONER: The Limits of American Capitalism TB/1305

FRANK H. KNIGHT: The Economic Organization TB/1214

FRANK H. KNIGHT: Risk, Uncertainty and Profit TB/1215

ABBA P. LERNER: Everybody's Business: *Current Assumptions in Economics and Public Policy* TB/3051

ROBERT GREEN MC CLOSKEY: American Conservatism in the Age of Enterprise, 1865-1910 △ TB/1137

PAUL MANTOUX: The Industrial Revolution in the Eighteenth Century: *The Beginnings of the Modern Factory System in England* ° △ TB/1079

WILLIAM MILLER, Ed.: Men in Business: *Essays on the Historical Role of the Entrepreneur* TB/1081

RICHARD B. MORRIS: Government and Labor in Early America △ TB/1244

HERBERT SIMON: The Shape of Automation: *For Men and Management* TB/1245

PERRIN STRYKER: The Character of the Executive: *Eleven Studies in Managerial Qualities* TB/1041

Education

JACQUES BARZUN: The House of Intellect △ TB/1051

RICHARD M. JONES, Ed.: Contemporary Educational Psychology: *Selected Readings* TB/1292

CLARK KERR: The Uses of the University TB/1264

JOHN U. NEF: Cultural Foundations of Industrial Civilization △ TB/1024

Historiography & Philosophy of History

JACOB BURCKHARDT: On History and Historians. △ *Introduction by H. R. Trevor-Roper* TB/1216

WILHELM DILTHEY: Pattern and Meaning in History: *Thoughts on History and Society.* ° △ *Edited with an Introduction by H. P. Rickman* TB/1075

J. H. HEXTER: Reappraisals in History: *New Views on History & Society in Early Modern Europe* △ TB/1100

H. STUART HUGHES: History as Art and as Science: *Twin Vistas on the Past* TB/1207

RAYMOND KLIBANSKY & H. J. PATON, Eds.: Philosophy and History: *The Ernst Cassirer Festschrift. Illus.* TB/1115

ARNALDO MOMIGLIANO: Studies in Historiography ° △ TB/1283

GEORGE H. NADEL, Ed.: Studies in the Philosophy of History: *Selected Essays from History and Theory* TB/1208

JOSE ORTEGA Y GASSET: The Modern Theme. *Introduction by Jose Ferrater Mora* TB/1038

KARL R. POPPER: The Open Society and Its Enemies △
Vol. I: *The Spell of Plato* TB/1101
Vol. II: *The High Tide of Prophecy: Hegel, Marx and the Aftermath* TB/1102

KARL R. POPPER: The Poverty of Historicism ° △ TB/1126

G. J. RENIER: History: Its Purpose and Method △ TB/1209

W. H. WALSH: Philosophy of History: *An Introduction* △ TB/1020

History: General

WOLFGANG FRANKE: China and the West. *Trans by R. A. Wilson* TB/1326

L. CARRINGTON GOODRICH: A Short History of the Chinese People. △ *Illus.* TB/3015

DAN N. JACOBS & HANS H. BAERWALD: Chinese Communism: *Selected Documents* TB/3031

BERNARD LEWIS: The Arabs in History △ TB/1029

BERNARD LEWIS: The Middle East and the West ° △ TB/1274

History: Ancient

A. ANDREWES: The Greek Tyrants △ TB/1103

ADOLF ERMAN, Ed. The Ancient Egyptians: *A Sourcebook of Their Writings. New material and Introduction by William Kelly Simpson* TB/1233

MICHAEL GRANT: Ancient History ° △ TB/1190

SAMUEL NOAH KRAMER: Sumerian Mythology TB/1055

NAPHTALI LEWIS & MEYER REINHOLD, Eds.: Roman Civilization. *Sourcebook I: The Republic* TB/1231

NAPHTALI LEWIS & MEYER REINHOLD, Eds.: Roman Civilization. *Sourcebook II: The Empire* TB/1232

History: Medieval

P. BOISSONNADE: Life and Work in Medieval Europe: *The Evolution of the Medieval Economy, the 5th to the 15th Century.* ° △ *Preface by Lynn White, Jr.* TB/1141

HELEN CAM: England before Elizabeth △ TB/1026

NORMAN COHN: The Pursuit of the Millennium: *Revolutionary Messianism in Medieval and Reformation Europe* △ TB/1037

G. G. COULTON: Medieval Village, Manor, and Monastery
TB/1022

CHRISTOPHER DAWSON, Ed.: Mission to Asia: *Narratives and Letters of the Franciscan Missionaries in Mongolia and China in the 13th and 14th Centuries* △
TB/315

HEINRICH FICHTENAU: The Carolingian Empire: *The Age of Charlemagne* △
TB/1142

GALBERT OF BRUGES: The Murder of Charles the Good. *Trans. with Intro. by James Bruce Ross*
TB/1311

F. L. GANSHOF: Feudalism △
TB/1058

DENO GEANAKOPLOS: Byzantine East and Latin West: *Two Worlds of Christendom in the Middle Ages and Renaissance*
TB/1265

EDWARD GIBBON: The Triumph of Christendom in the Roman Empire *(Chaps. XV-XX of "Decline and Fall," J. B. Bury edition).* § △ *Illus.*
TB/46

W. O. HASSALL, Ed.: Medieval England: *As Viewed by Contemporaries* △
TB/1205

DENYS HAY: Europe: The Emergence of an Idea
TB/1275

DENYS HAY: The Medieval Centuries ° △
TB/1192

J. M. HUSSEY: The Byzantine World △
TB/1057

ROBERT LATOUCHE: The Birth of Western Economy: *Economic Aspects of the Dark Ages.* ° △ *Intro. by Philip Grierson*
TB/1290

FERDINAND LOT: The End of the Ancient World and the Beginnings of the Middle Ages. *Introduction by Glanville Downey*
TB/1044

ACHILLE LUCHAIRE: Social France at the Time of Philip Augustus. *New Intro. by John W. Baldwin*
TB/1314

MARSILIUS OF PADUA: The Defender of the Peace. *Trans. with Intro. by Alan Gewirth*
TB/1310

G. MOLLAT: The Popes at Avignon: 1305-1378 △
TB/308

CHARLES PETIT-DUTAILLIS: The Feudal Monarchy in France and England: *From the Tenth to the Thirteenth Century* ° △
TB/1165

HENRI PIRENNE: Early Democracies in the Low Countries: *Urban Society and Political Conflict in the Middle Ages and the Renaissance. Introduction by John H. Mundy*
TB/1110

STEVEN RUNCIMAN: A History of the Crusades. △
Volume I: *The First Crusade and the Foundation of the Kingdom of Jerusalem. Illus.*
TB/1143
Volume II: *The Kingdom of Jerusalem and the Frankish East, 1100-1187. Illus.*
TB/1243
Volume III: *The Kingdom of Acre and the Later Crusades*
TB/1298

SULPICIUS SEVERUS et al.: The Western Fathers: *Being the Lives of Martin of Tours, Ambrose, Augustine of Hippo, Honoratus of Arles and Germanus of Auxerre.* △ *Edited and trans. by F. O. Hoare*
TB/309

J. M. WALLACE-HADRILL: The Barbarian West: *The Early Middle Ages, A.D. 400-1000* △
TB/1061

History: Renaissance & Reformation

JACOB BURCKHARDT: The Civilization of the Renaissance in Italy. △ *Intro. by Benjamin Nelson & Charles Trinkaus. Illus.* Vol. I TB/40; Vol. II TB/41

JOHN CALVIN & JACOPO SADOLETO: A Reformation Debate. *Edited by John C. Olin*
TB/1239

ERNST CASSIRER: The Individual and the Cosmos in Renaissance Philosophy. △ *Translated with an Introduction by Mario Domandi*
TB/1097

FEDERICO CHABOD: Machiavelli and the Renaissance △
TB/1193

EDWARD P. CHEYNEY: The Dawn of a New Era, 1250-1453. * *Illus.*
TB/3002

G. CONSTANT: The Reformation in England: *The English Schism, Henry VIII, 1509-1547* △
TB/314

R. TREVOR DAVIES: The Golden Century of Spain, 1501-1621 ° △
TB/1194

G. R. ELTON: Reformation Europe, 1517-1559 ** ° △
TB/1270

DESIDERIUS ERASMUS: Christian Humanism and the Reformation: *Selected Writings. Edited and translated by John C. Olin*
TB/1166

WALLACE K. FERGUSON et al.: Facets of the Renaissance
TB/1098

WALLACE K. FERGUSON et al.: The Renaissance: *Six Essays. Illus.*
TB/1084

JOHN NEVILLE FIGGIS: The Divine Right of Kings. *Introduction by G. R. Elton*
TB/1191

JOHN NEVILLE FIGGIS: Political Thought from Gerson to Grotius: 1414-1625: *Seven Studies. Introduction by Garrett Mattingly*
TB/1032

MYRON P. GILMORE: The World of Humanism, 1453-1517. * *Illus.*
TB/3003

FRANCESCO GUICCIARDINI: Maxims and Reflections of a Renaissance Statesman (Ricordi). *Trans. by Mario Domandi. Intro. by Nicolai Rubinstein*
TB/1160

J. H. HEXTER: More's Utopia: *The Biography of an Idea. New Epilogue by the Author*
TB/1195

HAJO HOLBORN: Ulrich von Hutten and the German Reformation
TB/1238

JOHAN HUIZINGA: Erasmus and the Age of Reformation. △ *Illus.*
TB/19

JOEL HURSTFIELD: The Elizabethan Nation △
TB/1312

JOEL HURSTFIELD, Ed.: The Reformation Crisis △
TB/1267

ULRICH VON HUTTEN et al.: On the Eve of the Reformation: *"Letters of Obscure Men." Introduction by Hajo Holborn*
TB/1124

PAUL O. KRISTELLER: Renaissance Thought: *The Classic, Scholastic, and Humanist Strains*
TB/1048

PAUL O. KRISTELLER: Renaissance Thought II: *Papers on Humanism and the Arts*
TB/1163

NICCOLÒ MACHIAVELLI: History of Florence and of the Affairs of Italy: *from the earliest times to the death of Lorenzo the Magnificent.* △ *Introduction by Felix Gilbert*
TB/1027

ALFRED VON MARTIN: Sociology of the Renaissance. *Introduction by Wallace K. Ferguson*
TB/1099

GARRETT MATTINGLY et al.: Renaissance Profiles. △ *Edited by J. H. Plumb*
TB/1162

MILLARD MEISS: Painting in Florence and Siena after the Black Death: *The Arts, Religion and Society in the Mid-Fourteenth Century.* △ *169 illus.*
TB/1148

J. E. NEALE: The Age of Catherine de Medici ° △
TB/1085

ERWIN PANOFSKY: Studies in Iconology: *Humanistic Themes in the Art of the Renaissance.* △ *180 illustrations*
TB/1077

J. H. PARRY: The Establishment of the European Hegemony: 1415-1715: *Trade and Exploration in the Age of the Renaissance* △
TB/1045

BUONACCORSO PITTI & GREGORIO DATI: Two Memoirs of Renaissance Florence: *The Diaries of Buonaccorso Pitti and Gregorio Dati. Ed. with an Intro. by Gene Brucker. Trans. by Julia Martines*
TB/1333

J. H. PLUMB: The Italian Renaissance: *A Concise Survey of Its History and Culture* △
TB/1161

A. F. POLLARD: Henry VIII. ° △ *Introduction by A. G. Dickens*
TB/1249

A. F. POLLARD: Wolsey. ° △ *Introduction by A. G. Dickens*
TB/1248

CECIL ROTH: The Jews in the Renaissance. *Illus.*
TB/834

A. L. ROWSE: The Expansion of Elizabethan England. ° △ *Illus.*
TB/1220

GORDON RUPP: Luther's Progress to the Diet of Worms ° △
TB/120

FERDINAND SCHEVILL: The Medici. *Illus.*
TB/1010

FERDINAND SCHEVILL: Medieval and Renaissance Florence. *Illus.* Volume I: *Medieval Florence* TB/1090
Volume II: *The Coming of Humanism and the Age of the Medici*
TB/1091

R. H. TAWNEY: The Agrarian Problem in the Sixteenth Century. *New Intro. by Lawrence Stone*
TB/1315

G. M. TREVELYAN: England in the Age of Wycliffe, 1368-1520 ° △
TB/1112

VESPASIANO: Renaissance Princes, Popes, and Prelates:
*The Vespasiano Memoirs: Lives of Illustrious Men of
the XVth Century. Intro. by Myron P. Gilmore*
TB/1111

History: Modern European

FREDERICK B. ARTZ: Reaction and Revolution, 1815-
1832. * *Illus.*   TB/3034
MAX BELOFF: The Age of Absolutism, 1660-1815 △
                                                    TB/1062
ROBERT C. BINKLEY: Realism and Nationalism, 1852-
1871. * *Illus.*   TB/3038
EUGENE C. BLACK, Ed.: European Political History, 1815-
1870: *Aspects of Liberalism*   TB/1331
ASA BRIGGS: The Making of Modern England, 1784-
1867: *The Age of Improvement* ○ △   TB/1203
CRANE BRINTON: A Decade of Revolution, 1789-1799. *
Illus.   TB/3018
D. W. BROGAN: The Development of Modern France. ○ △
Volume I: *From the Fall of the Empire to the Dreyfus
Affair*   TB/1184
Volume II: *The Shadow of War, World War I, Be-
tween the Two Wars. New Introduction by the Au-
thor*   TB/1185
J. BRONOWSKI & BRUCE MAZLISH: The Western Intellectual
Tradition: *From Leonardo to Hegel* △   TB/3001
GEOFFREY BRUUN: Europe and the French Imperium,
1799-1814. * *Illus.*   TB/3033
ALAN BULLOCK: Hitler, A Study in Tyranny. ○ △ *Illus.*
                                                    TB/1123
E. H. CARR: German-Soviet Relations Between the Two
World Wars, 1919-1939   TB/1278
E. H. CARR: International Relations Between the Two
World Wars, 1919-1939 ○ △   TB/1279
E. H. CARR: The Twenty Years' Crisis, 1919-1939: *An
Introduction to the Study of International Rela-
tions* ○ △   TB/1122
GORDON A. CRAIG: From Bismarck to Adenauer: *Aspects
of German Statecraft. Revised Edition*   TB/1171
DENIS DIDEROT: The Encyclopedia: *Selections. Ed. and
trans. by Stephen Gendzier*   TB/1299
WALTER L. DORN: Competition for Empire, 1740-1763. *
Illus.   TB/3032
FRANKLIN L. FORD: Robe and Sword: *The Regrouping of
the French Aristocracy after Louis XIV*   TB/1217
CARL J. FRIEDRICH: The Age of the Baroque, 1610-1660. *
Illus.   TB/3004
RENÉ FUELOEP-MILLER: The Mind and Face of Bolshe-
vism: *An Examination of Cultural Life in Soviet
Russia. New Epilogue by the Author*   TB/1188
M. DOROTHY GEORGE: London Life in the Eighteenth
Century △   TB/1182
LEO GERSHOY: From Despotism to Revolution, 1763-
1789. * *Illus.*   TB/3017
C. C. GILLISPIE: Genesis and Geology: *The Decades be-
fore Darwin* §   TB/51
ALBERT GOODWIN, Ed.: The European Nobility in the
Eighteenth Century △   TB/1313
ALBERT GOODWIN: The French Revolution △   TB/1064
ALBERT GUÉRARD: France in the Classical Age: *The Life
and Death of an Ideal* △   TB/1183
CARLTON J. H. HAYES: A Generation of Materialism, 1871-
1900. * *Illus.*   TB/3039
J. H. HEXTER: Reappraisals in History: *New Views on
History and Society in Early Modern Europe* △   TB/1100
STANLEY HOFFMANN et al.: In Search of France: *The
Economy, Society and Political System in the Twenti-
eth Century*   TB/1219
A. R. HUMPHREYS: The Augustan World: *Society,
Thought, & Letters in 18th Century England* ○ △
                                                    TB/1105
DAN N. JACOBS, Ed.: The New Communist Manifesto
and Related Documents. Third edition, revised
                                                    TB/1078

LIONEL KOCHAN: The Struggle for Germany: *1914-45*
                                                    TB/1304
HANS KOHN: The Mind of Germany: *The Education of a
Nation* △   TB/1204
HANS KOHN, Ed.: The Mind of Modern Russia: *Historical
and Political Thought of Russia's Great Age* TB/1065
WALTER LAQUEUR & GEORGE L. MOSSE, Eds.: Education and
Social Structure in the 20th Century. ○ △ *Vol. 6 of the
Journal of Contemporary History*   TB/1339
WALTER LAQUEUR & GEORGE L. MOSSE, Eds.: International
Fascism, 1920-1945. ○ △ *Volume 1 of* Journal of Con-
temporary History   TB/1276
WALTER LAQUEUR & GEORGE L. MOSSE, Eds.: The Left-Wing
Intellectuals between the Wars 1919-1939. ○ △ *Vol-
ume 2 of* Journal of Contemporary History TB/1286
WALTER LAQUEUR & GEORGE L. MOSSE, Eds.: Literature
and Politics in the 20th Century. ○ △ *Vol. 5 of the
Journal of Contemporary History*   TB/1328
WALTER LAQUEUR & GEORGE L. MOSSE, Eds.: The New
History: *Trends in Historical Research and Writing
since World War II.* ○ △ *Vol. 4 of the* Journal of Con-
temporary History   TB/1327
WALTER LAQUEUR & GEORGE L. MOSSE, Eds.: 1914: *The
Coming of the First World War.* ○ △ *Volume 3 of*
Journal of Contemporary History   TB/1306
FRANK E. MANUEL: The Prophets of Paris: *Turgot, Con-
dorcet, Saint-Simon, Fourier, and Comte*   TB/1218
KINGSLEY MARTIN: French Liberal Thought in the
Eighteenth Century: *A Study of Political Ideas from
Bayle to Condorcet*   TB/1114
ROBERT K. MERTON: Science, Technology and Society in
Seventeenth Century England ¶ *New Intro. by the
Author*   TB/1324
L. B. NAMIER: Facing East: *Essays on Germany, the
Balkans, and Russia in the 20th Century* △ TB/1280
L. B. NAMIER: Personalities and Powers: *Selected Es-
says* △   TB/1186
L. B. NAMIER: Vanished Supremacies: *Essays on Euro-
pean History, 1812-1918* ○   TB/1088
NAPOLEON III: Napoleonic Ideas: *Des Idées Napoléoni-
ennes, par le Prince Napoléon-Louis Bonaparte. Ed.
by Brison D. Gooch*   TB/1336
FRANZ NEUMANN: Behemoth: *The Structure and Practice
of National Socialism, 1933-1944*   TB/1289
FREDERICK L. NUSSBAUM: The Triumph of Science and
Reason, 1660-1685. * *Illus.*   TB/3009
DAVID OGG: Europe of the Ancien Régime, 1715-
1783 ** ○ △   TB/1271
JOHN PLAMENATZ: German Marxism and Russian Com-
munism. ○ △ *New Preface by the Author*   TB/1189
RAYMOND W. POSTGATE, Ed.: Revolution from 1789 to
1906: *Selected Documents*   TB/1063
PENFIELD ROBERTS: The Quest for Security, 1715-1740. *
Illus.   TB/3016
PRISCILLA ROBERTSON: Revolutions of 1848: *A Social
History*   TB/1025
GEORGE RUDÉ: Revolutionary Europe, 1783-1815 ** ○ △
                                                    TB/1272
LOUIS, DUC DE SAINT-SIMON: Versailles, The Court, and
Louis XIV. ○ △ *Introductory Note by Peter Gay*
                                                    TB/1250
HUGH SETON-WATSON: Eastern Europe Between the
Wars, 1918-1941   TB/1330
ALBERT SOREL: Europe Under the Old Regime. *Translated
by Francis H. Herrick*   TB/1121
N. N. SUKHANOV: The Russian Revolution, 1917: *Eyewit-
ness Account.* △ *Edited by Joel Carmichael*
Vol. I TB/1066; Vol. II TB/1067
A. J. P. TAYLOR: From Napoleon to Lenin: *Historical Es-
says* ○ △   TB/1268
A. J. P. TAYLOR: The Habsburg Monarchy, 1809-1918: *A
History of the Austrian Empire and Austria-Hun-
gary* ○ △   TB/1187
G. M. TREVELYAN: British History in the Nineteenth Cen-
tury and After: *1782-1919.* ○ △ *Second Edition* TB/1251

C. G. JUNG & C. KERÉNYI: Essays on a Science of Mythology: *The Myths of the Divine Child and the Divine
Maiden* TB/2014

DORA & ERWIN PANOFSKY : Pandora's Box: *The Changing
Aspects of a Mythical Symbol.* △ Revised edition.
Illus. TB/2021

ERWIN PANOFSKY: Studies in Iconology: *Humanistic
Themes in the Art of the Renaissance.* △ *180 illustrations* TB/1077

JEAN SEZNEC: The Survival of the Pagan Gods: *The
Mythological Tradition and its Place in Renaissance
Humanism and Art.* △ *108 illustrations* TB/2004

HELLMUT WILHELM: Change: *Eight Lectures on the I
Ching* △ TB/2019

HEINRICH ZIMMER: Myths and Symbols in Indian Art and
Civilization. △ *70 illustrations* TB/2005

Philosophy

G. E. M. ANSCOMBE: An Introduction to Wittgenstein's
Tractatus. º △ *Second Edition, Revised* TB/1210

HENRI BERGSON: Time and Free Will: *An Essay on the
Immediate Data of Consciousness* º △ TB/1021

H. J. BLACKHAM: Six Existentialist Thinkers: *Kierke-
gaard, Nietzsche, Jaspers, Marcel, Heidegger, Sartre* º △
TB/1002

CRANE BRINTON: Nietzsche. *New Preface, Bibliography
and Epilogue by the Author* TB/1197

MARTIN BUBER: The Knowledge of Man. △ *Ed. with an
Intro. by Maurice Friedman. Trans. by Maurice Friedman and Ronald Gregor Smith* TB/135

ERNST CASSIRER: The Individual and the Cosmos in
Renaissance Philosophy. △ *Translated with an Introduction by Mario Domandi* TB/1097

ERNST CASSIRER: Rousseau, Kant and Goethe. *Introduction by Peter Gay* TB/1092

FREDERICK COPLESTON: Medieval Philosophy º △ TB/376

F. M. CORNFORD: Principium Sapientiae: *A Study of the
Origins of Greek Philosophical Thought. Edited by
W. K. C. Guthrie* TB/1213

F. M. CORNFORD: From Religion to Philosophy: *A Study
in the Origins of Western Speculation §* TB/20

WILFRID DESAN: The Tragic Finale: *An Essay on the
Philosophy of Jean-Paul Sartre* TB/1030

A. P. D'ENTRÈVES: Natural Law: *An Historical Survey* △
TB/1223

MARVIN FARBER: The Aims of Phenomenology: *The
Motives, Methods, and Impact of Husserl's Thought*
TB/1291

MARVIN FARBER: Phenomenology and Existence: *Towards a Philosophy within Nature* TB/1295

HERBERT FINGARETTE: The Self in Transformation: *Psychoanalysis, Philosophy and the Life of the Spirit* ¶
TB/1177

PAUL FRIEDLÄNDER: Plato: *An Introduction* △ TB/2017

J. GLENN GRAY: The Warriors: *Reflections on Men in
Battle. Intro. by Hannah Arendt* TB/1294

WILLIAM CHASE GREENE: Moira: *Fate, Good, and Evil in
Greek Thought* TB/1104

W. K. C. GUTHRIE: The Greek Philosophers: *From Thales
to Aristotle* º △ TB/1008

G. W. F. HEGEL: The Phenomenology of Mind º △
TB/1303

F. H. HEINEMANN: Existentialism and the Modern Pre-
dicament △ TB/28

ISAAC HUSIK: A History of Medieval Jewish Philosophy
JP/3

EDMUND HUSSERL: Phenomenology and the Crisis of
Philosophy. *Translated with an Introduction by
Quentin Lauer* TB/1170

IMMANUEL KANT: The Doctrine of Virtue, *being Part II
of the* Metaphysic of Morals. *Trans. with Notes &
Intro. by Mary J. Gregor. Foreword by H. J. Paton*
TB/110

IMMANUEL KANT: Groundwork of the Metaphysic of
Morals. *Trans. & analyzed by H. J. Paton* TB/1159

IMMANUEL KANT: Lectures on Ethics. § △ *Introduction by
Lewis W. Beck* TB/105

IMMANUEL KANT: Religion Within the Limits of Reason
Alone. § *Intro. by T. M. Greene & J. Silber* TB/67

QUENTIN LAUER: Phenomenology: *Its Genesis and Pros-
pect* TB/1169

MAURICE MANDELBAUM: The Problem of Historical
Knowledge: *An Answer to Relativism. New Preface
by the Author* TB/1338

GABRIEL MARCEL: Being and Having: *An Existential
Diary.* ^ *Intro. by James Collins* TB/310

GEORGE A. MORGAN: What Nietzsche Means TB/1198

H. J. PATON: The Categorical Imperative: *A Study in
Kant's Moral Philosophy* △ TB/1325

PHILO, SAADYA GAON, & JEHUDA HALEVI: Three Jewish
Philosophers. *Ed. by Hans Lewy, Alexander Altmann,
& Isaak Heinemann* TB/813

MICHAEL POLANYI: Personal Knowledge: *Towards a Post-
Critical Philosophy* △ TB/1158

WILLARD VAN ORMAN QUINE: Elementary Logic: *Revised
Edition* TB/577

WILLARD VAN ORMAN QUINE: From a Logical Point of
View: *Logico-Philosophical Essays* TB/566

BERTRAND RUSSELL et al.: The Philosophy of Bertrand
Russell. *Edited by Paul Arthur Schilpp*
Vol. I TB/1095; Vol. II TB/1096

L. S. STEBBING: A Modern Introduction to Logic △ TB/538

ALFRED NORTH WHITEHEAD: Process and Reality: *An
Essay in Cosmology* △ TB/1033

PHILIP P. WIENER: Evolution and the Founders of Pragmatism. *Foreword by John Dewey* TB/1212

WILHELM WINDELBAND: A History of Philosophy
Vol. I: *Greek, Roman, Medieval* TB/38
Vol. II: *Renaissance, Enlightenment, Modern* TB/39

LUDWIG WITTGENSTEIN: The Blue and Brown Books º
TB/1211

Political Science & Government

JEREMY BENTHAM: The Handbook of Political Fallacies:
Introduction by Crane Brinton TB/1069

C. E. BLACK: The Dynamics of Modernization: *A Study
in Comparative History* TB/1321

KENNETH E. BOULDING: Conflict and Defense: *A General
Theory* TB/3024

CRANE BRINTON: English Political Thought in the Nineteenth Century TB/1071

ROBERT CONQUEST: Power and Policy in the USSR: *The
Study of Soviet Dynastics* △ TB/1307

EDWARD S. CORWIN: American Constitutional History:
*Essays edited by Alpheus T. Mason and Gerald Gar-
vey* TB/1136

ROBERT DAHL & CHARLES E. LINDBLOM: Politics, Economics, and Welfare: *Planning and Politico-Economic Systems Resolved into Basic Social Processes* TB/3037

JOHN NEVILLE FIGGIS: The Divine Right of Kings. *Introduction by G. R. Elton* TB/1191

JOHN NEVILLE FIGGIS: Political Thought from Gerson to
Grotius: *1414-1625: Seven Studies. Introduction by
Garrett Mattingly* TB/1032

F. L. GANSHOF: Feudalism △ TB/1058

G. P. GOOCH: English Democratic Ideas in the Seventeenth Century TB/1006

J. H. HEXTER: More's Utopia: *The Biography of an Idea.
New Epilogue by the Author* TB/1195

SIDNEY HOOK: Reason, Social Myths and Democracy △
TB/1237

ROBERT H. JACKSON: The Supreme Court in the American
System of Government △ TB/1106

DAN N. JACOBS, Ed.: The New Communist Manifesto *and
Related Documents. Third Edition, Revised* TB/1078

DAN N. JACOBS & HANS BAERWALD, Eds.: Chinese Communism: *Selected Documents* TB/3031

HANS KOHN: Political Ideologies of the 20th Century
TB/1277

ROY C. MACRIDIS, Ed.: Political Parties: *Contemporary Trends and Ideas* TB/1322

ROBERT GREEN MC CLOSKEY: American Conservatism in the Age of Enterprise, 1865-1910 TB/1137

KINGSLEY MARTIN: French Liberal Thought in the Eighteenth Century: *Political Ideas from Bayle to Condorcet* △ TB/1114

ROBERTO MICHELS: First Lectures in Political Sociology. *Edited by Alfred de Grazia* ¶ ° TB/1224

JOHN STUART MILL: On Bentham and Coleridge. △ *Introduction by F. R. Leavis* TB/1070

BARRINGTON MOORE, JR.: Political Power and Social Theory: *Seven Studies* ¶ TB/1221

BARRINGTON MOORE, JR.: Soviet Politics—The Dilemma of Power: *The Role of Ideas in Social Change* ¶ TB/1222

BARRINGTON MOORE, JR.: Terror and Progress—USSR: *Some Sources of Change and Stability in the Soviet Dictatorship* ¶ TB/1266

JOHN B. MORRALL: Political Thought in Medieval Times △ TB/1076

JOHN PLAMENATZ: German Marxism and Russian Communism. ° △ *New Preface by the Author* TB/1189

KARL R. POPPER: The Open Society and Its Enemies △
Vol. I: *The Spell of Plato* TB/1101
Vol. II: *The High Tide of Prophecy: Hegel, Marx and the Aftermath* TB/1102

JOHN P. ROCHE: American Political Thought: *From Jefferson to Progressivism* TB/1332

HENRI DE SAINT-SIMON: Social Organization, The Science of Man, and Other Writings. *Edited and Translated by Felix Markham* TB/1152

CHARLES I. SCHOTTLAND, Ed.: The Welfare State TB/1323

JOSEPH A. SCHUMPETER: Capitalism, Socialism and Democracy △ TB/3008

BENJAMIN I. SCHWARTZ: Chinese Communism and the Rise of Mao TB/1308

CHARLES H. SHINN: Mining Camps: *A Study in American Frontier Government.* ‡ *Edited by Rodman W. Paul* TB/3062

PETER WOLL, Ed.: Public Administration and Policy: *Selected Essays* TB/1284

Psychology

ALFRED ADLER: The Individual Psychology of Alfred Adler. △ *Edited by Heinz L. and Rowena R. Ansbacher* TB/1154

ALFRED ADLER: Problems of Neurosis. *Introduction by Heinz L. Ansbacher* TB/1145

ARTHUR BURTON & ROBERT E. HARRIS, Eds.: Clinical Studies of Personality
Vol. I TB/3075; Vol. II TB/3076

HADLEY CANTRIL: The Invasion from Mars: *A Study in the Psychology of Panic* ¶ TB/1282

HERBERT FINGARETTE: The Self in Transformation: *Psychoanalysis, Philosophy and the Life of the Spirit* ¶ TB/1177

SIGMUND FREUD: On Creativity and the Unconscious: *Papers on the Psychology of Art, Literature, Love, Religion.* § △ *Intro. by Benjamin Nelson* TB/45

C. JUDSON HERRICK: The Evolution of Human Nature TB/545

WILLIAM JAMES: Psychology: *The Briefer Course.* *Edited with an Intro. by Gordon Allport* TB/1034

C. G. JUNG: Psychological Reflections △ TB/2001

C. G. JUNG: Symbols of Transformation: *An Analysis of the Prelude to a Case of Schizophrenia.* △ *Illus.*
Vol. I TB/2009; Vol. II TB/2010

C. G. JUNG & C. KERÉNYI: Essays on a Science of Mythology: *The Myths of the Divine Child and the Divine Maiden* TB/2014

KARL MENNINGER: Theory of Psychoanalytic Technique TB/1144

ERICH NEUMANN: Amor and Psyche: *The Psychic Development of the Feminine* △ TB/2012

ERICH NEUMANN: The Archetypal World of Henry Moore. △ *107 illus.* TB/2020

ERICH NEUMANN: The Origins and History of Consciousness △ Vol. I *Illus.* TB/2007; Vol. II TB/2008

RALPH BARTON PERRY: The Thought and Character of William James: *Briefer Version* TB/1156

JOHN H. SCHAAR: Escape from Authority: *The Perspectives of Erich Fromm* TB/1155

MUZAFER SHERIF: The Psychology of Social Norms TB/3072

Sociology

JACQUES BARZUN: Race: *A Study in Superstition. Revised Edition* TB/1172

BERNARD BERELSON, Ed.: The Behavioral Sciences Today TB/1127

ABRAHAM CAHAN: The Rise of David Levinsky: *A documentary novel of social mobility in early twentieth century America. Intro. by John Higham* TB/1028

KENNETH B. CLARK: Dark Ghetto: *Dilemmas of Social Power. Foreword by Gunnar Myrdal* TB/1317

LEWIS A. COSER, Ed.: Political Sociology TB/1293

ALLISON DAVIS & JOHN DOLLARD: Children of Bondage: *The Personality Development of Negro Youth in the Urban South* ¶ TB/3049

ST. CLAIR DRAKE & HORACE R. CAYTON: Black Metropolis: *A Study of Negro Life in a Northern City.* △ *Revised and·Enlarged. Intro. by Everett C. Hughes*
Vol. I TB/1086; Vol. II TB/1087

EMILE DURKHEIM et al.: Essays on Sociology and Philosophy: *With Analyses of Durkheim's Life and Work.* ¶ *Edited by Kurt H. Wolff* TB/1151

LEON FESTINGER, HENRY W. RIECKEN & STANLEY SCHACHTER: When Prophecy Fails: *A Social and Psychological Account of a Modern Group that Predicted the Destruction of the World* ¶ TB/1132

ALVIN W. GOULDNER: Wildcat Strike: *A Study in Worker-Management Relationships* ¶ TB/1176

CÉSAR GRAÑA: Modernity and Its Discontents: *French Society and the French Man of Letters in the Nineteenth Century* ¶ TB/1318

FRANCIS J. GRUND: Aristocracy in America: *Social Class in the Formative Years of the New Nation* △ TB/1001

KURT LEWIN: Field Theory in Social Science: *Selected Theoretical Papers.* ¶ △ *Edited with a Foreword by Dorwin Cartwright* TB/1135

R. M. MAC IVER: Social Causation TB/1153

ROBERT K. MERTON, LEONARD BROOM, LEONARD S. COTTRELL, JR., Editors: Sociology Today: *Problems and Prospects* ¶ Vol. I TB/1173; Vol. II TB/1174

ROBERTO MICHELS: First Lectures in Political Sociology. *Edited by Alfred de Grazia* ¶ ° TB/1224

BARRINGTON MOORE, JR.: Political Power and Social Theory: *Seven Studies* ¶ TB/1221

BARRINGTON MOORE, JR.: Soviet Politics—The Dilemma of Power: *The Role of Ideas in Social Change* ¶ TB/1222

TALCOTT PARSONS & EDWARD A. SHILS, Editors: Toward a General Theory of Action: *Theoretical Foundations for the Social Sciences* TB/1083

ARNOLD ROSE: The Negro in America: *The Condensed Version of Gunnar Myrdal's An American Dilemma* TB/3048

GEORGE ROSEN: Madness in Society: *Chapters in the Historical Sociology of Mental Illness.* ¶ *Preface by Benjamin Nelson* TB/1337

KURT SAMUELSSON: Religion and Economic Action: *A Critique of Max Weber's The Protestant Ethic and the Spirit of Capitalism.* ¶ ° *Trans. by E. G. French. Ed. with Intro. by D. C. Coleman* TB/1131

12